The Law and Politics of Police Discretion

Recent Titles in Criminology and Penology

The Criminal Elite: Professional and Organized Crime
Howard Abadinsky

Born to Crime: The Genetic Causes of Criminal Behavior
Lawrence Taylor

Auxiliary Police: The Citizen's Approach to Public Safety
Martin Alan Greenberg

Punishment and Restitution: A Restitutionary Approach to Crime and the Criminal
Charles F. Abel and Frank H. Marsh

The Law and Politics of Police Discretion

Gregory Howard Williams

Contributions in Criminology and Penology, Number 4

Greenwood Press
Westport, Connecticut · London, England

Library of Congress Cataloging in Publication Data

Williams, Gregory Howard.
The law and politics of police discretion.

(Contributions in criminology and penology, ISSN 0732-4464 ; no. 4)
Bibliography: p.
Includes index.
1. Police discretion—United States. 2. Law enforcement—United States. I. Title. II. Series.
KF5399.W56 1984 345.73'052 83-22741
ISBN 0-313-24070-1 (lib. bdg.) 347.30552

Library of Congress Catalog Card Number: 83-22741
ISBN: 0-313-24070-1
ISSN: 0732-4464

First published in 1984

Greenwood Press
A division of Congressional Information Service, Inc.
88 Post Road West
Westport, Connecticut 06881

Printed in the United States of America

10 9 8 7 6 5 4 3 2 1

To Sara, Natalia, and Zach

Contents

Preface

From my early work as a deputy sheriff, over twenty years ago in Muncie, Indiana, to the present, I have been interested in the issue of police discretion. This book is an effort to try to focus on one aspect of that discretion—the decision to arrest. Although the issues discussed here are not new, there has been a general reluctance to deal openly and directly with them. It is my hope that this book will aid in opening up discussion about police discretion, especially in the arrest decision, and help bring public attention to a very important question regarding the appropriate range of police power.

It would be impossible to list everyone to whom I am indebted for their contributions to my knowledge about the police, nonetheless, I would like to thank some of those who have aided me in this work. I was able to prevail upon many of my colleagues at the University of Iowa College of Law to read the manuscript at various stages. I am particularly grateful to Professors Ronald Allen, Richard Kuhns, Peter Shane, and Robert Clinton for their comments. Other faculty members, too numerous to mention, were always willing to discuss particular aspects of the work or to offer encouragement, and I appreciate the scholarly atmosphere they fostered. Especially important in enhancing that atmosphere was Dean N. William Hines. Dean Hines was always willing to provide assistance to facilitate completion of the book, and I appreciate his support in this project and over the years.

I had the advantage of having colleagues from other universities read parts of the book. Professors Herman Goldstein and Frank Remington of the University of Wisconsin School of Law, two nationally recognized experts on the police, were especially kind in helping me crystallize my thoughts about the police, and I appreciate the fact that they took time out of busy schedules to read parts of the manuscript and visit with me on my trips to the University of Wisconsin. Dean Harvey Perlman of the University of Nebraska School of Law also read a segment of the book at an early stage and offered much appreciated comments. Professors Eric Sirulnik and Robert Park of the George Washington University School of Law and Professor John A. Morgan, Jr., of the Department of Political Science at George Washington University read the entire manuscript at an earlier stage and offered useful comments.

My research assistants, Mat Petrzelka, Brian Regan, and Delena Edwards, provided help in checking footnotes and gathering cases and materials, and I thank them for their work. A special debt of gratitude is due Nancy Whetstine for the always cheerful manner and special care with which she prepared the numerous revisions of the manuscript. Deb Brinegar was likewise very helpful in the preparation of the manuscript. David Lasocki provided much appreciated editorial assistance.

An earlier version of chapters 3 and 4 appeared as "Police Discretion: The Institutional Dilemma—Who Is In Charge?" *Iowa Law Review* 68, no. 3 (March 1983), 431–93. Copyright 1983 University of Iowa (Iowa Law Review). Chapter 2 is drawn from work that will appear as "Police Rulemaking Revisited: Some New Thoughts on an Old Problem" in a symposium, Discretion in Law Enforcement, in *Law and Contemporary Problems* 48, no. 2 (Spring 1985), copyright 1985, Duke University School of Law. A condensed version of chapter 3 also appears in "The Politics of Police Discretion" in Carl F. Pinkele and William C. Louthan, eds., *Discretion, Justice, and Democracy: A Public Policy Perspective* (Ames, Iowa: Iowa State University Press, 1984).

Most importantly, I would like to thank my friends and colleagues over the years in and out of law enforcement and more recently those on the Iowa Law Enforcement Academy Council and the Iowa State

Advisory Committee to the United States Commission on Civil Rights for their willingness to spend time with me discussing their ideas about the police. However, since I didn't always follow the comments or suggestions that were given, I must take responsibility for all errors or omissions that appear in this book.

Finally, I would like to thank the most important people in my life, Sara, Natalia, and Zach Williams, for their love and support.

The Law and Politics of Police Discretion

Introduction 1

> The three traffic tickets issued to the son of Waterloo's police chief and then withdrawn, spawning a controversy here, will not be reinstated. . . . [1]
>
> One Mesquakie [Indian] complained that "There is a white man's law; it's for the white man and protects the white man."
>
> . . . .
>
> Bill Neville, owner of Bill's Place, felt the police in Tama were repressive and overreacted. He asserted that they would arrest Indians who had too much to drink but would not arrest whites for similar offenses.[2]

Throughout America there has been a resurgence of interest in the police. Allegations of police brutality and excessive use of force have captured public attention and have become significant issues of national concern.[3] Nonetheless, as the above excerpts indicate, there is another aspect of the police function that, while not receiving extensive public attention, has even greater importance for society: the exercise of police discretion in enforcing criminal laws. To be sure, many law enforcement decisions involve only limited choices for the police. If a major felony such as murder or kidnapping occurs, the police act immediately to investigate and, if possible, to solve the crime and make an arrest. However, for less important, "low visibility"[4] crimes such as public intoxication and disorderly conduct, police reaction will vary. In one study of police and adult offenders, it was observed that police decided not to make arrests for 43 percent of all felonies and 52 percent of all misdemeanors judged by observers as situations where probable cause sufficient for an arrest existed.[5] Thus, even though the law may be violated and the violators known, an arrest may or may not be made; an officer may simply not act or may invoke an alternative remedy that is not officially sanctioned.[6] In his study of discretion, Professor Kenneth Culp Davis found the police to be among the most important policymakers in our society.[7] According to Davis, the police make "far more discretionary determinations in individual cases than do any other class of administrators." He estimated that discretionary enforcement "may account for about half of all the discretionary power that is exercised in individual cases in our entire legal system."[8]

Some scholars maintain that arrest decisions should be and are influenced solely by legal considerations.[9] However, in an article on discretionary decision making by the police, Charles W. Thomas and W. Anthony Fitch identify five characteristics that play a part in the arrest decision: race, age, sex, socioeconomic status, and demeanor of a person.[10] In fact, other criminal justice scholars argue that in making an arrest it is very important to consider factors in addition to violation of the law. Arthur Niederhoffer, a veteran of twenty years' experience with the New York City Police Department, thinks that

> [i]t is the *individual policeman's responsibility* to decide if and how the law should be applied, and [the officer must search] for the proper combination of cues on which to base his decision. These are derived from the typical sociological variables: class, education, clarity of role prescriptions, reference groups, self-conception, and visibility.[11]

Consistent with the Niederhoffer view, Professor Raymond Parnas found in his study of police response to domestic disputes that each officer handles a situation in a manner determined by his individual background, personality, and experience.[12] Although the police are not expected to make arrest decisions in a vacuum, the public is obviously concerned about the extent to which individual prejudices and dislikes determine an officer's response to an arrest situation.

Technically, the police have no explicit statutory authority to exercise this discretion. In fact, some scholars have argued that there are specific legal and political injunctions against such decision making.[13] As a practical matter, however, the police could not arrest all violators even if they so desired. Lack of sufficient resources alone precludes such action.[14] Consequently, the police exercise discretion, and the public expects them to do so. Nonetheless, concerns should not lessen the public's interest in how that discretion is exercised.

There has been some interest in finding what factors influence police arrest decisions. Some have argued that the police condone greater intragroup violence in minority neighborhoods where they think that citizens are inherently more violent,[15] and that arrests of blacks and Hispanics for low-visibility crimes are frequently for harassment purposes.[16] Other studies have concluded that, although decisions to arrest might not be knowingly influenced by racial factors, they may be influenced by other equally disturbing considerations. One of the best examples of these studies is Jerome Skolnick's *Justice without Trial*,[17] in which he concluded that, while a police officer may not be racially motivated, "[h]e may . . . appear to be discriminating against the Black, when in fact he may be mainly implementing departmental goals by deciding against the poor, the unemployed, and the residentially unstable, many of whom are Black."[18]

Owing to limited and conflicting research, it is impossible to state conclusively that law enforcement decisions are based on legally impermissible considerations. There is, however, sufficient evidence to conclude that "the law is administered inconsistently [in a way] which both creates an impression of discrimination and allows for the introduction of personal prejudices into police practices."[19] Largely because of the concern about the perception and reality of the exercise of police discretion, several national studies and writers have called attention to the importance of analyzing the need to limit discretionary powers of the police.[20] According to Professor Davis:

> The strongest need and the greatest promise for improving the quality of justice to individual parties in the entire legal and governmental system are in the areas where decisions necessarily depend more upon discretion than upon rules

> and principles and where formal hearings and judicial review are most irrelevant. . . . We must try something that neither the legal philosophers down through the centuries nor our current study groups of the organized bar have tried—we must try to find ways to minimize discretionary injustice.[21]

In addition to the studies done and the reports issued, calls for guiding and focusing police discretion have been made by prominent public officials. Over ten years ago, the Chief Justice of the United States Supreme Court expressed his anxiety over the lack of control of police discretion. In an address to graduates of the FBI Academy, Chief Justice Warren Burger said:

> It is often overlooked that no public officials in the entire range of modern government are given such wide discretion on matters dealing with the daily lives of citizens as are police officers. . . . No law book, no lawyer, no judge can really tell the policeman on the beat how to exercise this discretion perfectly in every one of the thousands of different situations that can arise in the hour-to-hour work of the policeman. Yet we must recognize that we need not choose between no guidelines at all and perfect guidelines. . . . [There is a] need for carefully devised basic standards to guide the exercise of this discretion and . . . for careful and comprehensive training of officers before they are thrust into situations that would often baffle the wisest judge.[22]

Unfortunately, few have taken up the challenge to consider and devise standards to control police discretion.

This failure to act is unfortunate. The lack of standards for control over the police has the potential to create public skepticism about the uniformity and impartiality of law enforcement and can seriously erode the public confidence and support necessary for the police to function effectively. A widely shared attitude that individual police officers are virtually free to enforce the law according to their personal whims and desires can have disastrous implications for the political system. A perception of uneven law enforcement has the ability to isolate community groups. Recent studies of police/community relations, conducted by various state advisory committees to the United States Commission on Civil Rights, found deeply held differences of opinion about how the law is enforced.[23] For example, in one study native American members of a small midwestern community perceived that local law enforcement decisions were influenced by racism and class considerations, and these perceptions influenced the native American citizens' attitudes toward the police as well as toward local government generally.[24]

In light of the focus and attention on the issue, it is disappointing that so little has been done. The lack of remedial action by the police, while regrettable, is not surprising. Action by police departments to establish limits on their discretion would require that police officials deal openly with such thorny issues as full enforcement and resource allocation—issues that most police executives would prefer to avoid.[25] However, rather than admit that the failure to act is due to a strong desire to maintain the *sub rosa* posture of police arrest decisions, support for the failure to act is frequently articulated in another way. For example, the argument is often made that the police do not have sufficient authority to develop guidelines to control arrest decisions. The claim is that neither statutory law, court decisions, nor the political structure of American government provide support for official efforts to control selective enforcement of the law.

This argument, while designed to deflect attention from the real issue of governmental accountability of police decision making, has sufficient merit to warrant closer investigation. Consequently, one of the goals of this book is to determine whether the police as a political entity, whose powers, duties, and functions are circumscribed by state and federal constitutions, can exercise sufficient power within the framework of those constitutions to develop specific rules and guidelines to control arrest decisions. In addition to analyzing the relevant state and federal constitutional provisions it is important to look to the statutory basis of modern police agencies. This requires an examination of the historical development of the American police to ascertain how the police have developed as an institution of government, the original scope of their power and authority, how that power and authority has evolved, and the implications that development has for selective enforcement decision making.

The police, as enforcers of the law, are obviously the most important institution in deciding which laws will be enforced. But even assuming it is clear that they have sufficient political and constitutional authority to undertake rule making, there is no assurance that they will do so. Their lack of action to control the exercise of arrest discretion is clear, and one must not be overly sanguine about any immediate change. Thus, it is important to see if there are other ways to bring police decision making under control.

What is often overlooked is that other institutions of government have specific responsibility for controlling law enforcement. For example, state legislatures are constitutionally charged to enact the criminal statutes the police enforce; prosecutorial offices have the political as well as legal responsibility to determine whether arrests made by the police will be prosecuted; state courts review arrest decisions of the police to assess their conformance to statutory law and constitutional principles; and local governing bodies have direct political control of the police.

Needless to say, there are other state and federal agencies that can influence the arrest decisions of the police, but their influence is statutorily as well as politically indirect and not as constant as that of state legislators, judges, prosecutors, and local government officials.[26] Obviously, the governor of a state is likely to be able to effect the passage of criminal laws to be enforced at the local level, but law enforcement, in the main, is a local function in which governors rarely intervene.[27] The same is true with the office of the state attorney general. Although the attorney general frequently represents the state in criminal cases appealed from the local levels, he rarely has specific authority over local law enforcement decisions.[28]

State legislatures have been identified as the most appropriate institution to control police arrest decisions.[29] It is useful to understand why—since many writers and studies have clearly focused on the need for legislative action—the legislatures have done so little. Is it because police discretion is not a priority issue and has no political constituency, or is it because developing criminal law legislation (such as the circumstances in which gambling laws will not be enforced) involves legislatures in difficult moral judgments that are not politically popular? This book attempts to address these questions by reviewing the findings of the work that has been done, supplementing that with limited interviews of legislators who have had substantial involvement with the passage of criminal justice legislation, as well as by assessing the institutional authority of legislatures and how they have acted on law enforcement issues.

This book also reviews the role of the courts as institutional bodies with policy-making power and political responsibility and analyzes how the courts have treated criminal law enforcement questions. In spite of inherent institutional limitations on the courts' ability to act, recent decisions of the Supreme Court indicate a real interest in the problem of police discretion. The recent Supreme Court decisions in *Delaware v. Prouse*,[30] *Brown v. Texas*,[31] *Michigan v. DeFillippo*,[32] and *United States v. Caceres*[33] all raise important questions about law enforcement discretion. It is important to analyze those cases to ascertain the implications they have for action to control arrest discretion.

Finally, it is necessary to look at two other policy-making bodies which can have direct legal and political impact on police work: prosecutorial offices and local governing bodies. Again, the object of this analysis is to discover the present role of these policy-making bodies as well as the role they might undertake to influence arrest decisions. Prosecutorial offices and local governing bodies rarely have been reviewed when discussing ways to control police arrest decisions. Nonetheless, prosecutors, by virtue of their institutional duty to decide which cases to prosecute, substantially influence police arrest policy. Local government agencies, by determining the level of police resources, likewise can have a substantial impact on police arrest decisions and thus deserve close review.

In addition to reviewing the primary institutional obstacles to efforts to control law enforcement, it is important to understand the extent to which proposals and models have been developed to foster action to control arrest discretion. Drawing upon the problems identified earlier, this work concludes by evaluating existing models and suggesting some alternatives. Proposals to address the problems of law enforcement policy making generally fall into one of two categories. Either they deal with the administrative and political problems of establishing an agency to develop guidelines or they discuss guidelines to control arrests for specific crimes. Unfortunately, by and large the work that has been done is quite limited and suggestions for implementing solutions frequently seem to be added as an afterthought to general discussion of problems of police discretion. Consequently, although such proposals have provided some structure within which to address the problem, they have not been well developed or comprehensive.

In assessing law enforcement policy making one finds that, without a broad theoretical framework, proposals to control such policy making are likely to be inadequate. Therefore, it is necessary to draw from the disparate writing and thinking on criminal law enforcement and develop the comprehensive theoretical framework that is needed to address the basic systemic questions of discretionary law enforcement. In other words, unless we have a theoretical framework that ties the work of courts, legislatures, police, prosecutors, and local government together, proposals to control police discretion are doomed to fail.

Constitutional and Statutory Obstacles to Controlling Police Discretion ______________ 2

> [S]elective enforcement [of the criminal law] should be open and above board . . . [e]nforcement policy should be made through the kind of rulemaking procedure that has been highly successful in federal administrative agencies. . . . [1]

> I unequivocally reject the suggestion that the police should engage in rulemaking that directly affects the scope of the substantive criminal law. . . . Police rulemaking affecting the scope of the criminal law is clearly inconsistent with [our model of government].[2]

Criticism may certainly be directed at the police for their failure to develop policies to control criminal law enforcement. Scholars, however, have not provided the police with examples of appropriate ways to respond to such problems. In addition to having failed to provide any real guidance on ways to control arrest discretion, scholars continue to disagree on the basic question of whether the police have constitutional and statutory power to develop discretion-limiting rules and guidelines.

A version of this chapter appears as "Police Rulemaking Revisited: Some New Thoughts on an Old Problem," *Law and Contemporary Problems* 48, no. 2 (Spring 1985), copyright 1985, Duke University School of Law. Used by permission.

The debate between professors Kenneth Culp Davis and Ronald Allen exemplifies the extent of this disagreement. Professor Davis, in his book titled *Police Discretion*, asserts that local police departments have the legal authority to draft law enforcement rules.[3] Davis maintains that the police may develop such rules because there is an implicit delegation of power to do so by the state legislatures.[4] According to Davis' theory, state legislators have acquiesced in law enforcement policy making by failing to provide adequate funds for law enforcement agencies and by neglecting to amend or repeal laws that legislators know cannot be fully enforced. In addition, Davis contends that the constitutional principle of due process that mandates development of enforcement policy by administrative agencies also mandates development of such policy by law enforcement agencies.[5]

Although there was general acceptance of Davis' position in the academic community when it was first articulated, Professor Allen raised some serious questions regarding the constitutional basis for Davis' conclusion.[6] After looking closely at Davis' work, Allen concluded that law enforcement policy making is impermissible because it is inconsistent with our theory of government in that it amends or repeals the criminal law, which only the legislature can do.[7] To a substantial extent, the positions held by Allen and Davis represent a clash between theory and reality.

Davis is strongly influenced by the unlimited discretion the police exercise and the lack of governmental control over the police. In his desire to address a serious problem, he attempts to apply to police work the constitutional theory and body of law that have supported the development of enforcement policy by federal administrative agencies. His failure to amplify fully his points and to give additional consideration to some of the unique aspects of state and local law enforcement agencies, however, causes his theory to be deficient in several respects. For example, while Professor Davis discusses Fourteenth Amendment due process theory, he does not fully develop the separation of power and delegation problems at the state level nor does he analyze the unique problems one must confront in considering the police as an administrative agency.

Professor Allen, on the other hand, minimizes the practical problems of law enforcement. His approach is straightforward, but tends to be excessively principled and theoretical. Allen contends that the principles of separation of power and delegation simply do not permit the type of rule making contemplated by Davis and that the administrative agency analogy is inappropriate. Largely because of the different perspectives of the two writers, there is sharp disagreement on some points, while others are addressed inadequately or not at all.

Due to the significance of the issue of whether police can formulate enforcement rules, there is an urgent need to consider carefully the unanswered questions and the areas of disagreement. The purpose of this chapter is to analyze the strengths and weaknesses of the positions taken by Davis and Allen and to attempt to develop a more complete understanding of the constitutional and statutory basis for police rule making. Since "full enforcement"[8] statutes have been central to most of the discussion surrounding police rule making, it is important to analyze not only the language of the statutes but the context within which they were developed. Consequently, the starting point of this chapter will be an analysis of the language and history of those statutes.[9] Following that, constitutional principles of separation of power and delegation and their impact on police rule making will be discussed. Finally, the constitutional principles of due process and equal protection will be reviewed, with a focus on the significance that those principles have for developing law enforcement policy.

HISTORICAL DEVELOPMENT OF POLICE DISCRETION

Conspicuously absent in the debate between Allen and Davis is an understanding of the historical evolution of police discretion. Professor Davis, while discussing police discretion in the abstract in his book *Discretionary Justice*, seems to base his specific recommendations for action on his observation and evaluation of the Chicago Police Department.[10] Thus, he recommends changes to a large extent apparently because of what he saw as the basic unfairness of uncontrolled discretion exercised by members of one contemporary law enforcement agency. On the other hand, while Professor Allen talks about the need to "conceptually . . . locate the police in relation to other principal decision makers in the criminal law process,"[11] he, like Professor Davis, fails to consider the historical development of the police and the effect such history has on their present role.

The end result is that both professors Davis and Allen, drawing from their limited analyses, make some unwarranted assumptions and reach questionable conclusions. For example, Professor Davis argues that the police are very similar to federal administrative agencies and likewise have power to establish law enforcement policy, while Professor Allen responds that the police are an executive as opposed to an administrative agency and they exercise only ministerial and not discretionary powers. Professor Allen conceives of administrative agencies as bodies created to regulate how society functions in certain areas. He sees the police, on the other hand, called upon solely to enforce laws passed by the legislature. According to Professor Allen, "We do not say to the police: 'Here is the problem. Deal with it. We say: Here is a detailed code. Enforce it.' " Thus, Professor Allen sees a very different mandate given to the police than to administrative agencies.[12]

Because of Professor Davis' limited development of the administrative agency analogy, especially how the doctrine of separation of powers applies to police, Professor Allen's arguments take on more weight than might realistically be due them. In other words, the failure to develop the political theory of the police as an administrative agency enables Professor Allen to engage in a discussion of the separation of powers doctrine without articulating how the police have fit into that doctrine.

An analysis of the development of the police clearly shows that the police are an agency that has a long historical tradition of performing discretionary functions and, in fact, supervising peacekeeping relationships within their jurisdictions. History is not only replete with many examples of the police as an independent agency[13] exercising broad law enforcement powers, there are some examples of the police exercising legislative[14] and judicial[15] functions as well.

The police as we know them in modern America trace their origin to early England. The first significant law enforcement officer, the English sheriff, provides an example of how the police function—a function not strictly limited to that of an executive agency exercising only ministerial powers. The English sheriff was probably the most important person in the local community and his function was similar to that of a viceroy. "He received and interpreted the King's mandate not only in matters concerning the peace, but in military, fiscal and judicial affairs as well."[16]

The sheriff was not only the chief law enforcement officer, he was also judicial president of the shire and administrator of the royal demesne. Thus, the sheriff had the authority to exercise both judicial and executive powers. Largely because of his administrative duties as royal tax collector, the sheriff was generally an unpopular person.[17] This general unpopularity, combined with frequent occurrences of corrupt acts by sheriffs in the collecting of taxes, ultimately led to efforts to restrict the broad powers of the English sheriff.[18]

It is clear, however, that efforts to control the range of the sheriff's powers did not rest upon the feeling that the extensive power of the sheriff violated any particular theory or principle of government; rather, the concern was with the corruption of the officeholders.[19] In fact, during the time of the early attempts to limit sheriffs' powers, many of them were able to secure appointments as justices of the peace and continued to exercise both executive and judicial functions.[20]

A second example of an English law enforcement officer who had broad discretion is the constable. In the Middle Ages, the English constable served not only as a law enforcement officer but as a magistrate as well. He interpreted statutes, enforced them, and penalized violators.[21] Although the rise of the justice of the peace ultimately resulted in the eclipse of the magisterial powers of the constable and the sheriff, there continued for many years to be a much closer governmental relationship between those officers and the justice of the peace than with the executive arm of the government.[22]

The justices had extensive discretion in enforcing the laws, and, to assist them in the exercise of that discretion, they had the constable and the sheriff.[23] Both served for many years as adjuncts to the justices of the peace. By the sixteenth century, the justices were firmly entrenched and the broad powers of the constable and the sheriff had eroded. Nonetheless, the constables and the sheriffs still continued to perform a wide range of duties.[24] Even in the late 1800s, considerable discretionary power was left in their hands.[25] However, law enforcement duties in England by that time were largely taken over by Sir Robert Peel's "New System of Police."[26]

As in England, the primary law enforcement officer in colonial America was the sheriff. The American sheriff, like his English counterpart, possessed extensive power and authority. The political evolution of the sheriff's office in America, however, was quite different.

Like their English counterparts, the earliest sheriffs in America were agents of the king and appointed by the governor of the colony.

> For the most part the colonial sheriffs were closely modeled upon their English contemporary. The power of appointment was usually vested in the governor, and the sheriff's duties so distributed as to include not only the apprehension of offenders, the care of prisoners, and the execution of civil process . . . the conduct of elections, collection of taxes, custody of public funds, and other fiscal operations. In some cases the judicial function adhered to the office for a time, particularly in Virginia.[27]

Also as in England, the non–law enforcement duties performed by the sheriff were largely the reason for concern about their powers. According to one scholar, "this practice of frequent rotation in the office of sheriff was not so much based upon democratic doctrines, as upon the fact that the colonial sheriff . . . was often charged with the collection of taxes and proved dilatory in settling accounts for them."[28] The Americans dealt with the sheriff problem in quite a different way than did the English. In England, the attempts to control the corruption of the sheriffs resulted in limiting the broad powers of the office. Although a reaction to the same concern—to limit corruption—the approach in America was not so much to restrict the powers, but to ensure political accountability of the officeholder. In essence, it was felt that the sheriff could be controlled by making the position an elective office.[29] Thus, the trend in America was to increase political control by requiring election and limiting the sheriff's term and tenure in office, rather than establishing rigid boundaries within which the sheriffs were expected to function.

Attempts to classify the sheriff as an executive, legislative, or judicial agency and likewise to categorize his powers as being solely executive, legislative, or judicial are complicated by several factors. First, although the American sheriff functioned on the local or county level, he was, in most states, an elected official who had been specifically created by state constitutions. Thus, he had power over a discrete area but owed fealty and allegiance to the state at large. The sheriff had exclusive power to determine law enforcement priorities, and any controls over the sheriff were indirect. No state or local officials had specific control over the sheriff in the performance of his duties.[30]

Second, in addition to the control being indirect, the diffusion of such control over several levels of government resulted in very little actual influence over law enforcement decisions. County governments normally provided the sheriff's budgetary needs and support; state legislatures passed the laws to be enforced. While county governments could take the position that particular state laws were to be fully enforced in their locality, they could not require the sheriff to comply fully with their wishes. Of course one could argue that the power of the purse held by county governments could force a reluctant sheriff to adhere to the enforcement wishes of the county officials. That argument, however, reinforces the idea that sheriffs are policymakers operating within a particular sphere of influence and that criminal statutes, like other statutes, are frequently the subject of negotiation among political agencies.

Negotiation on law enforcement priorities appears to have been commonplace throughout American history. Historical examination of the response of two agencies that could conceivably force full enforcement of the law reveals that they rarely did so. Legislatures passed criminal statutes, but seldom did they review how those statutes were enforced in specific localities. The sheriffs were left to decide specific implementation of the laws. Furthermore, there are very few cases in which the courts have required full enforcement of the law. One plausible conclusion from all of this is that the drafters of the state constitutions that established the office of sheriff intended that sheriffs be politically independent, and publicly accountable officials whose selection to office and performance of duties would not be directly controlled by any state or local official.[31] That is not to say that they were to be considered completely autonomous; rather, sheriffs, like most other state and local officials, were expected to exercise broad powers within a framework of practical politics and statutory law. In spite of state constitutional revisions that have occurred across the nation, the position of the sheriff as an independent, elected state official basically has not changed.[32]

If sheriffs cannot be classified as legislative, executive, or judicial officials by virtue of which branch of government has direct control over their decisions in office, can they be so classified by the specific functions they have been given to perform? As a general proposition, the functions of the sheriffs have not changed substantially since the American Revolution.

Looking at the specific powers of the sheriffs one gets a better idea of the role they are expected to play in government, and a picture of the office as an independent government agency begins to emerge. The sheriff has duties as court administrator, jailer, peace officer, tax collector, and election supervisor.[33] None of those duties—not even that of peace officer—can in any practical sense be regarded as solely ministerial. All of these tasks required the sheriff to analyze facts within the context of relevant statutes and to make policy judgments regarding enforcement of those statutes.[34]

The argument that the office of sheriff is to exercise broad discretion is reinforced by the constitutional status of the office. It is reasonable to conclude that the framers of the early state constitutions felt that the sheriffs, like other arms of government, warranted an exception to the application of a rigid separation of powers theory. This was certainly true in other cases in which

> the principle of separation of powers was violated in practice by legislative exercise of judicial and executive functions; by the election of the executive councils by and from the legislatures; by the appointment of judicial and executive officers by the legislatures; by the presidency and vote of the vice-executive in the upper house; and by the exercise of judicial functions by the governor and his council.[35]

One can conclude from this curious state of affairs that any interpretation of state separation of powers provisions that fails to consider the separate constitutional status of the first law enforcement officer in America, the sheriff, is seriously deficient. Unfortunately, professors Allen and Davis overlooked the implications of the historical evolution of law enforcement in America by focusing exclusively on the present, most prominent law enforcement agency—the municipal police.[36] Although the origin of the municipal police may be somewhat different from that of the sheriff, they do share a common institutional function; thus their power and authority may well be based on similar theories regarding the allocation of power.

Because municipal police officers are rarely mentioned in state constitutions, a scholar focusing only on them does not encounter the problem of trying to counterbalance separation of powers provisions of state constitutions with those which establish sheriffs as independent agencies. While the existence of state constitutional provisions establishing the independent character of the office of sheriff does not fully clarify the intended scope of sheriffs' powers, it does argue against automatically assuming their duties are exclusively ministerial in nature.

As we have seen, the early sheriffs, both before and after ratification of the state constitutions, were assigned a variety of administrative tasks and responsibilities. In fact, sheriffs could be considered to have been one of the first independent administrative agencies. After examining the historical role of the sheriff, the administrative agency analogy drawn by Professor Davis becomes much more plausible. The administrative agency analogy is less clear, although not untenable, when the focus is on municipal police departments, because the development of American municipal police agencies was different from that of the sheriff's office. However, even if there is a difference between the establishment of the sheriff and municipal police, the basic approach in distributing law enforcement powers may well be quite similar.

Politics have had a major impact on the operation of law enforcement, but it has been dealt with in different ways at the county and municipal level. The openly political nature of the sheriff over the years has remained largely unchanged, but the political nature of the police has developed in another way. Early American police departments were first and foremost partisan political institutions: officers were selected on the basis of their political affiliation, and such selection strongly influenced how they performed their duties.[37] Because of the vast powers of societal control inherent in police work, there were constant struggles to see which political group would control the police.[38]

The fights for control of the police in New York City typify the struggles that occurred nationally.[39] Around 1857 in New York there were efforts to introduce Sir Robert Peel's concept of modern law enforcement, although it had strong political overtones. At that time legislation was introduced in the New York State legislature that consolidated the boroughs of New York City and created a board of police commissioners consisting of the mayors of New York and Brooklyn and five commissioners appointed by the governor.[40] This new legislation marked the introduction of direct state control over local law enforcement and "represented the maneuvering of a Republican legislature to obtain control over the affairs and particularly the patronage of a Democratic city."[41] That the move was political is demonstrated by the fact that the governor appointed four Republicans and one American party man as his five appointees.[42] Needless to say, this "reform" effort created great controversy, but there was little change until a Democratic governor was elected. Shortly after the election of a Democratic governor, the Republican-controlled state legislature passed a statute that gave the state legislature the power to appoint the members of the police board. It is unclear whether this action was the result of a desire by the Republican-controlled legislature to limit the power of a Democratic governor or to bring about bipartisan membership of the police board. Although partisan politics probably played a part in the New York State legislature's actions, establishing bipartisan agencies to oversee the police was an idea becoming increasingly popular.[43]

By the early twentieth century in New York, at least ten different state or local officers or commissioners had been used to supervise local police activities.[44] This ever-changing search for ways to exert political control over the police led one police scholar to lament that

> [i]n this blind search for the "ideal system," this belief in the efficiency of checks and balances, if only the proper combination can be discovered, continuity has been sacrificed, and the existing arrangements have again and again been overturned. In the 91 years in which the Metropolitan police organization of London has been in existence, but one substantial change has been made in its machinery of control, and that was in 1856, when, after six years of trial with a single-headed commission the act of 1829 providing for two commissioners was altered to fit the new condition. In the 75 years in which New York City may legitimately be said to have had a regular police force nine fundamental changes, involving distinct breaks with the past, have occurred in the framework of her organization.[45]

Attempts at state control of local law enforcement were obviously unpopular in the large cities. In fact, it is plausible that the real push for home rule may have been motivated in large part by a desire to avoid state control of local police. Whether the concern about control of the police motivated or succeeded the movement for home rule, there was a decline in direct state involvement in local law enforcement, and new means were adopted to control the police by the turn of the century. Fluctuations in control of the police and, particularly, intervention of state government in local law enforcement were not limited to New York. In 1860, the Maryland state legislature created a police board for the city of Baltimore consisting of four commissioners selected by the state legislature; the following year, the legislatures of Missouri and Illinois, respectively, created police boards for the cities of St. Louis and Chicago and stipulated that board members be selected by the governor and approved by the state senate. State-controlled boards were also introduced in California, Louisiana, Massachusetts, Michigan, Nebraska, and Ohio. State boards seem to have been instituted primarily because state officials wanted to limit Democratic influence in local law enforcement policy decisions, which frequently were in direct conflict with the policy objectives of Republican-controlled state legislatures.[46] Later on, to avoid politicalization of state police departments, some provisions were made in the states to ensure political party representation on those departments. For example, an Iowa statute provided that the commissioner of the highway patrol "is authorized to employ the members of said patrol; however, not to exceed one hundred twenty-five men, and not more than sixty percent of said patrol shall at any time be members of the same political party."[47]

In spite of all the fighting between state and local governments over control of the police, the police continued to exercise a wide range of duties that clearly included interpreting the laws to be enforced. The cries for reform that did exist seem in large part to have been a reaction to reports of police corruption and incompetence. By the end of the nineteenth century investigations placed all big-city departments "under suspicion."[48]

Although there were several reform movements, the common thread was an acceptance and expectation that police would exercise a large degree of discretion. One such movement called on police to be social workers, to work with the schools and other social agencies to prevent crimes.[49] In accordance with this, the first women police officers were hired to work with the newly established juvenile divisions, which were expected to have wide latitude in dealing with law enforcement violations by children.[50]

Recognition of the wide discretion police exercise was implicit in many of the reform movements around the turn of the century. The movement to professionalize law enforcement that solidified around

1920,[51] had two main features: social reform and administrative efficiency. Administrative efficiency was believed to be achievable by virtue of increased training—the need for which was recognized because the policeman "is in a very real sense a judge exercising enormous amounts of discretion and to a great extent determines the quality of criminal justice in any given American city."[52] The role of the police as social reformers also implicity conveyed the recognition of broad discretionary powers of the police. One example of this is the work of Fred Kohler, chief of the Cleveland, Ohio, Police Department. He trained his men to work from the premise that "some men fail through some unfortunate circumstances and are not criminal at heart"[53] and should be treated accordingly. To accommodate such men, Kohler set up "Sunrise Courts" so that honest hard-working men could attend their court sessions early enough so as not to interfere with their jobs or stigmatize them and their families, and in fact in some cases acted to divert potential arrestees out of the court system entirely.[54] Much of this activity across the nation was undertaken in spite of the so-called full enforcement statutes.

FULL ENFORCEMENT STATUTES

Professor Allen argues that the existence of so-called full enforcement provisions in some state statutes is explicit evidence that state legislative bodies intended to prohibit, and in fact did prohibit, local police departments from formulating discretionary arrest policies.[55] Upon close examination, however, the situation is more ambiguous than Professor Allen suggests.[56] An analysis of the full enforcement provisions in the total context of the legislation of which they are part shows them to be a minor part of legislation primarily designed to create independent police departments acting within general guidelines. The extreme and undue focus exclusively on the so-called full enforcement clauses may simply show the imaginative powers of scholars rather than substantive statutory limitations.

Nonetheless, because of the fact that questions have been raised about the effect of such statutes on police rule making, a close look at them is warranted. A significant number of the full enforcement statutes were enacted around the turn of the century. In fact, fourteen of the twenty-three states that Professor Allen cites as having full enforcement statutes enacted them between 1883 and 1925.[57]

The question that must be answered is why such a large proportion of the statutes were enacted during that period. As indicated earlier, during that time there was throughout the country considerable tension between state and local governments over who was going to control the police. Thus, one plausible explanation might be that the full enforcement provisions were an attempt to maintain some remnant of state control over local police departments.

A more plausible hypothesis, however, is that the legislation was a genuine attempt to foster the creation of politically independent, yet locally selected, police departments. State-controlled police systems had been implemented in twelve of the twenty-three American cities that had populations larger than 250,000. Those twelve cities were located in ten states. According to the census estimates of 1925, those cities included the following: Baltimore, Boston, Chicago, Cincinnati, Cleveland, Detroit, Indianapolis, Kansas City (Missouri), New Orleans, New York, San Francisco, and St. Louis.[58] Eight had some type of full enforcement legislation at that time, and six enacted such legislation within nine years of the return of police control to municipal governments. In fact, five of these ten states enacted full enforcement legislation within four years of the return of police supervisory control from the states to the cities.

State	**End of State Control of Police**	**Full Enforcement Legislation**
California	1900	1883
Indiana	1891–1901	1905
Illinois	1865	1874
Louisiana	1877	1928
Maine	1920	1920
Maryland	NA	NA
Michigan	1881	1895
Missouri	NA	1949
New York	1870	1888
Ohio	1902	1902

It appears that the so-called full enforcement legislation was an attempt to foster the creation of politically independent yet legislatively structured police departments. The theory that the various state legislatures were motivated to enact such legislation by their interest in developing more politically insulated municipal police agencies draws considerable support from a close analysis of the full enforcement statutes.

The language and general context of the statutes supports the proposition that the state legislatures were intent primarily on establishing general rather than specific operational control of local police. The major concern of the legislatures, so expressed in the statutes, was with the design and structure of local police agencies, and not with controlling police decision making. First, many of the full enforcement statutes were placed in the "political," as opposed to "criminal," sections of the state codes. For example, the New York legislature frequently incorporated full enforcement language into municipal charters.[59] Full enforcement legislation in California, Indiana, Michigan, Nebraska, Ohio, and fifteen other states was part of legislation primarily enacted to establish city and county governments.[60]

Only six state legislatures enacted full enforcement legislation as part of the criminal codes.[61] Had the legislation been in the criminal code, there would be greater reason to believe the full enforcement statutes should be viewed as explicit commands. Judging from the placement of the full enforcement statutes, however, it appears that the various state legislatures intended that the statutes constitute part of a larger legislative scheme outlining general duties and responsibilities of municipal government rather than specific requirements concerning law enforcement. Whether full enforcement statutes are placed in criminal or political sections of state codes, however, is not dispositive; a more important question is how the statutes have been interpreted by the courts.

Unfortunately, there is very little case law interpreting the legislation. In Iowa, for example, *Emmetsburg v. Gunn*[62] is the only reported case interpreting the full enforcement statute. *Emmetsburg*, however, gives little guidance on the full enforcement question. In addition, there has been only one Iowa attorney general opinion on the duties of peace officers.[63] The paucity of cases interpreting the full enforcement statutes is not peculiar to Iowa. The few cases that do exist provide very little in the way of doctrinal principles to guide interpretation of the statutes.[64] The common thread that does run through those cases supports the idea that the statutes are general rather than specific guidelines. In the cases that do address police discretion questions, there seems to be a general concern that when the police are confronted with flagrant misconduct some action should be taken, even though that action might not necessarily be to arrest offenders. Two cases from California typify this approach.

In *People v. Mullin*, a sheriff was removed from office because he failed to investigate the complaint of a minor female that she had been molested by her father, despite the sheriff having been provided with some corroborating evidence by an aunt and two other persons.[65] Circumstances such as those in *Mullin* would offend the sensibilities of the citizenry of any community, and the court may have been responding to strong public support to remove such a sheriff from office.[66] In a less egregious situation, however, there is likely to be much less controversy over how a law enforcement officer exercises discretion as long as the officer does something. For example, in *People v. Spear*, in spite of clear and violent infractions of the picketing laws, the court held that a California sheriff had not exceeded his discretionary powers by ordering the picketers to disperse rather than arresting offenders who had clearly violated the law.[67] It appears as though the *Mullin* and *Spear* courts made an ad hoc analysis of the facts in each case, thereby determining whether the police officer's actions warranted removal. These cases seem to typify courts' recognition that the police have some discretionary power in enforcing the law and they are expected to exercise that discretion. But it is clear that the courts expect the police to do something: they cannot refuse to act, especially when confronted with tangible evidence concerning law violations.

There are a few other cases that speak to the issue of selective enforcement of the law. In *Gowan v. Smith*, the plaintiff sought a writ of mandamus to compel the police commissioner of Detroit to enforce a law prohibiting the operation of saloons on Sundays. The Michigan Supreme Court held that the writ of mandamus would not issue to compel the performance of discretionary acts of an executive kind but only to require specific ministerial duties.[68] The court explicitly recognized the need for discretionary decision making by police officers. The Michigan Supreme Court stated:

> [T]he [police] commissioner is bound to use the discretion with which he is clothed. He is not only charged with the execution of the liquor laws of the state within the city of Detroit but he is likewise charged with the suppression of all crime and the preservation of peace. . . . It is entirely obvious that he

must exercise a sound discretion as to how those means shall be applied for the good of the community.[69]

It is important to note that the supreme court of Michigan in deciding the *Gowan* case did not refer for guidance to the Michigan full enforcement statute which was then in existence.[70] The focus of the court was a local Detroit ordinance controlling and regulating establishments that sold liquor.[71] Nowhere on its face did the ordinance purport to give the police any discretion whatsoever: yet a majority of the court found that the police commissioner could not be judicially required to enforce this law.

Another case typical of those supporting the exercise of arrest discretion and one that ignored the state full enforcement legislation is *Taylor v. City of Pine Bluff*.[72] In *Taylor*, the legislature, and by implication the police, was found to have the power to discriminate among similarly situated businesses in the enforcement of Sunday closing laws. Taylor, a Pine Bluff grocer, charged that the police adopted a policy of law enforcement instigated by the mayor and city council that resulted in the enforcement of state Sunday closing laws against grocery stores but not against "drugstores, hotels, filling stations, restaurants, funeral homes, bakeries, tourist courts, bus stations, city park concessions and sporting goods stores" despite the fact that the Arkansas statute made it clear that it is a violation for any store to be open or to retail any goods or merchandise on Sunday. Taylor unsuccessfully made the argument that the enforcement policy of the police was a denial of equal protection of the laws as the other businesses sold many of the same items as the grocery stores.

In a decision clearly designed to support police discretion, the Arkansas court rejected Taylor's claim and said: "It does not seem to us that the equal protection clause restricts the legislature to classifications based on the type of commodity being sold."[73] In an unusual opinion, the court went on to add that there might be reasonable grounds for the legislature to believe that "it is necessary and desirable to fill prescriptions on Sunday" and that the court "prefer[s] to give full effect to the presumption of constitutionality that attends every statute and to uphold the statutory classification in the absence of proof indicating there is no reasonable basis for the distinctions laid down by the legislature."[74]

The problem is that no distinctions were laid down by the legislature. The focus of the court is on what the legislature could do, not what they did. The issue in the case, however, is not the statute, but how it was applied by the police, a point the court addresses only very tangentially. The Arkansas Supreme Court apparently wants to ensure that the police have sufficient power to exercise discretion in the arrest decision, but the court never directly addresses that issue, so we are unclear on the breadth of that power.

The principal state case cited in opposition to the argument that the police can engage in law enforcement policy making is *Bargain City U.S.A. v. Dilworth*. *Bargain City* was for all practical purposes also a "Sunday Blue Laws" case, involving strong economic overtones, a fact scholars tend to overlook when discussing its ramifications. In *Bargain City*, the enforcement policy of the police commissioner of Philadelphia was attacked on the grounds that it was discriminatory in violation of the Fourteenth Amendment.[75] Although the Pennsylvania Supreme Court did not directly resolve the claim of discriminatory enforcement, the court stipulated the following facts: "1) The Police Commissioner had established a policy of enforcing the act only against employees of certain large retail establishments. 2) This enforcement policy was followed because of limited personnel. 3) There was no finding that the policy resulted from an evil or arbitrary design."[76] Since the court declared that the issue of discriminatory law enforcement abated when the police chief left office, there was no actual determination of the validity of the enforcement policy. Nonetheless, *Bargain City* is frequently cited as an opinion prohibiting the development of selective enforcement policy.[77] But upon close analysis it has limited utility. The primary limitation is subject matter. Sunday Blue Law cases have strong equal protection overtones—that is, the right not to be discriminated against solely on the basis of economic status. *Bargain City* dealt with an explicit policy to enforce the Sunday closing laws only against large department stores. Any arrest policy in which the decision to arrest is based solely on the economic status of the arrestee is constitutionally suspect.[78] On the basis of the subject matter and especially the limited treatment given to police discretion and its tangential relationship to the case, one can argue that the precedental value of *Bargain City U.S.A. v. Dilworth* is quite limited.

Another case typical of those limiting law enforcement policy making is *State v. Lombardi*.[79] The defendant was a sheriff who was found by a trial court to be guilty of willful dereliction of duty.[80] He had allegedly reduced charges against some persons who were initially charged with driving under the influence of alcohol, and he had permitted violations of the state liquor and prostitution laws to go uncharged.[81] The opinion places substantial limitations on police arrest discretion of law enforcement officers in Wisconsin.

The most recent case with direct relevance to the problems of selective law enforcement policy making is *Bruno v. Codd*. In *Bruno*, a group of twelve married women brought an action for declaratory and injunctive relief against the New York City Police Department, the Department of Probation, and the Family Court. With regard to the police, the women alleged that when New York City police officers were called to situations where a wife said she was being assaulted by her husband, the police uniformly refused to make an arrest, even if there was physical evidence of an assault.[82] Instead of making an arrest, police informed the wives they were unable to act because of departmental policy permitting arrests only for violation of protection orders issued by the Family Court.

The question that was presented to the court was whether such action was an abuse of police discretion. The concern was that the police had a virtually automatic rule that precluded arrest in any situation in which the victim was the wife of the assailant. The case was heard by both a trial and an appellate court. At the trial court, the police and the other defendants requested a summary judgment, which was denied. The case was appealed and a decision was handed down approximately one year later reversing the decision of the lower court to refuse to dismiss the complaint.[83]

In denying the motion for summary judgment, the lower court noted that it had the power to compel the police department defendants to perform the duty imposed upon them by law to exercise their discretion to arrest and to exercise it in a reasonable, non-arbitrary manner.[84] The court found that the police have a duty to protect battered wives that might even be considered a "special duty" of protection. The court determined that sufficient information was offered by the plaintiffs to present a factual question as to whether, by the pursuit of a discriminatory policy, the police failed to perform their duty of providing persons in the plaintiffs' positions with proper police service.

In the interim between dismissal for summary judgment and the appeal hearing, the police department entered into a consent decree with the plaintiffs. While the consent decree called for greater enforcement of the assault statutes, it did recognize that the police must have the ability to exercise some discretion in the enforcement of the criminal laws. One provision of the consent decree requires officers to make an arrest when there is reasonable cause to do so, but that provision applies only to felonies.[85]

An officer must have justification for failing to arrest when reasonable cause exists to believe a husband has committed a misdemeanor against his wife, and he may not consider as justification the fact that the victim is the wife of the misdemeanant, that she has no protection order, or that he thinks reconciliation is preferable. The reference to "justification" leaves the police with some discretion in deciding to arrest in the cases of misdemeanors and permits the development of some guidelines to determine arrest such as seriousness of injury and whether weapons were used.

The appellate court opinion in *Bruno v. Codd* is also important. While that court decided that the consent decree between the police and the plaintiffs mooted the initial complaint, a close reading of the appellate case indicates that had there not been such a consent decree, the court might not have been as willing as the trial court to limit the discretion of the New York City Police Department. The appellate court appeared to be disinclined to grant the relief sought because the issuance of an injunction would involve the court in what it viewed as such a broad invasion of executive authority as to risk the danger of unconstitutional encroachment.[86]

Because of the lack of case law interpreting the full enforcement statutes and the likelihood that the language of the statutes might provide more explicit direction to police officers, it is important to analyze a typical full enforcement statute. Such an analysis may serve to produce more accurate information on the institutional constraints on the police. As appears to be the case with modern American police, it may be that the spiritual genesis of American full enforcement laws came from England. Sir Leon Radzinowicz found in his study of early English criminal law that laws penalizing law enforcement officials for failure to arrest for specific crimes existed in early England. As an example, officers could be fined:

Twenty pounds for non-enforcement of the laws relating to hawkers and pedlars, bawdy houses, gaming-houses or disorderly houses not licensed for music and dancing.

Two pounds for failure to attend the prosecution of persons bound on recognizances to appear, failure to apprehend persons throwing fireworks, to execute the summons of a justice, to report persons keeping alehouses without licenses, or to enforce certain laws relating to the armed forces.

One pound for failure to assist the Officers of Customs and Excise, for failure to carry out the orders of a justice regarding vagrants or for neglecting to prosecute fraudulent bakers.

Three shillings for neglect of duty relating to drunkenness, idle and disorderly persons, rogues and vagabonds; and to road offenses, including the depositing of rubbish in the streets.

Five shillings for various instances of neglect in connection with the laws concerning the armed forces.

Two shillings in a great variety of cases: for the non-enforcement of laws against profanity; for not apprehending lunatics when required to do so by a justice; for refusal to search for gun-powder; the failure to apprehend drivers of vehicles who misbehaved themselves; for failure to return a list of persons required to repair highways, or to apprehend persons committing nuisances, or to execute a warrant for a justice.[87]

While the existence of these laws seem amusing to us today, they are instructive in several respects. First, by virtue of different fines for different offenses, the laws convey an expectation that law officers will exercise some discretion in choosing whether to enforce particular laws. Second, there is a clear judgment conveyed by the lawmakers that the enforcement of particular crimes has been determined to be more important than the enforcement of others, and not only do those crimes deserve use of enforcement resources, but failure to follow the lawmakers' judgment regarding the relative importance of the offenses will cause officers to suffer some economic deprivation. Of course one must be careful not to read too much into the underlying meaning and implication of these laws: they must be recognized as crude efforts to isolate and structure law enforcement discretion. Apparently, these statutes were not successful in controlling law enforcement officials and in fact appear to have been largely ignored. A fate, one might argue, substantially similar to that of the American full enforcement statutes. Nonetheless, let us turn now to the American full enforcement statutes.

IOWA FULL ENFORCEMENT STATUTE

1. 748.4 Duties. It shall be the duty of a peace
2. officer and his deputy, if any, throughout the
3. county, township, or municipality of which he is
4. such officer, or to which he is assigned or employed
5. under any mutual assistance arrangement or
6. intergovernmental agreement, to preserve the peace,
7. to ferret out crime, to *apprehend and arrest all*
8. *criminals*, and insofar as it is within his power, to
9. secure evidence of all crimes committed, and present
10. the same to the county attorney, grand jury or
11. magistrate and to file informations against all
12. persons whom he knows, or has reason to believe, to
13. have violated the laws of the state, and to perform
14. all other duties, civil or criminal, pertaining to
15. his office or enjoined upon him by law. Nothing
16. herein shall be deemed to curtail the powers and
17. duties otherwise granted to or imposed upon peace
18. officers.[88]

The Iowa full enforcement statute was enacted in 1909, although some earlier statutes did speak of the sheriff as the conservator of the peace.[89] A number of internal contradictions, gaps, and ambiguities arise in interpreting the statute. On a first reading, especially of the operative phrase "apprehend and arrest all criminals" it would seem that a peace officer does not have the authority to refuse to make an arrest of a "criminal." The word "shall" in line one mandates that peace officers "apprehend and arrest all criminals."[90]

One of the first questions is the construction that should be given to the term "criminal" as used in the full enforcement statute. Judge John F. Dillon, an eminent and often-quoted authority on municipal law, writing around the time many of the full enforcement laws went into effect, appeared to distinguish between types of crimes, and ostensibly of criminals, by virtue of the distinction he found in the requirements of arrests for felonies and misdemeanors. Dillon indicated that the clear trend of the cases was that "[a]n officer is justified in arresting without a warrant upon a reasonable suspicion of a felony," even though the person did not commit the felony within the officer's view, but an officer cannot arrest a person for a misdemeanor without a warrant "unless there is a breach of peace in his presence."[91] Thus, Dillon might conclude that a misdemeanant is not a "criminal" within the meaning of the full enforcement statute. Judge Dillon does express his understanding of the legal posture of police discretion in misdemeanor cases. There is clear evidence of an expectation of discretion in such arrests. According to Judge Dillon, a police officer had the authority

> to arrest upon view intoxicated persons while guilty of disorderly conduct or other persons violating the laws, and to detain them until they can be brought before a magistrate. If such officer releases an intoxicated person, whom he had arrested while conducting himself in a disorderly manner, upon on his promise to go directly home, he may lawfully retake him on his going into a bar-room before he is out of the officer's sight; and such arrest is justified whether it be regarded as a recaption of the original purpose, or as a new arrest for disorderly conduct still continuing.[92]

Apparently Judge Dillon, a proponent of the view strictly limiting the authority of municipal officers,[93] believed that the police were authorized to exercise discretion in the performance of their duties, particularly in making misdemeanor arrests, in spite of the specific admonishment of the full enforcement laws. Judge Dillon's views about the different treatment due misdemeanors become more important later in our discussion.

Problems of interpretation continue to arise when the statute is read as a whole. Arguments can be made that the mandates to (1) preserve the peace, (2) ferret out crime, (3) secure evidence of crime, and (4) perform all other duties, if strictly construed, conflict with the explicit requirement to "apprehend and arrest all criminals."

Consider the conflict between the phrases to "preserve the peace" and to "apprehend and arrest all criminals." Since the statute begins by requiring officers to "preserve the peace," that would arguably be the most important legislative objective.[94] In fact, that was virtually the only duty included in the original Iowa full enforcement statute, which was in existence for fifty-eight years.[95] But what does the phrase mean? The phrase would seem to convey a general principle regarding the duties of law enforcement officers. It can hardly be classified as a specific command to apprehend and arrest all offenders. The most logical meaning is that officers are to exercise discretion, and in some circumstances they have the authority to refuse to make an arrest if such action would not "preserve the peace."

Ironically, the latter interpretation is consistent with a position taken by Professor Allen. He apparently is of the opinion that if an officer is faced with a situation in which an arrest is warranted, yet such an arrest would cause a riot, the officer has the discretionary power not to make the arrest. To support his argument, he cites section 3.02 of the *Model Penal Code* and also concludes that his position is in accord with the common law.[96] Although that interpretation seems logical and appropriate, it does present some problems. There is specific language in the full enforcement statutes of eleven of the states he cites that calls for the police not only to "preserve the peace" but also to "suppress all riots, affrays and insurrections."[97] Thus, under a strict interpretation of those statutes that Professor Allen cites elsewhere,[98] his statement that the police may refuse to arrest a person if such arrest would cause a riot would seem to be in error. According to a strict reading of the full enforcement statutes, police are required *both* to arrest all criminals and to suppress all riots. But it is obvious that Professor Allen's liberal interpretation that the police are not to make arrests if to do so would cause a riot is a more plausible approach. Yet such an approach clearly requires the police to make a policy judgment in direct conflict with the explicit language of the statutes.

These are not the only problems that arise from a strict construction of the statutes. For example, the Iowa requirements to "ferret out crime" and "to secure evidence of all crimes committed" could, if read strictly, conflict with the duty to "apprehend and arrest all criminals." It is common for law enforcement agencies to be involved in investigations covering a long period of time during which information regarding law violations comes to the knowledge of the police.[99] Two important questions must be considered here. First, do the police have discretion to delay making an arrest? Second, do police have the discretion to forego arrest altogether in return for cooperation? For example, in an investigation of illegal drug trade, the police might obtain evidence showing minor criminal violations by relatively insignificant members of a drug ring but defer or totally forego their arrest to avoid alerting major suppliers and distributors who might escape. Immediate or even ultimate arrest of minor violators might defeat the main purpose—to arrest the major suppliers and distributors and to break up the ring. In other words, can the police decide to focus on major as opposed to minor violators? Removing major violators certainly seems conducive to the primary legislative goal of "preserving the peace."

Finally, a strict reading of the statute creates additional problems of viewing it as establishing only ministerial duties. In lines 13 and 14 there are statutory provisions calling for peace officers "to perform all other duties civil or criminal." In Iowa, peace officers have had over the years a number of other duties that clearly require the exercise of some discretion.[100] Therefore, we return to the question of how strictly the language of the statute should be construed. Canons of statutory construction would argue against treating explicit statutory language as irrelevant.[101] Furthermore, in many of the full enforcement statutes the mandate to "preserve the peace" is the first and arguably the most important law enforcement duty assigned.[102] Construing the phrase as irrelevant would be tantamount to asserting that the legislature did not intend to list "preserve the peace" as a duty of the police officer. This is undoubtedly a tortured construction.

The most reasonable interpretation of the phrase "preserve the peace" is that the legislature intended that the police do more than rigidly apply the laws. In the context of most of the statutes, the phrase clearly implies that the police are expected to exercise some discretion in the enforcement of the laws, and their paramount duty is not full enforcement but maintenance of order and prevention of crime. The language "to apprehend and arrest all criminals," when read alone, establishes a concrete duty to arrest all persons who have committed a crime. But when read in conjunction with the rest of the statute, it must be construed as a statement of policy, requiring the police to arrest when arrest serves the general purposes of the law—to preserve the peace. Sound policy should compel a reading of the statutes more as policy statements than as explicit legislative commands.

The idea that the statutes were intended to be policy statements is reinforced when one reviews the status of law enforcement nationwide at the time when those statutes were promulgated. Law enforcement by sheriffs was lax. One writer, attempting to analyze the office of the sheriff in Iowa in the early 1900s, believes that the statute was made specific to encourage sheriffs to become more active in law enforcement than they had been in the past.[103] Because sheriffs were assigned many other duties that were more financially rewarding than law enforcement, there was little interest among the sheriffs in becoming active law enforcement officers.[104] The same objective, to encourage sheriffs to become more active in law enforcement, seems to have existed in Ohio. An Ohio full enforcement statute provided that:

> Each sheriff shall preserve the public peace and cause all persons guilty of breach thereof, within his knowledge or view, to enter into recognizance with sureties to keep peace and to appear at the succeeding term of the common pleas court of the proper county and commit them to jail in case of refusal.[105]

In spite of this ''full enforcement'' provision, there was a general attitude among the Ohio sheriffs that this duty could be avoided, and apparently there were ''few successful prosecutions'' of sheriffs who failed to fully enforce the law.[106] In fact, police scholars have found that sheriffs in the United States at that time generally considered the law enforcement aspects of their jobs to be very unimportant and few took them seriously.[107]

A different but similar case can also be made in considering those full enforcement statutes that are directed primarily toward local police departments. As we have seen, many of those ''full enforcement'' statutes were promulgated around the same time that control of the police and many other municipal functions were being returned to the local communities. Consequently, it seems appropriate to view the grants of power returning control of the police to the local communities (of which the full enforcement statutes were frequently part) primarily as expressions of the general duties and responsibilities of the police. The statutes were enacted to guide local communities in further refining and developing the proper role of the police. As the previous analysis suggests, there is difficulty in interpreting the statutes as anything more than policy statements.

If such statutes were to be considered otherwise, it would be impossible to give them full effect. Thus, to the extent that the full enforcement clauses are or have ever been important in the consideration of the role of the police in the United States, they have to be considered primarily as an aspect of general policy statements providing guidance to law enforcement officials. In fact, one can argue that the general nature of those policy statements conveys an implicit understanding of the need for police to be able to exercise some discretion in carrying out their law enforcement duties.

SEPARATION OF POWERS

The preceding analysis shows the police to be a peculiar organization that does not fit neatly into any particular category of government agency. Although many municipal police officers are hired according to state guidelines,[108] they enforce state law and their duties are prescribed by the state legislature,[109] yet they are selected, funded, and supervised by municipal governments.[110] While the involvement of so many different institutions and levels of government would seem to anticipate a closely supervised ministerial agency, the practical result is a truly independent agency in most parts of this country. Thus, even if one were to conclude that full enforcement statutes implicitly recognize this unusual situation and expect discretion to be exercised by the police, there are still other questions concerning the legality of law enforcement policy making. Professor Allen has argued that "substantive rulemaking flies in the face not only of the language of the full enforcement statutes, but also the concept of government that the statutes manifest: the principle of separation of powers."[111]

At least two questions need to be addressed. The first one, a bit different from what Professor Allen suggests, is whether the full enforcement statutes, which according to my view contemplate discretion, violate state separation of powers provisions. Second, if I am incorrect in my analysis that the full enforcement statutes contemplate discretion, then the question becomes whether any statute authorizing or contemplating the exercise of police discretion is violative of state separation of powers principles. The principles of separation of powers are clearly enunciated in the federal and most state constitutions.[112] Typical of state constitution separation of powers provisions is the language found in the Iowa Constitution.

> The powers of the government of Iowa shall be divided into three separate departments—the Legislative, the Executive, and the Judicial: and no person charged with the exercise of power properly belonging to one of these departments shall exercise any function appertaining to either of the others, except in cases hereinafter expressly directed or permitted.[113]

The primary difference between federal and state constitutions is that the latter frequently tend to be more explicit in expressing the theory that one branch should not exercise the power of another.[114] Those who criticize the development of formal law enforcement rules have essentially taken the position that the development of such rules is, in effect, a usurpation of the legislative function by the executive branch and therefore a constitutional violation.[115]

As the Constitution drafters realized, the essence of democratic government mandates that separation of powers be maintained.[116] The question is, however, whether the separation of powers doctrine requires rigid adherence or whether it is a political doctrine that expresses an ideal that government should seek to achieve. In other words, does it express specific or general limitations on government? Other constitutional provisions and American history seem to indicate it is the latter rather than the former.

For example, drafters of the U.S. Constitution, while expressing the separation of powers principles in that document, did not rigidly adhere to it throughout their work. The Constitution clearly requires the executive branch to review and monitor some of the work of other branches and vice versa. The President has the power "to grant reprieves and pardons for offenses"[117] made crimes by the U.S. Congress, negotiate treaties,[118] and in extraordinary cases convene the Congress.[119] The U.S. Congress, on the other hand, has the power to disapprove certain presidential appointments,[120] to remove executive officers through the impeachment process,[121] and to override presidential vetoes.[122] What we have come to recognize in America is that no single branch of government possesses exclusive authority to act in any one area.

The framers of the U.S. Constitution apparently did not view the separation of powers doctrine as rigid and inflexible. They clearly intended, and in fact provided for, overlapping powers. They were persons with considerable practical political experience. Their primary goal in allocating power and authority was to avoid the location of too much power in any one branch of government.[123]

An essay from the *Federalist Papers* clearly states the pragmatic principles underlying their view of separation of powers. *The Federalist no. 47* essentially reinterprets Baron de Montesquieu's position that "There can be no liberty where the legislative and executive powers are united in the same person,"[124] by adding:

> he [Montesquieu] did not mean that these departments ought to have no partial agency in, or no control over, the acts of each other. His meaning as his own words import and still more conclusively as illustrated by the example in his eye can amount to no more than this that where the power of one department is exercised by the same hands which possess the whole power of another department the fundamental principles of a free Constitution are subverted.[125]

Obviously the drafters of the U.S. Constitution were much more concerned than Montesquieu with the practical impact of the doctrine of separation of powers on the normal operation of government. There was expected to be some overlapping of power in the functioning of government.

The U.S. Constitution and most state constitutions have recognized the inherent difficulty of attempting to classify powers rigidly as being legislative, executive, or judicial. The courts, rather than trying to divide the powers sharply, have tended to stress that the differences are frequently those of degree rather than kind. For example, Justice Holmes, in his dissenting opinion in *Springer v. Philippine Islands*, stated:

> great ordinances of the Constitution do not establish and divide fields of black and white. Even the more specific of them are found to terminate in a penumbra shading gradually from one extreme to the other. . . . It does not seem to need argument that however we may disguise it by veiling words we do not and cannot carry out the distinction between legislative and executive action with mathematical precision and divide the branches into water-tight compartments which I am far from believing it is, or that the Constitution requires.[126]

More recently Justice Jackson reaffirmed Justice Holmes' position. In *Youngstown Sheet and Tube Company v. Sawyer*, Justice Jackson states in a concurring opinion: "While the constitution diffuses power the better to secure liberty, it also contemplates that practice will integrate dispersed powers into a workable government. It enjoins upon its branches separateness but interdependence, autonomy but reciprocity."[127] The primary concern underlying the doctrine of separation of powers at the federal level is that no single branch of government wield excessive power, not that the executive exercise no legislative power or vice versa.

The approach to separation of powers at the state level was somewhat different. In what could be characterized as an anomalous approach, state constitutions, while frequently tending to be more explicit in stating the doctrine, were less inclined to follow it.[128] The separation of powers provisions, although expressed formally, were not given great deference when the drafters came to the business of distributing power.[129] Particularly significant is the fact that in early state constitutions the legislatures were given substantial amounts of executive and administrative control. As the court in *People v. Chase* said, "We are not unmindful of the well settled rule that there are many cases in which ministerial officers exercise quasi-judicial powers or discretions and yet the laws conferring such powers are held to be no violation of the constitutional provision under consideration."[130]

The vesting in the legislative bodies of substantial power other than to make laws was largely a reaction to the excessive power exercised by colonial administrators.[131] Thus, as far as the principle of separation of powers is concerned, there was a clear contradiction in most state constitutions. While recognizing and expressing the doctrine of separation of powers, many constitutions clearly established the legislature as the most powerful branch of the government.

However, over the long term, this distribution of power did not result in the evolution of the legislature as the dominant policymaker in state government.[132] As we will see in the next section, the practical needs of modern society have required that the legislature and the executive share policy making to ensure the efficient operation of government. Consequently, many constitutions were amended as there developed "a strong centralizing tendency in economic and political life" which resulted in greater focus on the role of the state executives.[133] As a general proposition, the pressing need for the sharing of executive and legislative authority has been embraced and in fact welcomed.[134] This development has caused one writer to state that "the history of separation of powers doctrine has apparently been one of rapid retreat, if not rout."[135]

The historical evolution of the separation of powers doctrine sketched above clearly supports the concept of dividing policy-making power among the branches of government. It is clear, as recognized by James Madison, that there was a danger inherent in vesting absolute policy-making power in one branch of government.[136] Thus, the idea that the state legislature has absolute power in controlling the administration of the criminal laws is contrary to the normal operation of federal and state government. In conclusion, it seems that Professor Allen's arguments that substantive rule making is inconsistent with separation of powers ignores three things: (1) the uncertain boundary between substance and procedure, (2) the necessity of administrative discretion to carry out any complex statute, and (3) the courts' long recognition of the impossibility of legislative prescience and foresight. This will be reinforced in the next section when we analyze the principle of delegation of powers and how it fits into the separation of powers concept.

DELEGATION OF POWER

The separation of powers doctrine is given greater meaning by a close look at the principle of delegation of power. We have found in the United States that the delegation of power to executive and administrative agencies is absolutely essential to the operation of government.[137] Therefore, it is important to gain a general understanding of that principle and how it has evolved on both the federal and state levels. More specifically, the task is to determine whether law enforcement policy making by the police is permissible as a matter of federal and state constitutional law.

Again we see a different approach taken by our two main protagonists. Professor Davis asserts there is substantial support for the proposition that the police can engage in rule making. Essentially, his position is that administrative agency officials are expected to amass a special expertise in their work and to use that expertise by developing rules and standards to control the activities of their subordinates. He further maintains that courts have generally given deference to the exercise of this expertise and that the same deference should be given to police executives. According to Davis, government agencies require a broad mandate to enable them to perform their duties, and this mandate necessarily includes the authority to develop rules.[138]

Professor Allen, on the other hand, sees a much more limited scope for delegated power. Because of the penal nature of the criminal law, Allen contends that delegation of policy-making power to police agencies is substantially limited. Furthermore, he claims that the federal cases cited by Professor Davis have very little support on the state level. Finally, Allen says that delegation of legislative power concerning criminal law has been permitted on the state level only in very limited and carefully defined circumstances—and the exercise of law enforcement policy making would not fall within those limitations.[139]

Largely because of the ever-increasing complexity of our society, the principle of delegation of power has been constantly evolving. Initially, the United States Supreme Court had a very limited view of the proper boundaries of delegated power, as evident in cases like *Field v. Clark*.[140] It quickly became clear, however, that limiting the executive function solely to fact finding hampered administrators in carrying out the required work of government; consequently, Congress increased the responsibility of administrative agencies, and the courts permitted broader delegation of legislative power.

The Supreme Court case of *Wayman v. Southard*[141] signaled the beginning of this trend. In *Wayman*, Chief Justice John Marshall made it clear that the Congress had the power to delegate powers that were not strictly and exclusively legislative. But it was eighty-five years before there was elaboration of how far Congress might go. In *United States v. Grimaud*,[142] the Supreme Court reviewed a statute establishing forest reservations on public lands.[143] The statute gave the Secretary of Agriculture power to make rules to regulate the use and occupancy of reservations and stipulated that violators of the rules promulgated by the Secretary were subject to criminal sanctions. The Supreme Court held this grant of power was a proper delegation of legislative power.

The Court reasoned that the legislature was the body making the acts criminal and establishing the penalty; the Secretary was merely determining the facts of a given situation and applying the law to them.[144] In short, we see that at a very early stage the Supreme Court established that it is within the legislature's power to delegate to the executive branch the authority to make rules to carry out the legislative purpose of a statute. In fact, it might be noted that *Field v. Clark* and the other early Supreme Court delegation cases were unrealistic descriptions of the administrative process even at that time. For example, to look at the foreign affairs function delegated expressly to the president in the nineteenth century as being merely mechanical would be misleading no matter how the court describes that function.

The federal courts have increasingly upheld both explicit and implicit granting of power and authority by Congress to administrative agencies.[145] In fact, the situation may be as one scholar suggests: "Every statute is a delegation of lawmaking power to the agency appointed to enforce it."[146] It is this evolution of power that Professor Davis looks to for support of his theory.[147]

FEDERAL DELEGATION OF POWER

Professor Davis cites the case of *Skidmore v. Swift*[148] as establishing the proposition that agency heads are expected to develop a special expertise in their work. *Skidmore* was a case brought under the Fair Labor Standards Act.[149] An important issue in *Skidmore* was the degree of deference courts should accord to the Administrator of the Wage and Hour Division in the interpretation of the Act. The issue arose because there was no statute or previous case that stipulated what, if any, deference courts should give to the Administrator's findings.[150] The Supreme Court held that:

> [T]he Administrator's policies are made in pursuance of official duty, based upon more specialized experience and broader investigations and information than is likely to come to a judge in a particular case. . . . We consider that the rulings, interpretations and opinions of the Administrator under this Act, while not controlling on the courts by reason of their authority, do constitute a body of experience and informed judgment to which courts and litigants may properly resort for guidance.[151]

According to Davis, the recognition by the Supreme Court of specialized experience possessed by administrators is significant and has direct relevance to the work of law enforcement officers.[152] The fact that law enforcement work frequently requires the ability to deal with complex and difficult personal and societal problems would seem to support Davis' view. The diversity of situations to which law enforcement agencies respond requires that the police develop a wide variety of strategies and tactics to ensure that public safety is maintained, while individual rights are not violated. If this work is done poorly or improperly, it can have substantial repercussions on the body politic. It seems beyond argument that law enforcement officers similar to those of the Wage and Hour Division in *Skidmore v. Swift* are expected to develop an understanding of likely problems in their areas of work.[153]

Of course, there is a substantial difference between developing expertise in an area and being permitted to use that expertise to produce and put into effect enforcement strategies. Nonetheless, the Supreme Court of the United States, according to Professor Davis, has taken the next step and held that it is entirely proper for the courts in appropriate circumstances to defer to the expertise of agency heads in developing enforcement strategies. He argues that *Moog Industries v. FTC* recognizes the complex policy-making functions that many administrative agencies face.[154]

In *Moog*, the Court addressed the issue of whether the court of appeals could postpone a valid cease and desist order of the Federal Trade Commission. Moog Industries claimed the order unfairly discriminated against it in that it "would suffer serious financial loss if prohibited from engaging in pricing practices open to its competitors,"[155] since similar orders had not been entered against those competitors. The Supreme Court held that the Federal Trade Commission alone was empowered to develop the enforcement policy best calculated to achieve the ends contemplated by Congress. In essence, the Court found that in formulating enforcement policy, an administrative "agency is called upon to exercise its specialized, experienced judgment."[156] According to Allen, the important fact for the court was that there was no allegation that the FTC was unprepared to move against other violators of the statute, and thus the issue of selective enforcement was not squarely before the court.[157]

While Professor Allen may be technically accurate in that the issue of selective enforcement was not directly before the court, his interpretation of *Moog* minimizes the language of the opinion indicating the breadth of discretion properly delegated to the Federal Trade Commission to formulate enforcement policies. According to the Court,

> Only the Commission, for example, is competent to make an initial determination as to whether and to what extent there is a relevant "industry" within which the particular respondent competes and whether or not the nature of that competition is such as to indicate identical treatment of the entire industry by an enforcement agency. Moreover, although an allegedly illegal practice may appear to be operative throughout an industry, whether such appearances reflect fact and whether all firms in the industry should be dealt with in a single proceeding or should receive individualized treatment are questions that call for discretionary determination by the administrative agency.[158]

The development of case law since *Moog* seems to rely on and reinforce the rule that administrative agencies have discretion to determine against whom they will enforce the laws—discretion that goes beyond the mere allocation of resources. Since *Moog*, the United States Supreme Court has continued to address the issue of the establishment of enforcement policy by administrative agencies.

In *FTC v. Universal-Rundle Corporation*, the Commission had previously found the corporation to have violated section II of the Clayton Act by discriminating in price between customers and had issued a cease and desist order prohibiting that practice. The respondent petitioned the Commission to stay its cease and desist order pending investigation of alleged industry-wide discount practices, claiming that enforcement against it alone would cause it substantial financial injury. After the FTC denied the petition, respondent instituted review proceedings in the Court of Appeals for the Seventh Circuit. The court of appeals, finding the Commission's denial of the stay to have been a "patent abuse of discretion" in light of respondent's evidentiary offering, set aside the Commission's order. The court of appeals also instructed the Commission to conduct an investigation to determine whether industry-wide proceedings might not be more appropriate than proceeding solely against the respondent.[159]

On appeal, the Supreme Court reversed the court of appeals finding of "patent abuse of discretion" and specifically held that the Commission's denial of respondent's petition was appropriate because the respondent's evidence did not prove that the practices of the respondent's competitors had an anti-competitive effect. More significantly for this analysis, the Court stated

> that even if a petitioner succeeded in demonstrating to the Commission that all of its competitors were engaging in illegal price-discrimination practices identical to its own, and that enforcement of a cease-and-desist order might cause it substantial financial injury, the Commission would not necessarily be obliged to withhold enforcement of the order. As we stated in *Moog Industries* . . . "the Commission alone is empowered to develop that enforcement policy best calculated to achieve the ends contemplated by Congress and to allocate its available funds and personnel in such a way as to execute its policy efficiently and economically."[160]

The principle of deference to agency enforcement policy was also affirmed in the case of *Butz v. Glover Livestock Commission Co.* In *Butz*, the Court of Appeals for the Eighth Circuit, after finding that the Judicial Officer of the Department of Agriculture had improperly issued a cease and desist order against respondent for willful violation of the Packers and Stockyards Act, set aside the Department's twenty-day suspension of respondent's registration under the Act.[161] According to the court of appeals, the suspension order was "unconscionable" because the resulting sanction was too severe and the issuance of the suspension order, in respondent's case, was contrary to a policy of "achiev[ing] . . . uniformity of sanctions for similar violations."[162]

The United States Supreme Court granted *certiorari* and found that the proper standard of judicial review of the Department's suspension order must accord with the "fundamental principle . . . that where Congress has entrusted an administrative agency with the responsibility of selecting the means of achieving the statutory policy the relation of remedy to policy is peculiarly a matter for administrative competence."[163] Following that standard, the Supreme Court reversed the decision of the court of appeals, holding that, because the Department's suspension order was not "unwarranted in law" or "without justification in fact," the Department had full authority to issue the suspension order.[164]

Moog and its progeny support the proposition that enforcement agencies are expected to develop enforcement policy. The important question is whether the discretion delegated to the agency is abused. Justice Brennan crystallizes this concern in his dissenting opinion in

McGautha v. California. Justice Brennan asserts that in many instances the focus of Congress has been "much less upon the definition of precise standards than on the creation of other means adequate to assure that policy is set in accordance with congressional desires and that individuals are treated according to uniform principles rather than administrative whim."[165] The issue, therefore, is not over whether agencies should be delegated the power to make rules, but rather whether the agency-developed rules are consistent with legislative policy and are uniformly applied.

According to Justice Brennan, in judicially determining the propriety of delegation of rule-making authority, the point is not whether an intelligible legislative policy was or was not correctly inferred from the state. Rather, such a policy, once expressly articulated, not only serves to guide subsequent administrative and judicial action *but also provides a basis upon which the legislature may determine whether power is being exercised in accordance with its will.*

The concern expressed by Justice Brennan over the uniformity and fairness of administrative rule-making procedures is evident in cases such as *Morton v. Ruiz*. In *Morton*, the Bureau of Indian Affairs (BIA) denied respondent general assistance benefits because a provision in the BIA manual limited eligibility to Indians living "on reservations."[166] After finding that the congressional appropriation was intended to cover welfare services "at least to those Indians residing 'on or near' the reservation" (respondent lived fifteen miles from an Indian reservation), the Supreme Court faced the issue of whether the Secretary of the BIA had followed proper procedures in creating the requirements that limited welfare payments to Indians who lived directly on the reservation.

Before resolving the issue, the Court stated that "[i]n the area of Indian Affairs, the Executive has long been empowered to promulgate rules and policies, and the power has been given explicitly to the Secretary and his delegates."[167] Even after recognizing this broad delegation of power, however, the Court did not give effect to the eligibility requirement because the Secretary, in establishing the eligibility requirements, had not employed procedures that gave adequate notice to the public. Finding that the Administrative Procedure Act and the BIA manual required publication of all substantive rules adopted by the BIA that affected individual rights and obligations, the Court held that "the conscious choice of the Secretary not to treat this extremely significant eligibility requirement, affecting rights of needy Indians, as a legislative-type rule, renders it ineffective so far as extinguishing rights of those otherwise within the class of beneficiaries contemplated by Congress is concerned."[168] In *United States v. Caceres*, the Supreme Court apparently limited the rule established in *Morton*. In *Caceres*, it was acknowledged that the Internal Revenue Service had violated its own electronic monitoring of face-to-face conversations. The violation had resulted in the tape recording of the respondent attempting to bribe an IRS agent. The Court held that the violation of the regulation did not require that tape recordings be suppressed because none of the respondent's rights had been violated.[169] The Court ruled *inter alia* that the violation of the regulation by the IRS did not implicate the due process provisions of the Constitution because the respondent, though "prejudiced in the sense that he would be better off if all monitoring had been postponed until after the Deputy Assistant Attorney General's approval was obtained," had not "reasonably relied" on the IRS regulation.[170] The basic rule established by *Morton*, however, is still followed by the courts of appeal.[171]

As in *McGautha*, the Court was primarily concerned that the power delegated to administrative agencies not be abused. While the exercise of substantive rule-making authority is expressly accepted, the delegation of powers doctrine is available to invalidate either substantive or procedural acts of the agency that are unfair or arbitrary.

These cases strongly support the arguments that administrative agencies are expected to develop expertise in their fields and, absent a clear abuse of discretion, such expertise is to be deferred to by the courts. As stated in *Morton*, the power of a federal administrative agency "necessarily requires the formulation of policy and the making of rules to fill any gap left implicitly or explicitly by Congress."[172]

The United States Supreme Court decisions are clear regarding the permissibility of delegating rule-making power to administrative agencies. The range of discretion needed to develop selective enforcement policies would seem to fall within the powers exercised by agencies on the federal level. However, as Professor Allen points out, "our concern is with delegation in the states."[173] It is his judgment that the delegation of powers doctrine has not been accorded the broad approval in the states that it has received in the federal system. Therefore, it is necessary to examine the development of the delegation of powers doctrine at the state level to determine whether the judicial approach toward rule making is sufficiently different at the state level to preclude the development of law enforcement policy.

STATE DELEGATION OF POWER

Delegation in Mississippi

Professor Allen makes the point that the scope of delegation of power is substantially different at the state level.[174] He begins his discussion of state delegation by referring to a case about which he says that, although it "does not state the majority position in the United States . . . there is significant support for [its] old fashioned view."[175] In *Howell v. Mississippi*,[176] the Mississippi Supreme Court reviewed a Uniform Controlled Substances Act passed by the state legislature. The Act classified controlled substances into five schedules but gave power to the state board of health to add, delete, or reschedule any substances subject to specific guidelines provided in the statute.[177] The board rescheduled amphetamines from schedule III to schedule II, and the effect of the change was to increase the minimum penalty for possession of amphetamines from one to two years. A defendant who was convicted of unlawful possession of amphetamines and sentenced to two years in prison argued on appeal that the statute that authorized the board to reschedule controlled substances was an unconstitutional delegation of power. The Mississippi Supreme Court agreed with the defendant and held "that the authority to define crimes and fix the punishment therefore is vested exclusively in the legislature, and it may not delegate that power either expressly or by implication."[178]

As Professor Allen says, *Howell* is an important case; however, there is considerable difficulty in analogizing it to law enforcement policy making. The goal in developing law enforcement rules is not to make conduct criminal which presently is not, nor is it to increase the penalties provided by criminal statutes, as was the allegation in *Howell*. *Howell* is a case involving substantive rule making that is not at issue in developing law enforcement rules.

In developing rules to control police arrest decisions, the goal is to ensure uniform and fair application of the criminal law—in other words, to ensure that police conduct in law enforcement is not arbitrary and capricious. The goal of criminal law enforcement policy making is not to abrogate or add to the penalties set by the legislature but to define more accurately the circumstances in which the law can realistically be enforced and to enforce all laws when it is possible in the manner in which the legislature expected such laws to be enforced.

Howell presents the situation in which the state board of health action did result in an increase in penalty. Furthermore, the action of the board was essentially the equivalent of reclassification of a crime from a misdemeanor to a felony.[179] While the court in *Howell* did not address the upgrading of the crime, the point is by no means inconsequential. Felonies are major crimes to which society attaches much greater significance, both morally and legally.[180] Thus, courts are likely to scrutinize more closely crimes that are classified (or reclassified) as felonies than they scrutinize crimes classified as misdemeanors. When agency action results in an increase in penalty for a law violation, the question of whether agencies have invaded the province of the legislature takes on much greater significance. Increasing penalties squarely raises the question of there being an inappropriate tampering with the explicit policy decisions of the legislature.

There are additional points of departure between police rule making and reclassification of crimes. From the standpoint of the individual (potential defendant), there is a practical difference. In the *Howell* type of case an individual defendant can complain about the fact that the administrative agency, not the legislature, has in essence upped the ante, but, absent clear violations of equal protection or due process[181] provisions, that same person cannot complain about decisions that result in the underenforcement of the law.

There are also differences from an institutional standpoint. There is a substantial difference between administrators increasing penalties for crimes and administrators deciding how and when laws are intended to be enforced. An inherent qualitative difference exists between changing the statute by increasing penalties, on the one hand, and trying to determine the circumstances in which the legislature expects a statute to be enforced on the other. The expectation of discretion in choosing an enforcement policy is also supported by a "necessity" argument which recognizes the practical problems faced in law enforcement decision making. By contrast, the exercise of discretion in *Howell* was not essential to the proper functioning of any governmental activity.

No one except the legislature can initially define crimes. But at the same time, many agencies of government and even the general public have an amplifying role to play in deciding the impact of the criminal laws. The role of the general public is seen in the expectation that grand juries are to serve as a shield to prosecutorial discretion,[182] and petit juries can nullify[183] the effect of the criminal law in some circumstances. What happened in *Howell* is quite different from this normal amplifying function.

The goal of criminal law enforcement policy making is to set standards to determine fairly and equitably within statutory limits when violators should be arrested. There is a substantial difference between this goal and what was done in *Howell.*[184] However, law enforcement policy making, as opposed to "rescheduling" controlled substances, does not increase the severity of crimes nor does it have any effect on the ability of the courts to assess penalties as specifically provided for by the state legislatures.

The closest that *Howell* comes to the real crux of criminal law enforcement policy making is to suggest a situation in which an agency might reschedule controlled substances downward, reducing the penalty and in essence overriding the original legislative directive. Such an analogy seems to be false because, again, the proper focus of law enforcement policy making is to determine circumstances in which laws can be enforced according to the intention of the legislature, and it has no impact on the penalty of those ultimately found guilty of violating criminal statutes.

Even if a parallel does, in fact, exist between *Howell* and law enforcement policy making, an important question remains as to whether "there is significant support for *Howell*'s old fashioned view."[185] Since the *Howell* decision, the clear consensus of both federal and state courts that have addressed the issue of whether a legislature may delegate to an agency the power to reschedule controlled substances has been that such delegation is permissible.[186] The significance of *Howell* must be questioned. In fact, many courts have permitted administrative agencies much broader powers than are necessary to validate police rule making.[187]

As Professor Allen admits, *Howell* does not express the majority position of the states on the delegation question.[188] A substantial number of state courts have determined that legislatures may delegate some power to administrative agencies to promulgate rules concerning the substantive criminal law.[189] However, Professor Allen's research has led him to conclude that such criminal law rule making has been permitted only in very narrow circumstances. According to him, it is permitted only when the subject matter requires particular skills or expertise that could not be demanded of the legislature or when the development of rules would require the legislature "to spend vast amounts of time on relatively inconsequential matters."[190] He concludes that developing criminal law enforcement policy would fall into neither category and thus would not be permitted.[191]

This conclusion cannot withstand close scrutiny. First, it is based on the assumption that law enforcement work does not require special skills or technical expertise. That assumption is questionable in light of the myriad duties modern police are called upon to perform and the highly specialized training they receive in most states.[192] In fact, one might argue that the legislatures have explicitly recognized the technical nature of modern police work by the tasks they have assigned to the police and by requiring that law enforcement officers receive specialized training before they undertake those tasks. Recently, there has been a significant increase nationwide in legislatively mandated training for law enforcement officers. For example, in Iowa there is an attempt to provide not only skills training but also work in sociology, psychology, and criminal law to aid officers in resolving the problems encountered in their work.[193] Legislatively mandated police training of this character clearly indicates an awareness that law enforcement requires considerable expertise.

Even Professor Allen implicitly admits that police officials are expected to have some technical expertise: how else would they engage in the resource allocation decisions he condones?[194] In fact, if one takes it to its ultimate point, the decision to allocate personnel to enforce public intoxication laws rather than traffic laws results in at least partial abrogation of traffic laws. Decisions as to the allocation of personnel involve thoughtful and knowledgeable reflection of community goals, police capabilities, and criminal law. The ability to engage in these activities clearly requires a highly sophisticated analysis of political, legal, and social factors. This process may not involve the exceedingly complex analysis required to determine the dangers of pesticides, for example; yet it clearly requires more than rigid adherence to the specific language of criminal law.

Unfortunately, Professor Allen does not fully develop what he regards as the second exception to the prohibition against rule making: that legislatures will permit rule making rather than spend vast amounts of time on relatively minor matters. He merely says it is not applicable to police work.[195] A closer look is required. Felonies can certainly be classified as matters that deserve close legislative attention, but minor or low-visibility crimes arguably present a different situation. In creating two major categories of crimes, felonies and misdemeanors, state legislatures have recognized that there are different levels of concern with criminal conduct, that some violations of the criminal law are less significant than others, and that the enforcement of some crimes deserves more attention than that of others. Most major crimes present the ''strongest force that we permit official agencies to bring to bear on individuals,''[196] but it is doubtful that minor crimes such as public intoxication and simple assault have the same degree of importance to society.[197]

Nonetheless, it is important that enforcement strategies on minor criminal violations be developed. While the crimes are ''inconsequential,'' in the sense that violations are likely to have a less significant effect on the basic moral structure of society, it is important to monitor them for at least two reasons. First, minor crimes require a substantial amount of law enforcement officers' time. It has been documented that more than one-half of the time officers spend enforcing the law is spent on these minor or low-visibility crimes.[198] Second, these crimes constitute such a large part of police work that there is a heightened need for uniformity in enforcement policy because lack of uniformity, generally perceived as such by the public, endangers crucial public support for law enforcement.[199] The conclusion one must draw with regard to these crimes is that the legislature has criminalized such conduct and stopped there. The ''emphatic denunciation''[200] of the community is absent and these minor crimes are designed primarily as ''order maintenance'' crimes.[201] They are not expected to be fully enforced but to be enforced when their violation conflicts with the general goal of order maintenance. Enforcement, especially of low-visibility crimes, requires an interpretation by the police of what the legislature intended for the police to do. Clearly, the legislature does not have the time to articulate fully the situations in which laws against low-visibility offenses or minor crimes should be enforced. It is abundantly clear that legislatures would generally prefer not to have to spend vast amounts of time detailing when a person should be arrested for public intoxication or whether an arrest for assault should be made in every case where a person is slapped. The police are expected to keep order and those offenses are designed to aid the police in that job.

Professor Allen's error is that, while he recognizes that some governmental matters—such as the task of overseeing sewers and running airports—can be delegated to an agency, he fails to see that similar parts of criminal justice administration are likewise delegable.[202] If one closely scrutinizes the criminal laws, one finds that low-visibility crimes are closer to the so-called trivial and mundane acts he recognizes as appropriately regulated through delegated power than to major crimes. For example, I seriously doubt that a person arrested for public intoxication would be viewed as more of a criminal than Professor Allen's example of one who "disposes of his garbage improperly or fails to close his bar on time."[203] The administrative or regulatory crimes distinguished by Professor Allen are very much akin to low-visibility crimes, and clearly in both the emphatic denunciation of the community is absent.[204] As Professor Allen says, "there is more to the criminal process than mere labeling" and, by looking beyond the labels, one discovers a class of crimes that meets the requirements he outlines for a constitutionally permissible delegation of power.[205]

Delegation in Iowa

The thrust of *Howell* is limited and arguably means only that a state legislature cannot delegate power to a state agency to reclassify drugs if such reclassification would result in an increase in penalty.[206] While Professor Allen points out that *Howell* is not illustrative of the approach most states take toward the question of delegation, he does cite eight cases from six states as significant support for the proposition established by *Howell*.[207]

Professor Allen concedes that there are some states that do not fit within his model.[208] It seems appropriate, therefore, in light of the unsettled nature of state law on this subject, to review the development of the law in one of the states that admittedly does not fit Professor Allen's thesis.

One state he characterizes as not fitting within his model is Iowa. When one looks at the development of the delegation doctrine in Iowa, one finds as expected that a strong case can be made that a statute requiring law enforcement policy making would be constitutionally permissible. Analysis of Iowa case law indicates that the Iowa Supreme Court's position on delegation has evolved through at least four stages, each a bit more expansive in delegating power to administrative agencies.[209] The first stage in Iowa is commonly characterized as the "finding of facts" period.[210] The approach during this period is exemplified by two cases: *Hubbell v. Higgins* and *Goodlove v. Logan*.[211] In *Hubbell*, the Iowa Supreme Court upheld a statute authorizing a hotel inspector to use his discretion to determine whether hotels had "approved fireproof construction" and particular "sanitary conditions."[212] According to the Iowa Supreme Court, the delegation of this power was permissible because the law did not permit the inspector to act arbitrarily but rather authorized him to find whether the facts warranted application of the statute. In *Hubbell*, there was an implicit understanding that some decisions as to whether a law was violated will of necessity be vested in an administrator—but those decisions must be limited.

The importance of placing limits on discretionary powers of administrators was reinforced in *Goodlove v. Logan*. In that case, the Iowa Supreme Court invalidated a statute permitting the state highway commission to promulgate rules for highway safety. Under the statute, the highway commission had enacted a rule that made it illegal to stop a car upon a paved highway except in particular circumstances.[213] The court held that the legislature had exceeded its authority by delegating power to the highway commission to enact rules and regulations concerning the use of highways. In so holding, the court stated that any statute that delegated to an agency the power to determine "whether there shall be any law and second what the law shall be" would exceed the scope of legislative powers.[214] Neither *Hubbell*, *Goodlove*, nor any other case during that period defined the boundaries of the powers that could be delegated.

The second or "filling-up-the-details," period was a step in that direction.[215] The Iowa Supreme Court began to concentrate on the distinctions between legislative power and a "subsidiary power to fill up the details" of a general statute to effectuate legislative policy. The second period is exemplified by *State v. Manning*. In *Manning*, the Iowa Supreme Court reviewed the power granted to the state budget director to approve all money transfers sought by municipal officers. The allegation was made that the State Budget Act was an unconstitutional delegation of power because "it sets up no standard of conduct to guide the budget director in passing judgment . . . [on] the transfer of funds."[216] The Iowa Supreme Court held, however, that the Act was valid because it was permissible for the legislature to delegate to an agency the authority "to work out the details of administering the will of the legislature as expressed by the statute."[217] This broad range of delegation was held to be permissible because the legislature was compelled to discover new means of delegation due to the increasing "complexities of business, governmental and economic existence."[218]

There was some concern over the wide range of choice permitted under the "filling-up-the-details" approach, and courts began looking for more legislative guidance in statutes that delegate power to administrative agencies. In most cases, the search was for express guidelines or standards to direct administrators in the exercise of delegated authority.[219] The Iowa Supreme Court expressed some concern about standards in *Manning*,[220] but it was not until *State v. Van Trump*[221] that this concern became predominant.

State v. Van Trump signals the beginning of the "standards" stage. In *Van Trump*, the court analyzed "the nature of the authority" delegated under a statute that authorized the Iowa conservation commission to adopt rules and regulations "for the proper use and conservation of Iowa resources."[222] The violations of the commission's rules and regulations were to be penalized as misdemeanors.[223] Finding "no sufficient 'yardstick' or statement of legislative policy in the broad grant of power to the conservation commission," the court held that the rules were without authority and void.[224]

It must be noted, however, that while the Iowa Supreme Court would not permit the delegation of "strictly and exclusively legislative" duties, the court did *not* narrow the scope of delegation held permissible in *Manning*. Rather, the court stated that

[N]o government, embodying the principles of separation of power, could function if the legislature were prohibited from conferring power or authority of any character upon executive or administrative officials.

. . . when the legislature lays down an intelligible and complete declaration of policy which is definite in describing the subject to which it relates or to the field wherein it shall apply, and the character of regulation which is intended to be imposed, it is proper to leave to a non-legislative body the manner in which that general policy shall apply to varying situations.[225]

The Iowa Supreme Court, therefore, while requiring that the legislature establish a clear general policy, recognized that the nature of democratic government left the three branches with overlapping functions. The concern of the court was not over delegation *qua* delegation but that the power of the administrative agency be carefully circumscribed. According to *Van Trump*, delegation was permissible if, and only if, the potential for arbitrary and capricious administrative action was legislatively eliminated.

The Iowa Supreme Court quickly retreated from the rigid position developed in *Van Trump* and began to follow much more literally the approach taken in *Manning*, which recognized that increasing governmental complexities demanded the delegation of powers to administrative agencies. The Iowa Supreme Court, approximately three years after *Van Trump*, expanded the presumption of validity of delegation of authority by the legislature and found quite general legislative directives to be constitutionally valid standards.[226] The adoption of the standards approach by the supreme court did not dispel all the concerns about keeping the power of agencies within bounds. The Iowa Supreme Court, like other courts, continued to stress the need for standards, but generally tended to invalidate delegation of power only if there was a lack of safeguards to protect the rights of those within the ambit of agency control. Moreover, if a court finds inadequate safeguards, the general trend has been to find that agency action was *ultra vires* rather than the exercise of an unconstitutionally delegated power. This approach saves the statute from being invalid while it gives the court power to monitor the actions of administrative agencies.

This trend has been most recently reinforced in *Warren County v. Judges of the Fifth Judicial District*. In *Warren County*, the Iowa Supreme Court upheld a statute that delegated to the chief judge of each judicial district having three or more part-time magistrates authority to order the substitution of a full-time magistrate for the incumbent part-time magistrates of a county, provided a majority of the judges of the judicial district had voted in favor of the substitution.[227] The court articulated factors that would be considered in determining the validity of delegation of authority: (1) whether public interest is best served by the delegation,[228] (2) whether it is impossible for the legislature to function in the area delegated to an agency,[229] and (3) whether, in lieu of standards, adequate safeguards are institutionalized to protect those affected by the agency's action.[230] The court found that the statute challenged in *Warren County* allowed for the use of the superior knowledge of chief judges, while "in fact limit[ing] the scope of the judges' authority as much *as practicalities allow*."[231]

Warren County indicates that the Iowa Supreme Court continues the effort to strive for "a common sense policy in determining the extent to which delegation may be permitted."[232] The court remains aware of the need for an administrative scheme which recognizes the increasing complexities of modern democratic government. The court stated, "[W]e look to the practical necessities of public interest and will consider as an important factor the difficulty or impossibility of calling for the legislature to function in a given area."[233]

The approach of the court in *Warren County* in establishing factors to determine what is acceptable rule making is similar to the one developed by Professor Allen. However, they seem likely to diverge in their conclusions. First, the Iowa Supreme Court in analyzing a statute delegating rule-making power to the police would probably ask whether public interest is best served by the delegation of authority. Professor Allen would probably argue it is not. But it appears that the Iowa Supreme Court, for one, might disagree with him. This is, of course, a public policy question. The courts are likely to leave it to the legislatures and to assume that the question is largely answered by the passage of legislation authorizing police rule making.

The second factor, "whether it is impossible for the legislature to function in the area delegated to an agency," would seem to be analogous to cases decided by the Iowa Supreme Court which have recognized the "practical necessities of public interest" in vesting more discretion in agencies concerned with public safety. In *State v. Rivera*, the court upheld a statute against claims of unconstitutional delegation on the grounds there was an enhanced need for administrative discretion in situations involving public safety.[234] Likewise, the Iowa case of *Spurbeck v. Stratton*[235] also recognized the exceptional need for administrative discretion in the area of public safety.[236]

Though *Rivera* dealt with the "safe and sane regulation of . . . motor vehicle transportation," it is instructive in connection with police rule making because of its explicit recognition that the legislature is not the sole repository of all expertise on public safety issues.[237] The attitude of the Iowa Supreme Court that the state legislature does not necessarily possess total expertise concerning problems of public safety is likely to lead to a second ground for disagreement between the Iowa courts and Professor Allen.

The third concern of *Warren County*—whether, in lieu of standards, adequate safeguards are to be institutionalized to ensure that the action of the agency is fair and impartial—is more difficult to analyze in the selective enforcement context. Because we have no history of formal rule development by the police, and because informal rules that are used are not susceptible to analysis, it is difficult to gauge whether present enforcement is impartial. However, one could make a strong case that the existence of formal rules developed under legislative authorization would substantially enhance the likelihood of institutional safeguards.

The recent case of *State v. Watts* sheds some additional light on the question of institutionalizing safeguards. In *Watts*, the Court considered the constitutionality of a statute that provided that any violation by a parolee of the rules established by the board of parole would be deemed a felony.[238] The defendant, who had been found guilty of violating the rules of his parole, contended that the statute set forth an unconstitutionally broad grant of power by allowing the board to define the conduct made criminal by the statute. The court, however, finding that the rule-making authority was properly delegated, held the statute constitutional. According to the court, while only the legislature has the power to create and define crimes, "The board of parole neither defines or creates a crime nor determines the punishment. The legislature itself prescribed that a violation of any rule or regulation or condition of a parole of the administrative agency granting the parole was a felony. . . . "[239] The court in *Watts*, while finding there were no substantive guidelines in the state *sub judice*, upheld that statute, which creates and empowers the parole board to make rules for parolees, on the grounds that "the procedure established for the exercise of the power furnishes safeguards to those who are affected by the administrative action."[240]

The development of law enforcement rules would not need to go as far as the process that was upheld in *Watts*. One could argue that the parole board in *Watts*, by setting specific conditions of parole, would be defining the crime.[241] The police, in drafting rules to control criminal law enforcement, would neither define nor create crimes. The legislature defines the elements of the crime and establishes the general policy of enforcement: the police merely interpret the policy and formulate rules that, when effected, ensure that the objectives of the legislature will be achieved.

While under law enforcement rules some persons might not be arrested for an act or omission that technically violates a criminal statute, the rules do not expand the scope of the legislatively enacted policy. Therefore, even if the rules adopted create a lesser probability of arrest than would occur by explicitly following the criminal statutes, the police are acting within their delegated authority.[242] Constriction of a statute, as discussed previously, is appropriate under both an "amplification" and "necessity" theory, while expansion of the statute clearly adds to legislative commands, punishes persons not intended to be punished or intended to be punished in a different way, and is thus impermissible.[243]

It would be not only unlikely but ironic if the Iowa Supreme Court should determine that the delegation of power to develop rules to control criminal law enforcement is unconstitutional. That conclusion would have the effect of stifling the development of safeguards against arbitrary administrative acts—the sorts of safeguards that the court recently has found to be so important.[244]

In analyzing how the delegation of powers doctrine has developed in Iowa, one finds the Iowa Supreme Court using a different approach from that suggested by Professor Allen. While the Iowa Supreme Court remains opposed to delegating the "purely legislative authority" of defining crime to administrative agencies, the court is willing to permit delegation of authority to make rules, provided the rules are within the general policy established by the legislature and adequate safeguards exist to protect against arbitrary administrative action.

It may be that this approach is not substantially different in other states as well, and the reason for early limitations on state administrative agencies may have been judicial concern with state agencies' lack of professionalism and resources, and the state courts' simultaneous awareness that the often part-time state legislatures were in no position to oversee the operation of state agencies effectively. The conditions have undergone rapid change, to the point where many state agencies are now as intelligently staffed and innovative as their federal counterparts.

In any event, we find in at least one state that the state delegation doctrine articulated by Professor Allen simply does not fit.[245] The question remains as to whether there is sufficient overlap in the delegation doctrines of the other states to indicate that the model proposed by Professor Allen may be inappropriate.

DUE PROCESS AND EQUAL PROTECTION

The preceding analysis makes it clear that a state statute delegating law enforcement policy-making power to local police would be, in at least one state, a constitutionally permissible delegation of legislative power. This is true even if the conclusion from the earlier discussion on full enforcement statutes, that such statutes implicitly grant discretionary authority to the police, is incorrect. However, since no state legislature has ever explicitly required the formal elaboration of enforcement policy by the police, police have not been required to engage in formal policy making. If the police are not explicitly required to develop such policies, it seems unlikely such policies will be developed.[246] A final question, then, is whether legal doctrines exist that might require or encourage the police to develop law enforcement policy.

As we have seen, Professor Davis believes that, in spite of the lack of explicit statutory approval, an implicit delegation of such power can be inferred from the criminal statutes.[247] As an initial proposition, he asserts that criminal statutes cannot be fully enforced for at least two reasons: first, the statutes as drafted provide no enforcement guidance; second, police agencies are not funded at a level that would make full enforcement possible. According to Davis, the state legislators recognize these problems; thus, selective enforcement rules are not only implicitly authorized but expected.[248] He adds that rule making might well be required, under the due process clause of the Fourteenth Amendment, primarily on the theory that citizens are entitled to notice of what conduct is proscribed.[249]

Professor Allen does not directly address this argument for criminal law enforcement policy making, but he sets forth a third reason that the police cannot engage in policy making—the rejection of the doctrine of desuetude,[250] which has a strong linkage with the due process doctrine. Desuetude provides that failure to enforce a statute over a long period of time, "coupled with open and widespread violation" of the statute, results in the equivalent of the repeal of the statute.[251]

According to Professor Allen, law enforcement policy making would abrogate some criminal statutes, so it is important to determine the extent to which desuetude has been accepted in America. To aid in that investigation, he turns to the work of Professor Arthur Bonfield, who states that "American courts have come to mouth the view that the vitality of an enacted law can *never* be impaired by a failure to enforce it. . . . Desuetude is summarily and completely written off as alien to our law."[252] Professor Allen goes on to add, "In the decade since Bonfield wrote, desuetude has fared no better: it was rejected in every case in which it was raised."[253] Professor Allen claims that since selective enforcement policy making would have a desuetude-type effect on some criminal statutes, it would be impermissible.[254]

Desuetude questions arise primarily in circumstances in which there is an attempt to enforce a criminal statute that up to that time has been almost totally unenforced.[255] Such a situation would seem unlikely to arise as a result of implementing police arrest policy where the goal is not to establish a position of total non-enforcement, but rather to attempt to define the circumstances in which every statute will be enforced. This distinction between law enforcement policy making and desuetude-type situations is important and indicates that, even if Professor Allen is correct in saying American law does not recognize desuetude, the doctrine of desuetude is of limited value in addressing the issue of criminal law enforcement policy making.

More important for the analysis of law enforcement policy making are other points raised by Professor Bonfield in his discussion of desuetude. Bonfield concluded from his research that although desuetude has not been accepted as part of our law, its relationship to American constitutional doctrines of due process, equal protection, and separation of powers makes "the current notion that in the United States statutes can never be abrogated by a failure to enforce them . . . seem to be an unfounded and overly broad generality."[256] Especially compelling for our present discussion is his analysis of equal protection and due process doctrines. His conclusion that some penal statutes might violate equal protection principles because they permit an administrative authority to wield complete power to define unlawful conduct has direct implications for law enforcement policy making.[257] Such absolute power exercised by either an agency or legislative body could foster the development of irrational and discriminatory enforcement practices.

Professor Bonfield also finds a "notice" problem with desuetude that is likewise applicable to criminal law enforcement policy making. Because general terms in statutes often leave criminal law enforcement decisions solely to law enforcement officers, citizens may not have knowledge of what conduct is practically as well as statutorily proscribed and consequently be deprived of their due process right to have notice not only of statutory proscriptions but enforcement practices as well.[258] To understand fully these equal protection and due process problems, it is important to review some of the basic principles of those doctrines.

Law enforcement as an equal protection concern first arose in the case of *Yick Wo v. Hopkins*.[259] In *Yick Wo*, the U.S. Supreme Court struck down a San Francisco city ordinance as violating the equal protection clause of the Fourteenth Amendment, even though no specific discriminatory intent could be discovered in the language of the statute. According to the Court,

> [t]hough the law be fair on its face, yet, if it is applied and administered with an evil eye and an unequal hand, so as practically to make unjust and illegal discriminations between persons in similar circumstances, material to their rights, the denial of equal justice is still within the prohibition of the Constitution.[260]

Finding that the enforcement authorities had utilized the ordinance to prohibit Chinese citizens from maintaining lawful business, the Court held that the law was unconstitutional.[261]

Yick Wo has come to stand for the proposition that purposeful discrimination on the basis of sex, race, or religious or political beliefs is a violation of equal protection.[262] If a person can prove that his arrest was made under an enforcement policy that deliberately and intentionally discriminates on the basis of any of those criteria, absent a rational basis for such discrimination, that arrest is likely to be found to violate the equal protection doctrine. While this doctrine would on the surface seem to provide protection against arbitrary enforcement policy and implicitly call for the development of uniform arrest rules, there appears to be a substantial divergence between the theory established in *Yick Wo* and the reality of treatment by the courts. This seems largely due to the fact that the party who alleges such discrimination must bear an unusually heavy burden of proof on the discrimination issue.[263]

More specifically, discovery of evidence to prove intentionally discriminatory enforcement practices in police work is extremely difficult because a veil of secrecy cloaks law enforcement decisions.[264] This is a major reason that a substantial proportion of all cases reaching the appellate court level which allege discriminatory law enforcement practices have resulted in the courts' finding no adequate proof upon which to sustain the accused's allegations.[265] The legal and practical problems encountered in proving that law enforcement practices are constitutionally invalid are crippling.

A typical case is *Matter of Di Maggio v. Brown*, in which over 100 ferryboat officers, appointed to their job under a New York State civil service law, appealed an administrative decision that penalized them for partaking in a strike in violation of a state law prohibiting strikes by government employees.[266] The officers contended that the enforcement of the law prohibiting civil servants from participating in strikes violated their constitutional guarantee to equal protection because during the preceding twenty years the law had been enforced in only two cases, though there had been strikes by public employees "too numerous to recall or record."[267]

The trial court dismissed the appeal without allowing the officers to prove their claims. Because the trial court had erroneously deprived the officers of the right to offer proof, the appellate court held that the case had to be remitted to trial. More significant to this analysis, the court also held that the officers would face a high standard of proof. Rather than requiring proof of "mere non-enforcement," the court held that

[i]t must be shown that the provisions of [the state law] were enforced against petitioners . . . pursuant to an intentional and invidious plan of discrimination by the Department of Marine and Aviation or by the City of New York. As the Supreme Court stated in *Ahsin v. Wittman*: "No latitude of intention should be indulged in a case like this. There should be certainty to every intent.[268]

In addition to the difficulties in proving discriminatory intent with "certainty," a defendant trying to assert an equal protection defense faces significant practical problems. First, the police rarely keep records of policy formulations, which might be reviewed to discover discriminatory intent. Furthermore, it is not unknown for law enforcement officials to hamper an accused person's attempt to prove an otherwise valid statute is being enforced in a purposefully discriminatory manner.

United States v. Steele is a case in point. In *Steele*, four persons were convicted of willful failure to complete their census questionnaires. The four appealed their convictions, contending that the census authorities had prosecuted only them because they had been leaders of a movement urging the public to avoid compliance with census requirements and had, therefore, been intentionally discriminated against. A regional census official alleged that the four appellants were the only persons known by the agency to have failed to comply with the census regulations. The appellants lacked evidence to prove that the census agency had knowledge of other violators, and the agency refused to supply internal data that might have shown such knowledge. In the end, the appellants did prove, through their own investigation, that at least six other persons failed to complete their census forms. The appellate court, upon review of the evidence, found that the census authorities should have been apprised of the fact that at least ten persons had violated the statute. Stating that "an enforcement procedure that focuses upon the vocal offender is inherently suspect," the court reversed the convictions because "the only plausible explanation of this record is the one urged by Steele."[269]

Finally, as previously noted in *Matter of Di Maggio v. Brown*, a claim of discriminatory enforcement may be undermined by the trial court's refusal to admit evidence proffered to show discriminatory enforcement practices. *People v. Harris*,[270] a case in which ten black defendants appealed their convictions under state gambling laws, is a stark example of this evidentiary barrier. In *Harris*, the petitioners made offers of proof that, if uncontroverted, tended to show that the state gambling laws were clearly being enforced in a discriminatory manner. Proof was offered to the trial court by the defendants of the following:

1. In 1957, 16 white persons and 276 blacks were arrested for gambling.
2. In 1958, 9 whites and 82 blacks were arrested for gambling.
3. In 1959, all those arrested for gambling were black.
4. The police chief was aware of and permitted gambling in three ''white'' men's clubs—including one of which he was a member.
5. According to one police officer, it was routine police procedure to patrol the ''colored'' section to find gambling violations, and there was no similar patrol in the ''white'' section.[271]

The trial court, after reviewing the offers of proof, determined that although ''there may be some slight inference of discrimination, the offer of proof falls far short of showing deliberate, intentional, discriminatory practice.''[272] Accordingly, the trial court rejected the offers of proof and fined each petitioner. The trial court's remarkably high standard for proving ''intentional, discriminatory practice,'' coupled with its rather summary evidentiary analysis, left the petitioners in a serious economic dilemma: appeal and claim error on the grounds of erroneous rejection of evidence incurring substantial attorney's expenses, or accept the conviction with a negligible monetary sanction. The petitioners chose the former, more financially burdensome, alternative. The appellate court, finding a clear prejudicial error in the rejection of the proffered evidence, reversed the judgment and ordered a new trial. According to the appellate court in *Harris*, ''the appellants should have been permitted to introduce any evidence they offered which tended to show actual intentional discrimination in the enforcement of the statute and ordinance in this instance. . . . [W]e are merely holding that it was inadmissible in appellant's efforts to prove that defense. It is wholly unsatisfactory to determine whether that defense was sufficient merely under offer of proof.''[273]

Recorded rules could also provide a basis upon which an accused person would be able to establish a discriminatory enforcement defense. Such a proposal would not even require shifting the stringent standard of proof to the government; however, upon proof that an officer intentionally violated an enforcement rule, the burden could shift to the state to prove that the arrest was not made with the intent to discriminate against the arrestee.

What this analysis shows is that an accused person, while theoretically provided a defense to prosecution under intentionally discriminatory practices, is met with debilitating legal and practical obstacles in asserting the defense. Specifically, the accused must face the problem that the police (or the prosecutor) rarely keep records of why specific law enforcement decisions are made, and, in the rare case in which agency records tend to prove invidious discriminatory intent, these same agencies often effectively deny an accused person's attempts to gain access to them.[274] Finally, the courts often erect barriers to admission of evidence that are the foundation of the claim of constitutionally invalid enforcement.

The existence of law enforcement rules would likely alleviate many of the present problems of effectuating equal protection principles. Well-drafted rules could provide a general enforcement policy with objective criteria to guide decision making. The call for establishment of standards, although it draws support from and is consistent with equal protection principles, goes beyond that doctrine and finds even greater sustenance in due process principles, particularly due process concerns with the "vagueness" of statutes. The position of the Supreme Court abhorring "vague" statutes is established, and it would seem vagueness in enforcement policy is at least as serious as vagueness in statutory language.[275]

Professor Davis analogizes statutory vagueness to vagueness of law enforcement policy. He finds much to draw upon in the case of *Papachristou v. City of Jacksonville*,[276] in which a Jacksonville vagrancy ordinance was held constitutionally void because it "fail[ed] to give a person of ordinary intelligence fair notice that his contemplated conduct [was] forbidden by the statute" and "it encourage[d] arbitrary and erratic arrests and convictions" by leaving unfettered discretion in the hands of the police.[277]

In *Papachristou*, the Court found that adequate notice had not been provided by the statute, and, thus, too much discretion had been left to police; the statute made criminal a multitude of acts far too broad and diverse to be objectively interpreted. Because of the ambiguity of the statute, the Court felt neither citizens nor police officers were provided with adequate standards. The vagueness of the statute thus deprived citizens of appropriate notice as to what was unlawful conduct and deprived the police officers of necessary standards to determine what actions were proscribed. Statutory vagueness, therefore, created a situation in which the police essentially were left to define criminal acts, resulting in a variable law enforcement policy.[278]

The fact that the vagueness of the statute in *Papachristou* failed to meet the notice requirement of the due process clause is of importance in analyzing law enforcement policy making. As stated by the United States Supreme Court in *Lanzetta v. New Jersey*: "No one may be required at peril of life, liberty or property to speculate as to the meaning of penal statutes. All are entitled to be informed as to what the state commands or forbids."[279] It would seem reasonable, at the very least, that the government be required under the due process doctrine to eliminate barriers to notice caused by unpredictable enforcement. There are other cases that support the theory that the principles embodied in the due process clause of the Fourteenth Amendment would support if not require that police agencies act according to uniform standards. Those cases show that the implementation of standards serves to eliminate arbitrary and capricious administrative action, to improve the quality of judicial review of administrative decision making, and to restore public trust in administrative action.

In *Hornsby v. Allen*, a case often cited as supporting a "standards" requirement under the Fourteenth Amendment due process clause, plaintiff appealed a municipal agency's decision denying her application for a liquor dealer's license. Plaintiff alleged that the procedure followed by the agency violated the due process doctrine. Finding that the plaintiff had alleged sufficient facts to prove that the administrative procedure did not comport with due process, the Fifth Circuit Court of Appeals held that the case had to be remanded to the district court. The appeals court instructed the district court that, if it found

> that no ascertainable standards have been established by the Board of Aldermen by which an applicant can intelligently seek to qualify for a license, then the court must enjoin the denial of licenses under the prevailing system until a legal standard is established and procedural due process provided in the liquor store licensing field.[280]

In the *Hornsby* situation, it is evident that no judicial review of a licensing decision can occur unless the agency supplies the reason for its decision and the facts supporting that reason. Without judicial review, an arbitrary licensing scheme could easily proceed unchecked. Some might argue that *Hornsby* is not directly applicable to criminal matters, as no criminal penalty can be imposed on an individual unless there is presentation of evidence supporting the charges against that person to an impartial tribunal assessing the evidence under a pre-existing legal standard. However, as the Supreme Court has determined in the search area, if one's due process rights can be effectively denied at the time of arrest, why cannot they be violated before arrest? It seems important to recognize that a lack of standards to control arrest decisions presents a good possibility that an individual's rights to be fairly selected to face criminal charges might be violated. It should be a matter of some concern that we are more interested in the deprivation of economic benefits (as in *Hornsby*) than in the deprivation of liberty, which could be the effect of the selection process in criminal cases.

A barrier often confronted by courts reviewing an administrative decision, challenged on due process grounds, is that there is no "procedure" to review. This lack of procedure available for judicial review has led many courts to require agencies to formulate standard-based procedure.[281] It seems that we may also need a procedure in criminal cases as well.

Elimination of covert, arbitrary administrative decision making is one benefit derived from the formulation of standard-based procedures. In *Holmes v. New York City Housing Authority*, the Second Circuit Court of Appeals expressly sought that benefit. The plaintiff in *Holmes* alleged that the authority annually admitted 10,000 families from a pool of 90,000 applicants to low-rent housing projects without processing the applications "chronologically, or in accordance with ascertainable standards, or in any other systematic manner."[282] The court, holding that the federal courts could assert jurisdiction under 42 U.S.C. Section 1983,[283] stated that there was merit in the plaintiff's claim that the authority has failed "to establish the fair and orderly procedure for allocating its scarce supply of housing which due process requires."[284] The evil feared by the court was the "intolerable invitation to abuse" created by the existence of uncontrolled discretion by an agency of government. According to the court, "For this reason alone due process requires that selection among applicants be made in accordance with 'ascertainable standards.' "[285]

A second related benefit derived from the formulation of standard-based procedure is improvement in the quality of judicial review. This interest was significant in the disposition of *Environmental Defense Fund v. Ruckelhaus*. The Environmental Defense Fund sought judicial review of an order of the Secretary of Agriculture that refused to suspend the federal registration of the pesticide DDT. The Secretary argued that "the suspension of any DDT registration is not warranted at this juncture," without explaining how that decision had been made. The court believed he had "an obligation to articulate the criteria that he develops in making each individual decision,"[286] and remanded the case to allow for the review of factors and information the Secretary analyzed in deciding to issue the order. In support of its holding, the court stated that

> judicial review alone can correct only the most egregious abuses. Judicial review must operate to ensure that the administrative process itself will confine and control the exercise of discretion. Courts should require administrative officers to articulate the standards and principles that govern their discretionary decisions in as much detail as possible. . . . When administrators provide a framework for principled decision making the result will be . . . to improve the quality of judicial review in those cases where judicial review is sought.[287]

The public perception of administrative rule making is improved by the implementation of standards. Not only do citizens who have dealings with government agencies have notice of what factors are dispositive, but also they are able to participate more fully in governmental decisions.[288] While the need for standards or rules to control administrative action generally has been recognized, that trend has yet to take hold in the administration of criminal justice. Even if the doctrines of equal protection and due process do not mandate police rule making, the principles of fair play and equal treatment embodied in them strongly support the development of law enforcement rules.

On the basis of the preceding section, a strong argument can be made for the proposition that the principles of due process and equal protection include within them support for requiring rules to control law enforcement decisions.[289] While such rules would not and could not amend the criminal statutes passed by the state legislature, they could provide a legal basis upon which agencies could act. Kenneth Davis sees this as a solution to controlling discretion in the arrest decision.[290] However, Professor Allen rejects this approach for three reasons: first, as a practical matter, he fears such rules would not be challenged in the court; second, he is concerned that the process of labelling the practice of rule making as developing interpretative rules in the way Davis suggests does not make the practice any more constitutional than it now is without such label; and third, the process of labelling avoids resolving the question of whether the police have the power to draft such rules.[291]

The first two concerns are most important; the third can be considered to have been dealt with by our discussion of equal protection, due process principles, and the full enforcement statutes, during which the proposition was developed that equal protection and due process principles and at least some full enforcement statutes would appear to support the development of law enforcement policy.

Professor Allen, quite appropriately, is concerned that there is unlikely to be review of police rules by external agencies. His concern has considerable merit, since at present informal rules are developed and carried out by individual officers, and there is virtually no check on the formulation or implementation of those rules by legislative, judicial, or prosecutorial agencies.

The implementation of formal rules would contribute to the demise of uncontrolled rule development. In the first place, formal rules would require police agencies to be much more careful in developing law enforcement norms. The process of articulating and implementing rules is a significantly more deliberate process than the invocation of informal, and largely individual, norms. Furthermore, as a practical matter, the existence of formal rules creates a situation where such norms are much more likely to be challenged than is present conduct.[292] Professor Allen disagrees with this view; he feels that "no individual will be affected adversely by such rules,"[293] and there will be no challenge. While it may be that a person who was not arrested would not challenge such rules, it seems highly likely that many people who are arrested under such law enforcement rules would question whether such rules violate equal protection and due process guarantees; that is, do the rules discriminate against particular individuals or classes of people, or was the process of developing and implementing the rules improper? As Professor Allen does in his article, one could raise questions about the constitutional power to develop such rules,[294] attack the procedure by which the rules were developed,[295] or question the impact of the rules.[296] But the challenge in the courts is only one way such rules are likely to be reviewed. The existence of explicit rules would mean that state legislators, local government officials, prosecutors, and courts could analyze specific enforcement policies and comment on them or, in the case of legislators, promulgate statutes changing them if they so desired. Actually, the existence of such rules would facilitate reform of criminal procedure, because the rules would give the courts concrete language to analyze and would provide a rare opportunity to evaluate police practices.

The development of such rules under the rubric of managerial instead of interpretative rules,[297] might provide a more accurate description of what the police are expected to do. The case law at both the federal and state level supports the proposition that administrative agencies are expected to have input into interpreting and implementing their statutory mandate. *Skidmore v. Swift and Co.*, an extremely important case on this point, held that "the rulings, interpretations and opinions of the Administrator under this Act, while not controlling upon the courts by reason of their authority, do constitute a body of experience and informed judgment to which courts and litigants may properly resort for guidance."[298]

Cases at both the federal and state levels have reaffirmed the principle of *Skidmore*. For example, in Iowa the case of *Holland v. State*, while holding that a particular rule violated statutory authorization, clearly established that state agencies could promulgate appropriate rules.[299] More closely analogous to the present concern is the action of the Iowa Supreme Court in *Wagner v. Northeast Farm Service*. In that case, the court indicated that policy guidelines that "fill in an implicit gap" in statutes by providing discretionary standards would be appropriate because only in such a way would it be possible to ensure the effective realization of the legislature's policies.[300]

At least one recent case can be cited in support of the proposition that agencies are required to develop rules to guide both their substantive and procedural activities. *Citizens, etc. v. Pottawattamie County Board of Adjustment* involved a dispute over the operation of a sanitary landfill. Specific administrative action was invalidated because the court found that the board failed to adopt rules as directed by both state statute and local ordinance. However, there is important language in the case that says "the weight of authority is to . . . condemn the failure to adopt procedural rules whether demanded by statute or not." The court goes on to cite a number of cases that deal with mixed substantive and procedural problems that show "the necessity for *some* rules to govern the conduct of proceedings" before agencies.[301] It is significant that the court went further and stated that although there was no statutory requirement for the board to make written findings, such "would be of great benefit to the trial court" in that "[t]hey would provide a ready basis for determining the reason for the Board's action, and would help immeasurably in determining whether the result was reasonable or was, as is frequently claimed, arbitrary and capricious."[302]

The court felt the need for written findings was so important that it stipulated in the holding of the case that all boards of adjustment were to make written findings of fact after the date the opinion was filed.[303] The same idea was expressed in *Sun Ray Drive-In Dairy v. Oregon Liquor Control Comm'n.* The Oregon Supreme Court stated:

> An administrative agency cannot properly perform its duty under the law unless employees at all levels work toward the same objectives under a clear direction of policy from the head of that agency. . . . The public is entitled to consistency of enforcement from the agency. That situation cannot be achieved in the absence of written standards.[304]

The core of the delegation doctrine in Oregon is the requirement that agencies promulgate standards to guard against arbitrary exercise of administrative power. These same principles apply to the police. When arrest powers are exercised without rules, they can violate due process.

Support at the state level for the development of rules to control law enforcement policy may be found in many state administrative procedures acts. For example, the Iowa Administrative Procedure Act (IAPA) can be interpreted as suggesting that state police agencies develop rules to control arrest policy. The IAPA not only gives state administrative agencies the power to make rules "of general applicability that implement, interpret, or prescribe law or policy . . . '' but seems to indicate that while agencies may not be required to divulge such rules, they are expected to make them.[305] Even Professor Allen is of the opinion that the Iowa Administrative Procedure Act may give the police the authority to develop law enforcement policy.[306]

Although the Act authorizes a state agency to establish law enforcement policy, the Act does not explicitly include within its purview local police departments; yet a persuasive argument can be made that local police departments are ''quasi state administrative agencies'' and thus included under the Act owing to the fact that they derive their power and authority from the state,[307] implement the will of the state legislature, and are selected and trained[308] according to state mandates. This line of thinking is consistent with the approach of one state supreme court.[309]

In fact, the inclusion of some, but not all, law enforcement officers who are responsible for enforcing state criminal laws within the purview of a state administrative procedure act is more than a little ironic. Most citizens are likely to have more contact with local police than with any state law enforcement agency, yet a uniform approach with regard to arrests is expected at the state but not the local level.[310] This is clearly an intolerable anomaly that cries out for rectification.

CONCLUSION

This survey of the constitutional and legal obstacles to the development of law enforcement rules shows that the police do have authority to develop rules to control arrest decisions and that police agencies should embrace and use that authority to provide greater uniformity in decision making. Courts should likewise recognize police rule making. While this authority may not be as broad as Professor Davis seems to suggest, it is clearly beyond the range of activity contemplated by Professor Allen.

Courts and the police need only to look to the institutional evolution of the police to support this conclusion. American police have always been expected to exercise discretion in the performance of their duties. This is not to imply that there has been no concern with how that discretion is exercised; rather, the concern has been that partisan politics not affect the exercise of discretion. The fear of politics intruding into law enforcement decisions is likely to have been one of the factors influencing passage of the so-called full enforcement statutes. Reviewing those statutes in their historical context leads one to the conclusion that those statutes were not so much directed against police decision making as they were primarily directed to the problems of controlling political influence of the police and providing structure for governmental institutions. Although the statutes may have had some impact on limiting the political influence on police action, they never totally controlled the arrest decisions of the officer on the street nor, as a practical matter, were they intended to do so. Discretionary decision making under those statutes was, and is, expected.

A review of state constitutional separation of powers and delegation principles likewise leads one to conclude that the police have the power to develop law enforcement rules. Analysis of those principles supports the proposition that, at the very least, the police can develop arrest guidelines to control police discretion in minor or low-visibility crimes, such as those regulated in the normal course of the work of administrative agencies.

Finally, the principles embodied in the constitutional doctrines of equal protection and due process support the development of law enforcement rules: the principles of equity and fairness implicit in those doctrines might require the police to have explicit uniform arrest guidelines. If the police do not have such guidelines, courts would appear to be clearly within the scope of their authority to interpret the due process and equal protection doctrines as requiring such guidelines. In other words, policy making by police not only is consistent with the constitutional principles but may well be required by the values embodied in those principles.

The Institutional Role in Controlling Police Discretion 3

In chapter 2 there was a close examination of the constitutional and statutory problems of developing specific policies to control police discretion. While there was some focus on full enforcement statutes and court decisions, limited attention was given to how political institutions *qua* political institutions can respond to the issue of selective enforcement. The extent of institutional power and authority to act is central to the discussion of police discretion. Undoubtedly, the legislatures and the police are the most important institutions in determining arrest policies, but they have failed to act. Thus, we need to look at the ways other agencies of government can and do influence police arrest policies. It is important to remember that there are several governmental institutions that have some responsibility for forming and shaping criminal law enforcement, that is, courts, prosecutorial offices, and local governing bodies. In fact, some scholars have argued that " . . . idealism or naiveté or both must be present in king size doses in order

Reprinted, with changes, from "The Politics of Police Discretion" in Carl F. Pinkele and William C. Louthan, eds., *Discretion, Justice, and Democracy: A Public Policy Perspective* (Ames, Iowa: Iowa State University Press, 1984); and "Police Discretion: The Institutional Dilemma—Who Is in Charge?" 68 *Iowa Law Review* 431 (1983), copyright 1983, University of Iowa (Iowa Law Review). Used by permission of the publishers.

to sustain the position that the legislature can or should play an exclusive role in the molding of criminal law policy."[1]

Unfortunately, the role of these other institutions of government that can directly influence police arrest decisions has largely been overlooked in the analysis of police discretion. Yet state legislatures enact the criminal laws that are to be enforced, prosecutorial offices decide which of the cases brought by the police will be prosecuted, courts review arrest decisions to assess their conformance to state laws, and local governing bodies fund and are politically responsible for local law enforcement agencies.

As suggested earlier, there are still other agencies that can and sometimes do influence law enforcement decisions. Most governors and state attorneys general by virtue of their political positions can undoubtedly exert some influence over local police agencies. However, such influence depends more upon their power of persuasion than their explicit legal authority. For example, a governor who has sufficient political influence in the state legislature could bring about the enactment of legislation to control police discretion should he or she desire to do so. But the lack of such action in the past suggests there is unlikely to be any change in the future, barring unforeseen developments.

It seems likely that if any action to guide arrest discretion will be taken, it will be by institutions such as the legislatures, courts, prosecutorial offices, and local governing bodies, which have direct input into police decision making. Thus, it is appropriate to gain a more comprehensive view of the ability of those institutions to influence and control police discretion—specifically arrest decisions. Therefore, this chapter will analyze the legal and political authority those institutions possess, what they have done to control criminal law enforcement, or, if they have done little or nothing, the reasons for inaction.

In more specific terms, the goal of this chapter will be to identify legal and institutional problems that are significant obstacles to the development of rules and guidelines to control arrest decisions and to try to assess whether inaction might be attributable to institutional structure. An analysis of the institutional structure of agencies is important because the relationship between public policy and the structure of government institutions is very close. In fact, there is considerable support for the proposition that institutions may be so structured as to facilitate certain policy outcomes and obstruct others.[2]

In addition to analyzing institutional structure, there are two other questions to ask: first, what are the law enforcement goals of these different policy-making bodies; and second, how might these goals be reconciled to produce a comprehensive and interdependent plan to control police discretion?

One way to begin is to analyze the policy outputs of the institutions and to compare that information with the results of interviews of persons who influence the development of policy. For example, with regard to the state legislatures, in addition to analyzing what the legislatures have done, it is necessary to interview major legislative policymakers to discover their perception as to what motivated legislative action or inaction. The analysis of policy output and perceptions, while possessing inherent limitations, can provide important information as to what factors are critical to the emergence of police discretion as a major institutional issue.

STATE LEGISLATURES

State legislatures have broad power and authority to enact criminal laws and control their enforcement. This authority to act is exercised under the "police power" of the state. The primary limitations on the state's police power to enact criminal statutes are federal and state constitutional provisions that protect specific individual rights.[3] Thus, as long as state legislatures do not enact legislation that unconstitutionally infringes on individual rights, they have a free hand to enact criminal law legislation. But having the power to act does not mean that action is automatically forthcoming.

The major obstacle to the development of formal arrest policy by the police is, according to Professor Kenneth Davis, that state legislative commands are ambiguous. First, according to Professor Davis, state legislatures enact penal statutes that seemingly mandate full enforcement of the laws. Second, the legislatures provide resources sufficient for only limited enforcement, and finally, they acquiesce in partial enforcement.[4] Unfortunately, the assessment of legislative action rarely goes beyond this analysis; few writers have asked why the state legislatures have taken such an approach. There has been no analysis of the kinds of policy directives that the state legislatures might realistically be expected to make or the practical and policy reasons that have motivated the legislatures to follow their present course of action.

Analysis of Legislative Action

Review of the work of state legislatures suggests that there are at least three major ways legislative attention can be directed toward controlling police discretion. First, the issue of police discretion can arise on its own as the subject of specific legislation. Second, the issue can surface as a supplement to other legislation. Third, the issue can be considered during criminal code revision. Specific legislative proposals directed solely to the control of police discretion are virtually nonexistent. Nor have real concerns about police discretion arisen as part of other legislation.[5] "Full enforcement" statutes,[6] on which many scholars erroneously rely as the definitive treatment of police discretion,[7] are a prime example of the degree of inattention given to police discretion problems when the issue is a part of other legislation.[8]

Except in a crisis atmosphere, the primary way in which criminal justice legislation and, inferentially, police discretion problems come before a state legislature is during major criminal code revision. In the last twenty years, approximately half the states have undertaken such revision.[9] Thus, a large number of states have had a specific opportunity to take action to limit the range of police discretion. It appears that state legislatures have not acted to control police discretion generally or arrest discretion specifically either during criminal code revisions or at any other time. But it is important to take a closer look at legislative action and analyze specifically how such concerns have in fact been addressed.

Attempting to answer the following seven questions would seem to be a good way to assess legislative action controlling discretion within the criminal justice system:

1. To what extent have there been attempts to remedy vagueness and ambiguity problems in full enforcement statutes?
2. To what extent have legislatures attempted revision of vague and highly discretionary statutes?

3. To what extent has there been decriminalization of largely unenforced and unenforceable statutes?
4. To what extent have legislatures undertaken the enactment of citation systems to guide officers' power to issue citations for law violations in lieu of making custodial arrests?
5. To what extent has there been enactment of criminal statutes that provide policy guidance for law enforcement?
6. To what extent have legislatures attempted to structure the discretion given to police officers to use deadly force?
7. To what extent has the discretionary power of other major actors in the criminal justice system been guided and structured?

An analysis of action on the first three questions provides information on how legislatures approach the issue of arrest discretion specifically. Action on the fourth, fifth, and sixth questions provides information on police discretion generally and shows the extent to which state legislatures have acted to solve the problem of police discretion in a broader context. Legislative treatment of the seventh indicator measures the legislatures' willingness to deal with problems of discretion in the criminal justice system generally. In the preparation of this work, the legislative actions of several states were analyzed within the framework of the seven questions.[10]

A look at the full enforcement statutes reveals an obvious lack of interest in altering that legislation. Despite the concerns expressed about uncontrolled police discretion,[11] several states incorporated full enforcement statutes into their revised criminal codes without providing substantive direction regarding expected law enforcement policy.[12] Other states, although repealing their full enforcement statutes, not only did not indicate what effect the repeal should have on the exercise of arrest discretion but apparently undertook such repeal without any consideration of the implication of the repeal.[13] Actually, the repeal or restructuring of full enforcement statutes may not be the most appropriate and direct way for legislatures to focus on the laws the police must enforce. A better approach might well be to provide more workable statutes that remedy problems of vagueness and overbreadth.

One concern about the overbreadth of criminal statutes is that the "very presence of . . . broadsweeping provisions on the statute books may in itself place a needless burden on local police."[14] To resolve this problem in Michigan, it was suggested that the vagrancy statute be replaced by provisions prohibiting specific acts, such as prostitution, loitering, and disorderly conduct.[15] The argument was made that the elimination of vagrancy-type laws "should serve both to promote more equal enforcement of the law and to facilitate more efficient police administration."[16] The point is well taken, but the degree to which enforcement problems are resolved by such action is questionable. In fact, a persuasive argument can be made that replacing the law on vagrancy with a disorderly conduct statute creates its own set of enforcement problems, as the constitutionality of disorderly conduct statutes themselves have been challenged with increasing frequency.[17]

Unfortunately, the approach of many legislative bodies has been to review overbreadth problems in statutes when there is concern about the constitutionality of specific statutes and not to deal with statutes that present less immediate problems. Recent attacks on the constitutionality of laws regulating private, consensual sexual behavior, such as adultery and sodomy, have generally resulted in the repeal of those laws. This has been the case in Iowa,[18] Minnesota,[19] and Missouri.[20] However, there has been no attempt to deal directly or comprehensively with other statutes that in the enforcement decision are highly discretionary.

Not only has there been virtually no effort to revise discretionary statutes that are not the subject of immediate constitutional attack, legislatures also have not attempted to delineate the policy objectives of criminal justice legislation when seeking to decriminalize specific conduct. Recent changes in the Iowa gambling statute are an example. While the statute clearly indicates that some forms of gambling are legally permissible,[21] the lack of policy directives concerning how and when the statute should be enforced created serious problems for local police. Even when the enforcement problems were brought to the attention of legislators, the legislators indicated very little concern about this lack of policy direction.[22]

Another way to gauge the extent to which state legislatures are concerned with the problems of police discretion in a more general sense is to look at the usage of citation systems in the various states. Statutes in approximately thirty-nine states permit state and local police departments in some situations to issue citations to law violators in lieu of making a custodial arrest.[23] A large proportion of these citation statutes give authority to issue citations for all simple misdemeanors, including traffic violations. Thus, by these statutes police are given discretion to determine who will be subjected to custodial arrest and who will be able to appear on their own before a magistrate. While it is likely that a major impetus of such statutes was to reduce demand on police resources and jail overcrowding, the statutes quite clearly convey an expectation of police discretion. What is important to understand is the extent to which that discretion is structured and controlled.

The American Bar Association, among others, has proposed a policy favoring issuance of citations in lieu of arrest or continued custody[24] and recommended that, while state legislatures should take the initial step in defining situations where pre-trial release should be mandatory, local law enforcement agencies should be able to supplement the state statutes with their own regulations guiding officers' discretion.[25] It is significant to observe that only five of the state statutes mandate the use of citations.[26]

The vast majority of the states merely authorize the use of citations. While one can argue that it might be improper to require police departments to use citations in lieu of custodial arrest, it seems appropriate to expect some guidance for those departments that do undertake to use citations. Nonetheless, it is quite rare for the citation statutes to include any guidelines for officers to consider when issuing citations. Again, the legislatures have failed to give policy guidance. Typically, the statutes do not clearly state when citations are to be issued, what crimes are citable, and how officers should decide who should receive a citation.[27] Thus, while the citation statutes on their face recognize and anticipate police discretion, the problems of implementation obviously were not given great consideration.

A related question is why, particularly since the use of citations could reduce the demand on police resources, so few police departments have embraced the use of citations. It appears that many look at the use of citations as an assault on their powers. While an officer would clearly be required to possess probable cause to arrest a person before he could issue a citation, some officers feel they have the prerogative of choosing how to channel an offender through the criminal justice system. Apparently some officers view the incarceration of arrestees as the only chance they will have to ensure that an arrestee will be subjected to some punishment, so efforts to limit the power of the police to "punish'' offenders are resisted.[28] In actuality it appears that greater use of citations in low-visibility crimes like simple misdemeanors would go a long way in reducing the potential for discrimination in the arrest decision, as the officer's ''punishment'' aspect of the offense would be removed and questions of police power and authority would be reduced. Jail as an immediate consequence would not be an issue. Furthermore, guidelines that switch the presumption from incarceration to release would further serve to control the limits of discretion yet would not handicap the ability of an officer to make an arrest when the officer felt an arrest was necessary.

In conclusion, while many states in enacting citation statutes can be characterized as having explicitly recognized the exercise of police discretion[29] by the officer in the field, the supervising officers, and others,[30] legislatures have for one reason or another deemed it either unnecessary or unwise to go any further. Thus, a tremendous void is left in this area. By not developing or requiring development of guidelines for the use of citations, another area of uncontrolled discretion and possible abuse is created.

An additional way to determine legislative concern about police discretion is to analyze statutes controlling the use of deadly force. Nationwide, a majority of the states have specific provisions governing the use of deadly force.[31] Approximately twenty-four states have codified the common law ''fleeing felon'' rule under which a law enforcement officer is justified in using deadly force to arrest any person suspected of committing a felony.[32] Primarily because of the considerable discretion inherent in the choice to use deadly force, provisions of the *Model Penal Code* have called for state statutes to require that the decision to use deadly force be based on a concern for immediate public safety rather than the commission of a felony.[33]

As a general proposition, legislatures have not acted to limit and control the use of deadly force. For example, the Missouri legislature, during a period of criminal law reform, rejected its advisory committee's suggestion to limit the use of deadly force to those situations in which an individual has committed a felony ''involving the use or threatened use of physical force against a person.''[34] The statute ultimately passed by the Missouri legislature permits an officer to use deadly force when he or she ''reasonably believes'' that such force is necessary.[35]

Of the states evaluated, over one-half dealt with the issue of the use of force, but few adhered to the standard of the *Model Penal Code* concerning the police decision to use force.[36] The end product of legislative action on the use of deadly force has to be described as one of maintaining extensive discretion. While legislative action on the use of deadly force is quite obviously different from legislative action on statutes to limit selective enforcement, action on deadly force statutes seems to reinforce the theory that police discretion as a general issue has not been given extensive consideration or extensive discretion is expected by the police in all situations in which there is a need for decisions to be made.

A final way to gauge state legislative attitudes toward police discretion generally is to evaluate the manner in which other discretionary problems have been treated during consideration of criminal justice legislation. The findings here are quite instructive. There has been considerable legislative focus on the need to control judicial discretion, especially in sentencing.[37] The focus seems to have been motivated primarily by public awareness and concern about the problem of disparate sentencing. For example, under the former Arizona Criminal Code, sentences were prescribed individually in each penal statute. The range of sentences permitted was broad, giving courts power to shape individually the punishment of offenders for the purpose of rehabilitation. Such discretionary power caused widespread disparity in sentencing.[38] The approach of the new code is to classify each offense and specify punishment for each class.[39] In each class the range of punishment is sharply limited to coincide with the punishment objectives of the code.[40] As part of sentencing reform, Arizona also adopted the increasingly popular presumptive sentencing method in which minimum, maximum, and normative sentences are established for offenders.[41] While individual judges may, within certain ranges, raise or lower penalties and thus depart from the presumptive sentence, such departure requires specific support.[42]

A review of the questions used to gauge legislative action on police discretion shows very little action on police discretion problems. Such action has been neither sustained nor uniform and can be characterized as ambiguous at best. For example, some legislatures have repealed the full enforcement laws but apparently not because of concern with problems of police discretion. Also, while many state legislatures appear to have recognized the need for some discretion with regard to the use of citations, rarely have legislatures made efforts to structure and guide that discretion. It appears that other legislatures have addressed enforcement problems in some ambiguous criminal statutes and limited the discretion of some criminal justice officials, but only in rare situations.

Accounting for Legislative Inaction

What accounts for the lack of legislative activity to control police discretion? Professor Wayne Francis, in his seminal work on state legislative issues, argues that four factors substantially determine legislative action on public issues. The factors can be loosely classified as interest, conflict, resources, and expected impact.[43] Professor Francis argues that, by assessing the degree to which the four factors are present, the likelihood of legislative action on an issue can be ascertained.[44]

Analyzed according to the Francis model, police discretion legislation, not surprisingly, fails to emerge as an important issue to legislators. First, although it is quite easy to arouse interest in the topic of crime generally, no organized interest groups seek legislative action to control police discretion, especially in the arrest decision.[45] As Professor Herbert Packer stated, "The criminal law, after all, is not a subject that provides a very solid base of political appeal. It affects no powerful interests; it has no constituency."[46] Obviously, because it is so difficult to develop interest group activity on criminal law issues generally, it may be expected that concerns about arrest discretion will fare poorly in competition for a place on the legislative agenda.[47] Second, there appears to be little "conspicuous" public conflict on arrest discretion. This is not to infer that no public conflicts exist on other police discretion issues, as that is surely not the case—witness the recent outcry in many communities concerning use of deadly force and use of chokeholds by the police. But rarely have arrest issues been characterized as discretionary matters subject to the attention of legislatures.[48] This is supported by Francis' low ranking of the "courts-penal-crime" policy area on both the interest (twentieth of twenty) and conflict (seventeenth of twenty) scales.[49] Analysis of the resources and expected impact factors likewise reveals that police discretion legislation cannot be considered important according to the Francis scale.[50]

There is, however, a fifth factor that may have a significant impact on legislation: the degree of expertise that the legislature has on an issue affects its decision to deal with it. In limited interviews with state legislators, they frequently raised questions about the legal and political problems of deciding who should make the rules controlling arrest discretion and the difficulties of the legislature in providing such rules, in determining what factors should be considered in drafting rules, and deciding how such rules could be monitored.[51] Thus, an additional consideration that affects police discretion legislation is legislative inability to respond to the problems effectively.

Assuming that state legislatures desire to act to control arrest discretion, do they possess sufficient expertise and understanding of the problem to accomplish any real work in this area? Are the broadly drafted criminal laws the best that can be expected? The legislatures certainly have been offered little help on this issue by criminal law scholars. A significant shortcoming of the studies and articles on police discretion problems has been the tendency to consider the issue generally and not to provide specific principles, guidelines, or models to aid legislative bodies in the development of law enforcement policy making. Scholars provide extensive treatment of general propositions, but, as Justice Holmes once stated, ''No general proposition is worth a damn.''[52]

Typical of the general treatment on this subject is the landmark work on criminal law legislation by Professors Frank Remington and Victor Rosenblum.[53] While their article superbly illuminated a number of shortcomings of criminal law reform and could be considered a landmark work on the development of criminal law legislation, the authors gave little prescriptive advice for legislators. The same deficiency is also evident in other works on criminal law reform. Professor Wayne LaFave, for example, viewed the legislature's failure to consider how a law is to be enforced as a major shortcoming of penal code revision, but he was less than clear about how a legislature could provide enforcement guidance. LaFave gave no substantive suggestions or specific guidelines or principles to assist legislators in penal code reform. According to LaFave, legislative failure to deal with enforcement problems reflects a legislative policy judgment that it is more important to give prosecutors sufficient tools to accomplish their task of proving criminal charges than to deal with police enforcement problems.[54]

A few proposals on how to solve the problem of excess police discretion have been made. Unfortunately, the proposals have not been well developed or comprehensive and thus do not provide guidance for legislative action. Joseph Goldstein, for example, recommends the development of "Policy Appraisal and Review Board[s]."[55] He suggests that the boards be established by state legislatures to provide an investigative function "to assist commissions in drafting new codes in reappraising basic objectives of the criminal law and in identifying laws which have become obsolete." While his recommendations are useful, he fails to develop the broader theoretical considerations involved in his selection process. Finally, rather than dealing with the particularly sensitive institutional problem of state agency involvement in local law enforcement, he chooses to give his board an advisory function and to limit its investigations to enforcement of state laws.[56]

Stephen Schiller's proposal for "Enforcement Policy Boards" is more developed from an administrative point of view. However, Schiller does not discuss the real or theoretical problems of public participation in the formulation of discretionary enforcement policy making, and he does not address the problems of public dissemination of law enforcement policy statements.[57]

Wayne Schmidt's proposal for a "statewide law enforcement administrative council" addresses the imbalance in the literature on police rule-making proposals by developing a model statute for state legislatures. He has some excellent suggestions concerning the administrative structure for a statewide rule-making agency. However, he does not focus primarily on arrest discretion, and his proposal does not provide a theoretical framework to respond to concerns about the legal and political problems that are likely to arise from the approach he suggests.[58]

Other writers, instead of sketching institutional structures for agencies, have tried to outline rules to guide the enforcement of specific laws.[59] The purpose of such an undertaking generally has been to fill a substantial void in police training. Police training programs largely have failed to give new recruits any guidance or training in the discretionary aspect of their work. Training manuals, to the extent they address discretion, provide very general statements such as: "Discretion in the interest of justice and in the achievement of departmental objectives is defensible, but there should be like treatment for all individuals irrespective of economic or social status in the community."[60] Frank Vandall made one of the few attempts to deal with the discretionary aspect of police work.[61] Vandall's approach is to develop scenarios that provide discussion material dealing with policy issues encountered in the arrest decision. His work is a good beginning, but it is limited in scope: the major focus is on domestic disturbances and street gatherings. There is a need to focus on additional crimes and to refine theoretically the work he has done.

At present, the institutional stimulus to make arrest discretion an important issue is simply not present because the conditions described by Francis that confer importance do not exist.[62] But it is significant that, even if the issue becomes important in the manner suggested by Francis, which is a strong possibility because of increasing interest group activity and the change in local government liability,[63] the lack of models to guide police discretion legislation will remain a major impediment to legislative action. The critical problem seems to be knowing what to do and how to do it. There is no theoretical framework to guide legislative discussion of issues such as who should make the rules—state or local agencies; the optimal degree of public knowledge of the rules or participation in their development; or what principles are important or relevant to consider in the rule-making process. The lack of prescriptive advice from the criminal justice system scholars is a serious deficiency.

COURTS

The courts are an institution of government with special responsibility for and an ability to address problems of police discretion. However, there are significant institutional limitations placed on the courts. They do not have the prerogative of picking and choosing issues they deem important to address. Cases might involve significant public policy issues, yet those issues may not be disputed or be directly relevant to issues before courts and thus are beyond their jurisdiction. A court that seeks to address matters not before it is subject to the serious accusation that it is overreaching its constitutional power and authority. There appears to be a strong desire among members of the judicial branch not to exceed their constitutional power and authority.[64]

The courts also have a special difficulty in effectively addressing the day-to-day problems of law enforcement. This was clearly expressed in *Terry v. Ohio* when Chief Justice Warren conceded: "[W]e approach the issues in this case mindful of the limitations of the judicial function in controlling the myriad daily situations in which policemen and citizens confront each other on the street."[65] In spite of the limitations faced by the judicial branch, the courts are clearly policymakers, and the most prominent policymaker among the judiciary is the Supreme Court of the United States.[66] For that reason, it is appropriate to begin examination of the role of the courts in controlling police arrest discretion by looking at the Supreme Court.

The Supreme Court's Approach to Police Discretion

According to Professor Anthony Amsterdam, there are four major reasons why the Supreme Court of the United States is not able to take a more definitive role in the development of general police discretionary policies. First, the Supreme Court does not have daily supervisory control over the police. Its authority is limited to the cases that are litigated. This substantially reduces the opportunity for the Court to develop any comprehensive policies on the discretionary practices of the police. Second, because of the Supreme Court's heavy case load and other pressing matters of great national significance, the Court can consider and decide no more than three or four cases a year involving the issue of police discretion. A third limitation is the lack of statutes or police department regulations to be evaluated, which forces the Court to focus on the individual conduct of officers in specific cases.[67] Finally, even if the Supreme Court's findings enable it to develop case law addressing police practices, those decisions must be filtered down through several levels of government before they can begin to affect the conduct of the officer on the street. There is little assurance that policy established by the Supreme Court will be implemented by patrol officers.

In spite of the inherent limitations of its position, the Supreme Court has recently addressed some problems of police discretion in the broader sense of that term. In some recent cases, the Court has recognized that police are to exercise discretion and grappled with the extent of that discretionary power. In *Foley v. Connelie*, the Supreme Court recognized the discretionary power of the police and held that, because of the significant public responsibilities of the job, the selection process used by police departments could be above the norm required for jobs in the private sector.

Foley was an alien eligible in due course to become a naturalized citizen and was lawfully in this country as a permanent resident. He applied for appointment as a New York State trooper and was denied the right to take competitive examinations pursuant to New York Executive Law Section 215(3) which provides that "[n]o person shall be appointed to the New York State police force unless he shall be a citizen of the United States." Foley brought a class action suit before a three-judge district court which found the statute constitutional. He then appealed to the U.S. Supreme Court. Foley claimed the New York statute violated his rights under the equal protection clause of the U.S. Constitution. The question as framed by the Supreme Court was whether it would apply strict scrutiny analysis in determining the constitutional validity of the statute as it does for all alienage classifications, except classifications affecting positions held by either elective or non-elective "officers who participate directly in the formulation, execution, or review of broad public policy."[68]

The Court felt the test it must use was to examine the job and "determine whether it involves discretionary decision making, or execution of a policy, which substantially affects members of the political community." After examining the job, the Court upheld the statute *sub judice*, applying a less rigid rational basis test because

> [p]olice officers very clearly fall within the category of "important nonelective . . . officers who participate directly in the . . . *execution* . . . *of broad public policy*." *Dougall*, 413 U.S. at 647 [emphasis added]. In the enforcement and execution of the laws the police function is one where citizenship bears a rational relationship to the special demands of the particular position.

The Court felt that while

> [p]olice officers in the ranks do not formulate policy, *per se* . . . they are clothed with authority to exercise an almost infinite variety of discretionary

powers. The execution of the broad powers vested in them affects members of the public significantly and often in the most sensitive areas of daily life. . . . [The] police may, in the exercise of their discretion, invade the privacy of an individual in public places, e.g., *Terry v. Ohio*, 392 U.S. 1 (1968). They may under some conditions break down a door to enter a dwelling or other building in the execution of a warrant, e.g., *Miller v. United States*, 357 U.S. 301 (1958), or without a formal warrant in very limited circumstances; they may stop vehicles traveling on public highways, e.g. . . .

. . . .

Clearly the exercise of police authority calls for a very high degree of judgment and discretion, the abuse or misuse of which can have serious impact on individuals. The office of a policeman is in no sense one of "the common occupations of the community" that the then Mr. Justice Hughes referred to in *Truax v. Raich*, 239 U.S. 33, 41 (1915). A policeman vested with the plenary discretionary powers we have described is not to be equated with a private person engaged in routine public employment or other "common occupations of the community" who exercises no broad power over people generally.[69]

While the Court has recognized that the police have certain inherent discretionary powers, the recent difficulty has been to decide how to control those powers. For instance, in the case of *Delaware v. Prouse*, a Delaware law enforcement officer stopped an automobile and seized marijuana that was in plain view. During a hearing on a motion to suppress the use of the marijuana as evidence, the arresting officer testified that prior to stopping the vehicle he had not observed either a traffic or equipment violation or any suspicious activity. The officer further testified that in making the decision to stop he was not acting pursuant to any standards, guidelines, or procedures.[70]

The issue before the Supreme Court was whether the action of the officer constituted an unreasonable seizure under the Fourth and Fourteenth Amendments to the United States Constitution.[71] In other words, was it permissible for the officer to make such a stop when there was neither probable cause to believe that a crime had been committed nor even reasonable suspicion that the car was being driven contrary to the laws governing the operation of motor vehicles in the state of Delaware? The position of the Supreme Court in *Prouse* was similar to that in *Terry v. Ohio*,[72] which held that, at the very least, reasonable suspicion is required before an individual can be stopped.[73] In *Prouse*, the Court held that there must be "at least articulable and reasonable suspicion"[74] or "some other substantial and objective standard or rule" to make a stop permissible.[75]

In perhaps the most important statement on discretion in the case, Justice White made clear the Court's concern about unbridled police discretion: "This kind of standardless and unconstrained discretion is the evil the Court has discerned when in previous cases it has insisted that the discretion of the official in the field be circumscribed, at least to some extent."[76] While the Court is concerned about the stop of a citizen based upon the casual judgment of an individual officer, the decision in *Prouse* does include within it an invitation to recognize the need of the police to be able to use discretion in the type of problem the officer in *Prouse* was trying to monitor—highway safety. The specific need for such discretion is recognized in the Court's discussion of ways in which stops based on more than an individual officer's unsupported decision might be permissible. Specifically, the Court indicated that "checks that involve less intrusion or that do not involve the unconstrained exercise of discretion" are permissible. The majority listed as possible alternatives: the questioning of all oncoming traffic at roadblock-type stops, truck weigh stations, and inspection locations.

The Court seems to be attempting to show that it fully understands the need, at least in some instances, to stop vehicles even though reasonable suspicion that a crime had been committed does not exist. However, the Court feels that such stops must be based on a plan of action developed at a supervisory level in a police department. This plan must not permit the singling out of particular individuals without some appropriate and neutral selection criteria.

The concern with uncontrolled police discretion was also a central issue in *Brown v. Texas*. In *Brown*, the Court reviewed the validity of a stop under a Texas penal code provision that made it a crime to refuse to identify oneself on the request of a law enforcement officer. Zachary Brown was observed in an alley in El Paso, Texas, and police officers stopped him because he "looked suspicious." As in *Prouse*, the Court tried to balance law enforcement needs with individual rights. The Court held in *Brown* that the privacy rights of an individual should not be subject to the unfettered discretion of officers in the field. Seizure of a person must be based on specific, objective facts that indicate that society's legitimate interests require the seizure of that individual,[77] or, as stated in *Prouse*, the seizure must be made pursuant to a standard or rule embodying implicit limitations on the conduct of individual officers.[78]

The Supreme Court in *Brown* and *Prouse* established some outer limits on the power of the police to stop citizens. The Court was clear on the general point that uncontrolled police discretion is undesirable and that articulable, objective facts or a specifically approved plan will be required to validate police field encounters. But it is unclear how far the Court itself is willing to go to control police discretion. In neither *Brown* nor *Prouse* did the Court develop what would constitute specific, articulable, and objective facts. Nor did the Court in either case fully develop its thinking on what kind of plan for stopping cars or persons on the basis of less than reasonable suspicion might be constitutionally acceptable.

The Court obviously is concerned about the existence of unfettered discretion, but, as a policy-making body, it is limited in what it can do to control such discretion. Nonetheless, some basic thoughts guide the Court's thinking on police discretion. First, the Court presently appears to be more concerned than in the past about the discretionary activities of the police.[79] The amount of time and effort spent by the Court on basically "minor" cases reinforces this point.

Second, there is a general concern that the police should not exercise excessive discretion, but it is recognized that there are problems in drawing the line between excessive and permissible discretion. Clearly, the Court will apply minimal Fourth Amendment standards to control unfettered police discretion. However, the Justices seem to prefer that the police departments and local communities themselves develop "substantial and objective standard[s]"[80] to control the police. It appears that if such standards exist, considerable effort will be made by the Court to uphold them. In *Prouse*, the Court indicated that, although it was acting because of its concern about the "unbridled discretion" of the police, the action of the Court did "not preclude the State of Delaware or other States from developing methods for spot checks that involve less intrusion or that do not involve the unconstrained exercise of discretion."[81]

Third, the Court desires to assist the police in ferreting out crime and is willing to be as flexible as constitutionally permissible. In *Brown* and *Michigan v. DeFillippo*,[82] at least part of the Court's refusal to hold the "stop and identify" ordinances unconstitutional must have been a strong preference for state and local governments to act to control police discretion. The failure to hold the Texas statute invalid in *Brown* may be attributable in part to the general reluctance of the Court to go further than it must in overturning constitutionally deficient arrests.[83] But the refusal of the Court to invalidate the arrest in *DeFillippo*[84] seems to express a policy preference that the states have flexibility in controlling police discretion even though such flexibility might sometimes result in inappropriate ordinances.

Nonetheless, there do appear to be limits beyond which the Court will not go, in spite of its apparent interest in generating activity at the state level to limit and control the range of police discretion. While the Supreme Court successfully avoided deciding the constitutionality of "stop and identify" ordinances in *DeFillippo*[85] and *Brown v. Texas*,[86] it ultimately addressed that issue in *Kolender v. Lawson*.[87] Although the Court did not decide that "stop and identify" ordinances were inherently unconstitutional, the majority found that legislative failure to clarify what was "credible and reliable" identification under the statute resulted in the statute being facially unconstitutional.[88] The explicit concern of the Court was that the failure of the legislature to provide guidance as to how officers were to interpret the statute permits those officers to engage in "a standardless sweep [that] allows policemen . . . to pursue their personal predilections."[89] The lack of guidelines in such statutes "vests virtually complete discretion in the hands of the police to determine whether a suspect has satisfied the statute."[90] Again, there is a clear call for guidance from agencies of government that have some responsibility for the police.

Lower Federal Courts

The recognition of the need for neutral standards or rules to control police discretion has been treated more extensively in the lower federal courts. Lower court judges have dealt with the need for rules and some judges have even made extra-judicial statements elaborating on the need for rule making.[91] The cases have fallen generally into one of three categories: those in which the police have developed internal rules on their own initiative;[92] those in which the courts have suggested the development of rules;[93] and those in which the courts have required the development of rules.[94]

A good example of the cases where rules have been developed by law enforcement agencies without being suggested or required is the case of *United States v. Perry*. In *Perry*, the Metropolitan Police Department of the District of Columbia, apparently concerned with the problem of eyewitness identification, established a regulation limiting the time for conducting "on and near the scene" identification of suspects arrested to within sixty minutes after the alleged offense. The regulation provided that suspects must have been apprehended in close proximity to the crime scene before an "on the scene" identification could be conducted. According to the court, this effort to ensure that crime scene confrontations did not violate constitutional standards was "a careful and commendable administrative effort."[95]

In other cases, the courts have suggested the need to develop guidelines to control police action. The Supreme Court set the tone in this area initially in *United States v. Wade*,[96] and that has been followed by other courts. In the year following *Wade*, three major appellate court decisions strongly suggested the need for the development of rules to control the action of the police. In *Clemons v. United States*, the court, as in *Wade*, confronted a pre-trial identification issue concerning the use of photographs. The court stated: "Any well run department will presumably prepare and enforce careful regulations in this regard for the guidance of its personnel as it will also do with respect to police station lineups."[97]

In 1969, the Court of Appeals of the District of Columbia decided the case of *Dancy v. United States*, which also involved an "identification" problem. The court stressed that the lack of any plans for identification procedures to protect the rights of criminal defendants was a real shortcoming of undercover operations carried out by the department. The court in *Dancy* was especially concerned with the "low level of authority within the Police Department at which the formulation of undercover agent policies was carried on. . . . "[98] Thus, in addition to concern about the need for explicit regulations and procedures, there was an implicit recognition that procedures should be developed by those primarily responsible and accountable for the operation of the police department.

Two other cases have suggested the need to control the action of law enforcement officials and strongly implied that well-developed rules that include efforts to protect suspects' rights might very well obviate the need for court action. In *United States ex rel. Guy v. McCauley*, the federal court for the Eastern District of Wisconsin was concerned with strip searches conducted by the Milwaukee Police Department.[99] The searches in the case were conducted by law enforcement officers and not physicians. The court found that the routine practice of the Milwaukee Police Department to search the body cavities of females was clearly as egregious as the forced vomiting which the U.S. Supreme Court found to "shock the conscience" in *Rochin v. California*.[100] To alleviate this offensive situation, the court suggested "the promulgation of written guidelines for individual officers by the police department."[101]

It is interesting to note that strip searches are another issue which, by virtue of attendant publicity on their wholesale use, has created an issue of such significance that several state legislative bodies have moved to structure the discretion of the police in this area. While strip searches are not totally prohibited, the situations in which they can be used have been substantially limited. For example, in one state, strip searches cannot be conducted on persons arrested for simple misdemeanors unless there is probable cause to believe that the person is concealing a weapon or contraband.[102] Furthermore, if such a search is conducted

1. [The officer] must have written authorization of the supervisor on duty.
2. A search warrant must be obtained for probing any body cavity other than mouth, ears or nose.
3. The search must be conducted in a sanitary place and in some instances must be performed by a doctor.
4. Subsequent to the search a written report must be completed which includes the written authorization for the search, the names of the person searched and the officers conducting the search, and a copy must be provided to the person searched.[103]

While legislation establishing the limits of strip searches is a good example of the type of activities legislative bodies can take to limit and guide police discretion in one area, there are two points worth underscoring. First, legislative action on strip searches is consistent with our earlier thesis that such action occurs only after there is specific public interest in an issue; and, second, such action to control police discretion is, at best, sporadic. This of course leaves issues that do not generate sufficient legislative or court interest untreated.

Another example of a case suggesting rule making to control discretion is *United States v. Barbera*. In that case, the United States Court of Appeals for the Second Circuit suggested that the Immigration and Naturalization Service itself undertake administrative rule making to ensure that policies regarding searches be clarified.[104] Apparently, rather than attempting to develop guidelines in accordance with the court decisions on "border searches," the Attorney General simply developed regulations that provided for the redelegation of his power to conduct border searches to any immigration officers. *Barbera*, like *Dancy*, seems to express a concern about low-level decision making, even when there has been formal acquiescence by higher-ups.

Finally, there have been several cases in which courts have specifically required police departments to develop rules to guide their actions. In an opinion written by Judge Skelly Wright for the District of Columbia Court of Appeals, the court required the Metropolitan Police Department of the District of Columbia to systematize procedures for preserving evidence. In *United States v. Bryant*, the government lost a tape recording of a conversation between the defendant and an undercover agent. The court held that "sanctions for nondisclosure based on loss of evidence will be invoked in the future unless the Government can show that it has promulgated, enforced, and attempted in good faith to follow rigorous and systematic procedures designed to preserve all discoverable evidence gathered in the course of a criminal investigation."[105] Judge Wright further stated that agencies should draft rules suited to guide investigations and that such rules would be subject to review. The court referred to what it characterized as "an incipient but powerful trend in the law . . . a new judicial willingness to require promulgation of and obedience to rules by administrative agencies."[106]

The Court of Appeals for the District of Columbia also required the police to undertake rule development in a 1975 case. In *Washington Mobilization Committee v. Cullinane* the court required the Metropolitan Police Department to develop rules and procedures guiding arrest policies during mass demonstrations.[107]

The decision in *Cullinane* apparently relied in part on *Council of*

Organizations on Philadelphia Police Accountability and Responsibility v. Rizzo. *Rizzo* illustrates both federal judicial interest in the development of rules by police departments and what the Supreme Court sees as the limits to the authority of federal courts to order rule formulation. The district court in *Rizzo* required the Philadelphia Police Department "to formulate and submit for approval a comprehensive program for improving the handling of citizen complaints alleging police misconduct."[108] An agreement was negotiated between the parties and thereafter incorporated into a final judgment by the district court. The United States Court of Appeals for the Third Circuit affirmed the relevant part of the district court's judgment.[109]

The Supreme Court of the United States reversed the court of appeals' decision in a five-to-three decision. The Supreme Court reversal cast considerable doubt upon the premise that federal courts can as a general proposition order local police departments to develop rules to control police action. It appears that unless there is a substantial showing that acts of individual officers are affirmatively linked to a specific policy or plan of a local police department, the concern of the Supreme Court that the principle of federalism be respected would likely preclude the Court from upholding federal judicial interference in the operation of local police departments.[110]

The *Rizzo* case limited the power of federal courts to require police departments to make rules regarding their internal operations, but there was some question as to the continued viability of *Rizzo*, as only four of the five members of the court that voted with the majority in *Rizzo* remained on the Court in 1979.[111] There was an attempt to test the holding of *Rizzo* in the fall of 1979 when the U.S. Department of Justice filed suit in federal district court in Philadelphia to raise many of the same issues identified in the first case.[112] The second case, *United States v. City of Philadelphia*, was dismissed by the federal district court in Philadelphia and that dismissal was affirmed by the U.S. Court of Appeals for the Third Circuit.[113]

In spite of the opinion of the Supreme Court in *Rizzo v. Goode*, there is a growing trend for courts to look for and suggest the development of rules by the police,[114] and there is still a strong interest by the Supreme Court in fostering the development of rules. This position was clearly evidenced in *United States v. Caceres*. The Court in *Caceres* appeared willing to give great weight to the internal development of rules in balancing the individual's right to privacy against the need of the government to perform its law enforcement function.[115] In addition, one might also argue that the case of *Papachristou v. City of Jacksonville* would support the proposition that specific standards might save some ordinances from a constitutional challenge.[116]

In conclusion, *Rizzo v. Goode* and the more recent case of *Lyons v. Los Angeles*,[117] in which the Supreme Court refused injunctive relief against the use of chokeholds by Los Angeles police officers, indicate that the Supreme Court will discourage federal court intervention in local police management. However, the Supreme Court does have an interest in encouraging the adoption of law enforcement guidelines and standards as is plainly evident from the specific request for a neutral plan in *Prouse*,[118] the willingness to permit occasional violations of administrative guidelines in *Caceres*,[119] and the specific holding in *Kolender* that the deficiency in the stop and identify ordinance was the failure of the legislature to define what constituted "credible and reliable" identification.[120]

Response to Police Discretion by State Courts

Primarily owing to the holding in *Rizzo v. Goode*, there is a substantial obstacle to federal court review of local law enforcement policies. Thus, if rules to control police discretion are to be judicially mandated, they are most likely to come from the state courts. However, as suggested in chapter 2, state court treatment of police discretion issues is extremely inconsistent. While a number of decisions recognize the discretionary powers of the police and would appear to support development of rules to control police arrest policies, a number of decisions have been interpreted to oppose such development.

Typical of the state cases supporting discretionary decision making by the police is *Gowan v. Smith*. *Gowan* dealt with the question of the validity of a writ of mandamus to compel the police commissioner of Detroit to enforce an ordinance prohibiting the operation of saloons on Sundays. The language of the ordinance did not give the police any discretion, yet a majority of the Michigan court found that discretion was inherent in the ordinance.[121] *Gowan* makes clear that the police have "discretionary executive power" in the enforcement of the criminal law and that the courts should avoid intruding on that power absent "gross and manifest abuse" of such powers.[122]

As developed in chapter 2, the principal state case cited in opposition to the argument that the police can engage in law enforcement policy making is *Bargain City U.S.A. v. Dilworth*. In *Bargain City*, the Sunday closing law enforcement policy of the Philadelphia police commissioner—under which only employees of large commercial establishments were arrested—was attacked on the ground that it was discriminatory in violation of the Fourteenth Amendment.[123] The case is of limited utility. We must not lose sight of the fact that the primary limitation is subject matter. *Bargain City* was for all practical purposes a "Sunday Blue Law" case involving strong equal protection overtones with specific economic impact. An arrest decision that is based solely on the economic status of the arrestee is inherently suspect.[124] The recent case of *Bruno v. Codd* reflects the lack of understanding and direction of the state courts on arrest decisions.[125] In *Bruno*, the court offers very little in the way of any substantive theoretical underpinnings on the issue. While the court's concern was, as it should be, that the police followed a rule that precluded arrest in any situation in which the victim was the wife of the assailant, the court offered little of the basis for its decision. The trial court simply noted that it had the power to compel the police department to perform the duty imposed on police by law: to exercise their discretion to arrest in a reasonable, non-arbitrary manner. While the court did find that the police had what might be considered a "special duty" to protect wives, the nature and the basis of that duty was never developed. The court found that sufficient evidence was offered by the plaintiffs to present a factual question concerning whether the police failed to perform their duty of providing persons in the plaintiffs' position with proper police service.[126] While it may be unfair to expect that a court deciding on a motion for summary judgment should do more than decide the issue, there was some hope that the appellate decision in the case might offer more substantive thinking.

In the interim between dismissal of the motion for summary judgment and the appeal hearing, the police department entered into a consent decree with the plaintiffs.[127] Nonetheless, in an even more frustrating failure to develop the legal basis of its gratuitous comment, the appellate court indicates that had there not been a consent decree, it would not have been as willing as the trial court to limit the discretion of the New York City Police Department. The appellate court was clearly disinclined to grant the relief sought because of what it viewed as a broad invasion of some undefined executive authority.[128]

No general trend can be drawn from the state court decisions. On the one hand, the position developed in *Bargain City* appears to limit the discretionary power of the police. Yet *Gowan* clearly supports the exercise of discretion in the arrest decision. The trial and appellate court in *Bruno*[129] convey the present ambivalence and lack of any theory to guide the courts in the control of police discretion. As in *Prouse* and *Brown*,[130] there is explicit recognition in *Bruno* that the police are expected to exercise some discretion in the course of their work, but the problem is to find the limits. In *Bruno*, as in the other cases, there was no real effort to find those limits. Examination of the case law reinforces the view that, even if the courts do find a need for law enforcement policy making, they are unlikely to provide much leadership in achieving it.

It is not likely that any change will occur in the future in the manner in which cases are selected and handled, nor is there assurance that the reluctance of the Supreme Court to permit federal courts to intervene in state law enforcement problems will change. Even if the courts are inclined to discuss the amount and extent of permissible discretion, there are no basic theories or models for the courts to use to evaluate police action. The lack of such means that trial courts are unable to ask appropriate questions of police departments or their officers regarding informal arrest policies. If theory and models existed, the courts could use them to gauge the discretionary actions of police officers. But in the final analysis it is clear that the courts are not going to provide leadership here. It is necessary to look elsewhere to deal with the problems of police discretion.

PROSECUTORS

The role of prosecutors in selecting cases for prosecution would appear, at least on the surface, to give them substantial input into the police arrest decision.[131] Nonetheless, there has been very little discussion of the role of prosecutors in influencing police arrest policies.

It seems that police discretion is not an issue of concern to prosecutors. For example, when selected prosecutors in Iowa were asked to identify the "major criminal justice issues that confront the state," none identified police discretion. Even when prosecutors were asked to rank police-related issues, police discretion continued to rank toward the lower end of the priority scale.[132] Why does police discretion have such a low priority? It appears that the institutional structure and power of the prosecutor's office serve to limit the significance of police discretion as a problem and the impetus to deal with it directly.

First, a separation of function dilemma exists between police and prosecutors. Even though police and prosecutors have overlapping functions, which include the making of arrest decisions,[133] there is a traditional reluctance for prosecutors to monitor police arrest policies. This situation seems largely from the political separation of the agencies. Most prosecutors are elected officials and are thus separate and distinct political entities from local law enforcement agencies. Even in states in which prosecutors are appointed, it is rare that persons who appoint prosecutors will have a similar power to appoint local police executives. Thus, the police and prosecutor are quite likely to have very different political constituencies, and therefore differing law enforcement goals, which may be reflected in their enforcement policies.[134]

A second and more compelling factor accounts for limited interest of prosecutors in police arrest decisions. Very simply, prosecutors, in deciding which cases to prosecute, have the authority, should they choose to exercise it, to overrule arrest decisions by dismissing cases. The control by prosecutors over which cases will be prosecuted does not provide them with absolute control over arrest policies and resource allocation decisions of the police, but their power to make charging decisions may contribute to their feeling that police discretion should not be a major concern. However, there are two problems with such an approach. First, according to Professor Herman Goldstein, prosecutors mistakenly assume that when they are reviewing the cases brought to them they are reviewing all of the violations discovered by the police. In fact, police do a substantial channeling of cases before they bring them to the prosecutors. Prosecutors like many others are not aware of the number of decisions made. Second, as a practical matter, the low-visibility crimes that are brought forward by the police are rarely the subject of intensive or systematic review by prosecutors. Thus, while prosecutors might delude themselves that their power to decide on the prosecution of offenses precludes the necessity for a closer review of police arrest decisions, as a practical matter that power operates as a sporadic and distant check on police discretion, especially in the enforcement of low-visibility crimes.

A third and possibly most important reason for the reluctance of prosecutors to become involved in the development of police arrest guidelines is their desire not to call attention to the discretionary aspects of the criminal justice system generally and to prosecutors' own discretionary powers in particular.[135] Prosecutors have been reluctant to draw attention to their discretionary powers because of a feeling that there would be significant public concern about the extent of that power.[136] This situation may, however, be changing. Prosecutors, on their own initiative, are beginning to develop guidelines to control their discretion. A serious concern about the informal institutional decisions that have guided charge selection and plea bargaining in many prosecutorial offices has resulted in the development of formal policies. For example, the California charging manual outlines in considerable detail the proper course for prosecutors to follow in selecting charges for criminal violations. It even lists proper bases for exercising the discretion not to charge and develops the reasons not to charge in sufficient detail that a prosecutor can have at hand a practical and useful guide to aid in decision making.[137]

More recently, the United States Department of Justice released publicly and to all United States Attorneys, "Materials Relating to Prosecutorial Discretion." While the Attorney General took particular pains during the transmittal of the materials to point out that they were "not to be construed as Department of Justice 'guidelines' " and that they did not "impose obligations on United States Attorneys," the materials do provide concrete recognition of the need to develop some uniformity in the selection of charges and the charging decisions among the United States Attorneys.[138] Like the California charging manual, the Justice Department "Materials" attempts to distinguish appropriate and inappropriate factors for consideration in decisions to prosecute.[139]

Initially, efforts to control prosecutorial discretion most frequently occurred in offices with large numbers of prosecutors in which there was serious concern that charging and plea-bargaining decisions were made without any control or supervision. Previously, review of such decisions would occur only in cases of very serious crimes. Furthermore, any review that did occur generally would be informal.[140] The need to control prosecutorial discretion has begun to be recognized not only in large prosecutorial offices but in smaller offices throughout the nation.

If prosecutors are willing to limit their own discretion to ensure that their decisions are uniform and fair, it would seem that the other institutional reasons for their failure to monitor police arrest decisions may no longer be as compelling.

In fact, the county attorney's office in Polk County, Iowa, has attempted to limit and control police discretion in at least two ways. First, it has attempted to persuade the police to refrain from making arrests for low-visibility crimes when officers do not personally observe the criminal behavior.[141] This is apparently because of the difficulty of proving these violations in court without at-the-scene observations of officers. Second, the Polk County attorney's office has encouraged local law enforcement agencies to use their discretion to issue citations rather than to make custodial arrests in the enforcement of low-visibility crimes. The office has made it clear that "the rule should be to issue a summons for all simple misdemeanors unless a violator does something which warrants custodial arrest."[142] In other words, if a person is subject to arrest for disorderly conduct or public intoxication, that person should be released after issuance of a citation unless there is a fear that the disorderly behavior will continue absent an arrest, or there is no one to take the intoxicated person home or the intoxicant will probably not stay at home when taken there. The use of citations is a point of some controversy between the police and prosecutors.[143]

The extent to which prosecutors can force changes in police policies comes out vividly when looking at the citation issue. As detailed above, the Polk County attorney's office has been concerned that local police departments have failed to use the citation procedure as permitted by the state code. The Des Moines Police Department, for example, did in fact issue guidelines calling for the use of citations in lieu of custodial arrest. But examination of these guidelines reveals different approaches taken by the police and prosecutors on the use of citations. Des Moines Police Department regulations state:

Item 1—The citation shall be used whenever it is lawful to make an arrest for a misdemeanor under the following conditions:

a. If, in the officer's opinion, there is *no doubt* that the offense will not continue or reoccur if a citation is issued; or that the defendant *will appear* in court on the appointed date and time; or there is not an outstanding warrant or detainer issued against the individual, the officer may issue a citation.[144]

The prosecutors have asked the police to exercise their discretionary powers to issue citations. Unfortunately, the police have acted by developing rigid guidelines to control the issuance of these citations. The guidelines developed by the Des Moines police are not likely to result, and apparently have not resulted, in many citation arrests being made. Thus, the policy objectives of the prosecutors are thwarted, yet the prosecutors are unable to order the police to take a different approach than that which they have taken.

Because major institutional obstacles to prosecutorial review of police arrest decisions are being removed, a new era of cooperation between police and prosecutors may be under way. This trend can be expected to have significant implications for the development of police arrest policies. However, if substantial changes are to be made, there needs to be explicit delineation of the role of prosecutors in the formulation of law enforcement policies. Because of the different political bases of these institutions, prosecutors have limited ability to direct change by the police.

LOCAL GOVERNMENT

Traditional Reluctance of Local Government to Involve Itself in Law Enforcement

Limited local government involvement in police affairs is typical nationwide. Studies have found an alarming lack of interest by city officials in controlling the dealings of local police, especially their arrest decisions.[145] In a national study by the United States Commission on Civil Rights, in which the central focus was on the "institutional mechanisms which impact upon police conduct,"[146] a major concern was the lack of local government oversight of police activity. It is indeed rare that city officials deem it appropriate to monitor police arrest decisions. The pervasive attitude appears to be that hiring good officers and providing adequate training obviate the need for local government officials to review arrest decisions.[147]

City officials seem to embrace this position largely because of the lack of organized interest groups pushing for efforts to control police arrest policies.[148] This is not to imply that the public lacks interest in other aspects of police work; that is surely not the case. From time to time, concerns about the use of force and ways to limit discretion in that area have certainly been raised in many communities.[149] However, there has been little focus on discretion in the arrest decision by these same groups. A perceived concern about arrest decisions among interest groups might change the approach of the city officials. But even assuming there were such a change, two factors suggest that governmental efforts to control the police may not be forthcoming or may be substantially limited in scope. First, legitimate interest in law enforcement policy making is frequently mistaken for an attempt to interject partisan politics into the development of such policy.[150] Second, normal techniques of supervision and evaluation of local administrative agencies are not directly transferable to efforts to review activities of law enforcement agencies.[151]

In the United States, there have been generally negative results when state and local political officials have become involved in law enforcement.[152] During the early 1900s, involvement of local government officials in the internal operation of police departments was substantial, and it was clear that many law enforcement decisions were, to a large extent, partisan political decisions.[153] Because of strong public reaction against political control of law enforcement, the trend since that time has been to make special efforts to keep partisan politics out of law enforcement. This clearly has been the dominant attitude for the last twenty years. One study found a very determined effort on the part of local officials to stay out of police department work, particularly with respect to issues concerning development of law enforcement policy.[154] Unfortunately, the general feeling has been that local government review of police work is an either-or proposition: either local officials control the police and politics influences law enforcement policy or the police are left alone and politics do not affect law enforcement.[155] The choices do not seem to be as stark as that to this writer.

There are ways to moderate and supervise police activities without letting partisan politics influence such review and supervision.

Nonetheless, some argue that even if local government officials are able to overcome the traditional reluctance to monitor and review police activity, another obstacle must be surmounted. The argument goes that the responsibilities of the police differ fundamentally from those of many other locally oriented administrative agencies, and bringing the police under administrative control presents special difficulties because usual methods of supervision and evaluation are not appropriate.[156] Local governing bodies can easily evaluate the work of most municipal agencies because such work is largely ministerial. The various city agencies make recommendations for new sewage treatment plants, additional traffic lights, and street pavings, but the council decides whether the plants will be built, the lights installed, or the streets paved. The agencies then carry out the council's directives. The faithfulness with which they do so can be checked.

With regard to the police, it is a different story; rarely will city councils ask or will the police divulge their enforcement priorities, and even more rarely will the council indicate that the police are making too many or too few arrests. But there are some situations in which it is more difficult for city officials to evaluate the work of municipal agencies. For example, in education, welfare, and public health the agency tasks are much more than ministerial. Nonetheless, in spite of the difficulty of the task, city councils feel it is not only appropriate but highly desirable for them to monitor the direct action in health, education, and welfare. The approach toward the police is different. The same feeling of the appropriateness and necessity for control of the police does not exist.

Contributing to this point of view is a belief—one to which the police contribute—that local officials lack the expertise and knowledge to monitor police activity. The claims of lack of expertise and knowledge are similar to the ones made by many police agencies when the issue of civilian review boards was considered in many cities in the 1960s.[157] There is no doubt that considerable specialized knowledge is required in police work.[158] However, this does not mean that local officials cannot acquire sufficient knowledge of police operations to make intelligent evaluations of police work. The first step is to change the thinking as to the inappropriateness of such evaluations and to recognize that the police, like all other government agencies, are subject to monitoring and control, and that public officials who do not undertake such monitoring and control are seriously derelict in their duties.

Potential Municipal Liability and Local Government Involvement

Because there is such strong resistance by both public officials and the police to local government monitoring of police activity, it may be unrealistic to expect any change. While no voluntary efforts by local governments to monitor police activity appear to be on the horizon, a number of factors may in time compel a change of attitude by local government officials. Most significant are recent changes in municipal liability.

Traditionally, municipalities were not liable for the improper acts of their law enforcement officers. At the state level, although the sovereign immunity of the state from suit was not directly passed on to the local communities, a modified form of immunity developed over the years.[159] This immunity was primarily reflected in the distinction between governmental and proprietary functions. Local governments were liable for the improper acts of their agents only when those acts arose out of proprietary functions—when the local government was engaging in an activity that normally was done in the private sector, such as business.[160]

The view was that if local governments were competing with private enterprise, they should bear the same risks of doing business as those that were borne in the private sector. With regard to governmental functions, a different view was taken. In performing governmental functions, local governments were regarded as primarily motivated by the desire to provide a public service not performed by the private sector. A municipal government generally was immune from suit for the negligent performance of the "governmental" acts of its officers. Law enforcement functions invariably were classified as governmental functions; thus, for the most part, municipalities were immune from suit for acts or omissions arising from the failure of law enforcement officers to carry out their duties properly.[161]

Because of the traditional difficulty of bringing successful suits at the state level, many citizens turned to the federal courts and the civil rights statutes to remedy improper treatment by local police officials.[162] But, like efforts at the state level, that course of action had inherent weaknesses. Most notably, the Supreme Court of the United States held in *Monroe v. Pape* that a municipality was not a "person" and could not be held liable for acts of its employees that deprived citizens of their constitutional rights.[163]

Recently, however, there has been a remarkable evolution of the doctrine enunciated in *Pape*. The Supreme Court, in a reinterpretation of the legislative history of the Civil Rights Act, found that in some circumstances municipalities may be held liable for the "governmental" actions of employees. The Supreme Court in *Monell v. New York City Department of Social Services*[164] substantially overruled *Pape*[165] and began to open the door for suits against municipalities for the tortious acts of their employees.[166] This new theory of municipal liability, however, is limited. Rather than finding municipal liability after any showing of tortious action of a city employee or on the theory of *respondeat superior*,[167] the Court in *Monell* said that city liability would be found only if the action of the city employee could reasonably be said to represent official policy or informal governmental custom.[168]

Monell left some unanswered questions, most notably whether municipalities might have some type of qualified immunity from suit under 42 U.S.C. § 1983.[169] The Supreme Court in *Monell* hinted that such immunity was unlikely[170] and directly addressed the question in *Owen v. City of Independence*. In *Owen*, the Court held that a municipality may not assert the good faith of its officers as a defense to a liability suit.[171] More important, the Court said in *Owen* that section 1983 "was intended not only to provide compensation to the victims of past abuses, but to serve as a deterrent against future constitutional deprivations, as well."[172] Apparently, members of the Court felt that the threat of liability for damages may encourage those in policy-making positions to "*institute internal rules and programs* designed to minimize the likelihood of unintentional infringements on constitutional rights."[173] The Court added the following in a footnote:

> In addition, the threat of liability against the city ought to increase the attentiveness with which officials at the higher levels of government supervise the conduct of their subordinates. The need to institute system-wide measures in order to increase the vigilance with which otherwise indifferent municipal of-

ficials protect citizens' constitutional rights is, of course, particularly acute where the front line officers are judgment-proof in their individual capacities.[174]

Clearly, the Supreme Court is putting municipalities on notice that it is concerned about the lack of control by municipalities over their agents. The footnote has special importance for the relationship between the police and local government officials and may be interpreted to necessitate more activity at the local level to control police discretion. Lower federal courts are attempting to wrestle with many questions concerning the scope and extent of municipal liability for negligent training, supervision, and control of local police departments.[175] While some police departments may have taken refuge in the position of the Supreme Court in finding municipal liability only if the action of a city employee can be claimed to result from an official policy or informal custom, there is evidence that the courts are willing to go quite a way to find official policy or informal custom.

A case that clearly has significant implications for local police departments across the country is *Webster v. City of Houston*, which recognized an informal and covert practice of the Houston Police Department as establishing a "policy or custom" within the ambit of *Monell*.[176]

The testimony of the officers demonstrates that the use of a throw down weapon was well-nigh universal throughout the HPD. From their earliest days in the Police Academy, recruits surreptitiously learn to "protect themselves" by employing a throw down. Such protection may have influenced the officers, even if not intentionally, to use greater force than necessary or to resort to unnecessary force in borderline cases. In protecting themselves, the officers take away the innocent victim's constitutional right to be free of excessive force.[177]

The court found the police department liable for a killing resulting from this practice.

While the Houston case dealt with departmental policy on the use of deadly force, the distinct possibility that successful claims can be made that constitutionally protected rights have been violated in the arrest decision surely should cause municipalities to take a closer look at the function and operation of local police departments.

There is, however, another Supreme Court opinion that may diminish the impact of cases such as *Webster*. The Supreme Court in *Parratt v. Taylor* indicates that claims for the violation of federal civil rights under 42 U.S.C. § 1983 might not be heard in federal courts if there are alternative state court proceedings that would satisfy due process requirements.[178] The question that remains is how extensive is the holding in *Parratt*. It is possible to read the case narrowly to mean that the decision applies only to negligent deprivations of property, especially since that was the specific issue in the case. On the other hand, if construed in a broader sense it might be possible to conclude that violations of federal civil rights statutes that involve deprivations of life and liberty as well as property would be required to be tried in appropriately alternative state court proceedings if such existed. *Parratt* may be an opportunity for local police departments to avoid suit in federal court for violations of the federal civil rights of its citizens, but it might be premature to draw too much from the case as there is substantial conflict among the federal courts in interpreting it.

While the courts argue back and forth on such questions as appropriate damages[179] to award and forums to resolve violations of individual rights, it appears that immediate efforts must be made at the municipal level to prevent costly and extensive litigation. But what must be the nature of these efforts? At first blush it could be argued that mayors and city councils must more closely scrutinize police operations such as resource allocation decisions and police arrest policies. Even if they did, however, it is not clear that the end result would be substantially different. Most mayors and city council members would probably perceive that they are ill equipped to engage in such oversight. If city officials are to review police operations intelligently, they need to have a basic theory to guide them. At this point, there is no systematic way of reviewing the work of the police. No official enforcement policies are articulated, although informal policies are clearly followed.[180] Very simply, there is no way to determine whether the police have performed as expected because no standard of performance has been enunciated. Moreover, there is no systematic and institutionalized opportunity for local government input into law enforcement decision making. Even if an enforcement policy to judge performance existed, most city officials would have no way to evaluate the policy because of the lack of models against which to measure it.

Concern about the lack of models ultimately leads to the question of whether appropriate models can in fact be formulated. This chapter has demonstrated that the legislatures have not developed such models and that courts, prosecutors, and local government officials have not fashioned them on their own. Discussion of models is actually premature, however, because not only have models not been developed, the basic institutional theory that must guide their development has not been discussed. The next chapter will articulate and discuss that theory.

Formulating Models for Controlling Police Discretion — 4

Previous chapters have identified at least four major questions that must be answered if development of institutional models to control police arrest decisions is to be successful. First, what is the degree of responsibility of each institution—police, courts, legislatures, prosecutors, and local governing bodies—for the development of arrest policy? Should the police continue to develop arrest policy, but on a more formal basis? Should the other agencies develop policy? Should policy development be a joint endeavor? Second, who should participate in the process, and what offenses need to be examined? Third, what are, and how might one identify, politically satisfactory and legally appropriate guidelines for the enforcement of laws against specific crimes? Fourth, how might the guidelines be narrowed to specific rules? By attempting to answer these questions, one may gain a more accurate focus on how to create greater public accountability of law enforcement personnel as well as obtain the theoretical tools to control informal and uneven decision making.

PLACING PRIMARY RESPONSIBILITY FOR RULE MAKING

State legislatures are the most appropriate agency to undertake control in this area. But their reluctance to do so in the past is not likely to change in the future. In any event, assuming they eschew the role of active rule maker, legislatures have three basic options in choosing who should develop law enforcement policies. First, the state legislatures could decide that arrest rules are to be made by a state agency and then be applicable statewide. This choice would reinforce the state role in law enforcement. Second, the legislatures could permit local governing bodies or police agencies themselves to formulate selective enforcement rules. This approach would constitute a formal recognition of the local role in law enforcement. A third possibility could be some combination of state and local involvement in the rule-making process.

The major advantages of placing responsibility for rule development in a state agency are that it encourages uniformity in the application of state criminal law, centralizes responsibility for rule making, and facilitates the allocation of greater resources to finance and staff the police rule-making effort. Uniform application of the criminal law is a significant consideration in designating a police rule-making body. Although state agency development of rules does not guarantee the uniform application of such rules, it would ensure that the same rules are in effect statewide and substantially limit the ability of local law enforcement officers to put their own "gloss" on the rules. Centralizing rule development in a state agency also would have the advantage of concentrating policy-making authority and responsibility. One agency would be legally and politically accountable for the development of rules. Finally, centralization would enhance the likelihood of greater access to funds and personnel to assist in rule making.

A serious problem with placing rule-making responsibility at the state level is that a state agency is unlikely to possess sufficient public credibility and legitimacy to do its work. Simply creating, and granting power to, a new agency does not provide the immediate political credibility and legitimacy that would clearly be needed by an agency developing law enforcement rules. Action to control police discretion by a state agency is so novel that, if it is believed a state agency should be the rule-making body, serious thought should be given to selecting an existing state agency that already possesses substantial political credibility. Most states have several existing agencies that could undertake the police rule-making task, and normally the institutional role and purpose of those agencies is clear and has been publicly accepted.

In most states, there are at least three agencies that might be likely candidates for the policy-developing role: the state law enforcement training academy, the state crime commission, and the state attorney general's office. Law enforcement training academies normally are charged with developing and coordinating the training and education of law enforcement officers in a state.[1] State crime commissions are frequently charged "to ensure the maintenance of peace and good order" by coordinating law enforcement throughout a state.[2] The attorney general is the chief law enforcement officer in most states and thus generally has some ultimate responsibility for the actions of local law enforcement agencies.[3] All three agencies normally have some type of statewide mandate and are in a strategic position to monitor and control the development of law enforcement policy. However, each agency has a distinct political and legal basis.

Most law enforcement training academies have the responsibility to provide training to facilitate uniformity of law enforcement throughout the state.[4] Implicitly, the goal in establishing such training programs is uniform law enforcement by virtue of uniform training or, at the very least, the establishment of a minimum level of performance by local police officers. The trend in some states is to develop mandatory hiring in addition to training requirements.[5] So the mandate does exceed training. Should the state legislatures desire to place in one state agency the power to develop rules controlling police arrest practices and mandate that such rules be followed statewide, law enforcement training academies, by virtue of their present political power and legitimacy in many states, may be a good selection. There is general acceptance among the law enforcement community and the public of this clear intrusion of state law enforcement training academies into the selection and training of local officers. Most training academies have developed substantial goodwill throughout their states, although the goodwill has been achieved in part because the training academies have strictly construed their powers.

Selection of a state crime commission as the state agency to develop law enforcement policies would transmit different political messages to local agencies. Most state crime commissions have special strengths that would aid them in their role as rule-making bodies. They have "a continuing interest [in] and familiarity with the problems of [local] police departments through [their] involvement in developing solutions to [police] difficulties" and are "somewhat removed" from political influence.[6] However, the primary task of most state crime commissions has been the distribution of grant money on a statewide basis;[7] little of their work has involved the development of statewide operational policies. Their work has been largely of an advisory and suggestive nature—advising law enforcement agencies on technical and financial problems and suggesting ways in which to resolve them. If a state legislature makes the political judgment that it is a better course of action to encourage rather than to mandate rules, the choice of an agency like the state crime commission to develop model law enforcement policies would be appropriate.

An attorney general, in the capacity of chief law enforcement officer, may logically be considered as a potential rule maker. An attorney general is normally charged with providing what is, except for judicial decision, the most authoritative interpretation of state criminal statutes.[8] The use of the attorney general's office to make enforcement rules would be consistent with the recommendations of the American Law Institute's *Model Code of Pre-Arraignment Procedure*, which suggests that the chief law enforcement officer of the state issue regulations for the implementation of the criminal code.[9]

Use of the attorney general's office, however, presents some problems. First, in most states, the office is clearly a political one. The officeholder is not only a member of a partisan political party but also, because of the statewide nature of the office, a party member of considerable importance. Consequently, there has often been the public perception that decisions of the office are tinged with politics.[10] This factor alone might make it unlikely that a state legislature would consider increasing the law enforcement power and authority of state attorneys general. Second, in many states the office traditionally has only limited constitutional authority over local law enforcement; thus, legislative attempts to expand that power might prompt questions about whether the duties of the office had been expanded improperly. Finally, because of the wide range of responsibilities assigned to the office, the attorney general may have little actual knowledge of or interest in local law enforcement.

As candidates for the role of rule maker, the state law enforcement academy, crime commission, and attorney general all have certain advantages. Some of these advantages are derived from the specific nature of the respective agency's present responsibilities, and others result from inherent statewide authority and access to resources and expertise. But there are also significant disadvantages and obstacles to state control.

One disadvantage is the traditional reluctance of state agencies, the attorney general, the legislature, and even the governor to become involved in supervising local law enforcement.[11] A second disadvantage is the more practical problem of trying to accommodate the differing law enforcement needs that exist throughout a state. State agency resources would more likely be devoted to issues on which there was a general consensus rather than specific problems, which may vary from area to area. For example, if there was a need to deal with gambling violations in only one area of the state, it would be unlikely that the state agency would devote its resources to developing procedures and methodologies to deal with gambling enforcement problems. A final disadvantage of state development of local law enforcement policies is the strong resistance likely to come from local agencies[12] that view decisions about the enforcement of state criminal statutes as peculiarly local decisions.[13]

In light of these disadvantages, some scholars have suggested the development of rules at the local level.[14] A typical suggestion is to create local enforcement policy boards, which would review local law enforcement policy and formulate appropriate rules.[15] The primary reason for placing rule-making authority and responsibility at the local level is that it would reinforce the local role in law enforcement and affirm the attitude that such activity is local in nature. However, again, there are questions concerning political legitimacy, depending on which local agency makes the rules. Selection of the mayor or city council as the body primarily responsible for rule development would have the advantage of placing power in governmental institutions that have a history of making public policy decisions and of being held directly accountable for them. The problem, as previously indicated, is that mayors and city councils have refrained from developing their own law enforcement policies and have not reviewed the enforcement policies developed by the police.[16]

Most of those who have recommended development of rules at the local level have identified the police as the body most appropriate to make the rules.[17] But there are inherent problems in such an approach. The basic shortcoming is the lack of direct political accountability of the police. There is also the strong possibility that rules developed by the police would be perceived by the general public as beyond the scope of their powers and an abuse of police discretion.[18] Furthermore, local police agencies would be unlikely to have adequate funds for rule development, and there would be no incentives for police agencies to work together in formulating rules. This lack of collaboration would probably result in the development of inconsistent rules throughout the state.[19]

Each policy-making plan—local and statewide—has both advantages and disadvantages, and each has definite political costs and benefits. To achieve uniformity of the rules yet retain some local control over development of law enforcement policy, it might be appropriate for state legislatures to require local law enforcement agencies to develop rules and to have those rules reviewed at both the state and local levels. Municipal agencies, however, currently lack models and guidelines to assist them in review of police rules. To overcome this problem, a state agency could conduct studies on the law enforcement problems in the state and formulate guidelines for police agencies to consider in making rules. Municipal agencies could also use the guidelines to evaluate rules developed by the police.

After municipal action, the state agency could review the local rules to check for general compliance with state law.[20] This approach would encourage general uniformity in rules while maintaining a degree of flexibility to deal with problems unique to local communities. Because the state legislature has ultimate authority for the criminal laws of the state, it must have some input into and ultimate control over criminal law enforcement policy. Local rule making subject to state agency review seems the best compromise possible and would ensure the integrity of both state and local political processes.

In other contexts, there have been some recent attempts to deal with the problem of how to structure formulation of rules by local police agencies. Connecticut, in an attempt to bring about more control of high speed chases by the police, required most police departments in the state to adopt a policy controlling such chases. Under the Connecticut statute, there is no provision for state review of those policies.[21] On the other hand, the recent approach of the Iowa legislature is closer to the compromise suggested. Under a new statute that encourages issuance of citations in lieu of custodial arrests, local police departments may develop guidelines for the issuance of citations in all cases involving violation of simple misdemeanor offenses and most other crimes.[22] While the departments are not obligated to develop such guidelines, if they do so, they are to submit those guidelines to the Iowa Law Enforcement Academy Council for review. The Iowa Law Enforcement Academy Council after reviewing such guidelines is to submit its recommendations concerning guidelines to the general assembly.[23] This approach is one example of how local development of law enforcement rules with state agency review might be accomplished. It is interesting to note that in this latter case very few arguments have been made that placing responsibility for review of local law enforcement practices with a state agency usurps local police powers.

THE RULE-MAKING PROCESS

In addition to developing an institutional structure for formulating police arrest policies, there are four related issues to consider. First, if the police are the primary agency formulating the policies, how do other local institutions and the general public participate in the process? Second, which laws or police practices should go through the process? Third, are arrest policies to be publicly disseminated after they are drafted? Fourth, what should be the legal effect of the rules?

INPUT BY LOCAL GOVERNMENT OFFICIALS, THE PUBLIC, AND PATROL OFFICERS

Broad institutional participation at both state and local levels is critically needed. The major question, however, is the nature of such participation. The involvement of local government officials such as the mayor and city council would probably broaden the political support for and the legitimacy of formulated rules. In light of the limited involvement of mayors and council members in the past, it is unrealistic to expect any major changes in the future. Nonetheless, after the police have drafted rules, the dissemination of rules to these officials would invite reasoned and official response, while increasing the opportunity to broaden institutional consensus on the rules. Initially, because of the tradition against monitoring local police and feelings of lack of expertise, not much more than review and comment might be expected; however, that would be a substantial advancement over the present situation. This review and comment process would crystalize law enforcement issues and permit them to be dealt with directly.

It would also be important to involve prosecutors in the process of rule formulation. Prosecutorial agencies have the power, if they choose, to nullify arrest policies. If prosecutors choose not to prosecute persons arrested for violating criminal code provisions, does it make sense for the police to allocate resources to the enforcement of such laws? As a practical matter, most police departments are aware of local prosecutorial policy and follow it. But this can and often does present problems for the police. For example, an internal policy against prosecuting misdemeanors that are not personally observed by officers can create undesirable situations that, through no fault of the police, adversely reflect on them. An officer is placed in a dilemma when forced, for example, to explain to irate parents, on a Sunday outing in the park with their children, that prosecutorial policy does not permit the arrest of a person urinating in open view in the park unless the act is personally observed by the officer.[24] While it may be arguable that it is necessary for the police and prosecutors to have some conflicting policies, it is advisable that the conflicts be clearly delineated and that policy be made after due consideration of possible ramifications. The development of rules by the police with review and discussion by other local government agencies, especially prosecutors, would have the important advantage of compelling explicit policy statements from both police and prosecutors on their respective enforcement policy goals.

This broader review would also aid the police in understanding the enforcement style desired in a community and in selecting laws for rule development. Law enforcement styles vary from community to community and present an added dimension to the problem of developing arrest policies. This fact reinforces the need for widespread participation in the rule-making process. There is a need for explicit institutional and community input into the decision regarding the enforcement style[25] desired by the community. Studies have shown that the police attempt to enforce the law as they perceive influential community members desire it to be enforced, but the cues upon which the police make such judgments are largely informal and non-directive.[26] Development of formal arrest policies requires that more explicit cues and directions be given and that there be some community consensus on the enforcement styles desired.

Public hearings prior to the promulgation of enforcement policies might be one way to provide police agencies with information about the kind of law enforcement the public really wants.[27] Does the public want the criminal laws fully enforced? Do they want all drunks off the street or only the violent ones? Do they want all gamblers arrested or only those associated with organized crime? It is important to generate enforcement policy that explicitly considers community attitudes. Policy should represent a public consensus on desired law enforcement yet not simply reflect the values of dominant political forces in a community. Allowing community input in the rule-making process is likely to aid both in developing a public consensus on police rules and in enhancing the possibility that the public will accept and support law enforcement action consistent with the rules.

In view of their responsibility for the operation of police departments, the chief and his or her immediate subordinates will undoubtedly develop any rules that are made. The role that street patrol officers should and will play in the development of rules, however, is less clear. There is need to encourage participation from such officers. Obviously, they have important contributions to make regarding the practical application of the rules. Their knowledge of the day-to-day problems of the officer on the street will be more current than that of many police officials, and thus their involvement in the development of rules would increase the likelihood that significant enforcement problems would be addressed by the policy-making bodies.

Another reason for involvement of patrol officers is to minimize their resistance to the rules. It is likely, judging from recent events, that when police agencies move to structure the discretion of their personnel, there will be a strong negative reaction from the rank and file of the departments.[28] Patrol officers may view the efforts to develop rules as another attempt to limit their power and authority. Allowing representatives of patrol officers to participate in the rule-making process may help police understand that rules are not an attempt to eliminate their discretion but to guide it. This may help diminish the opposition from these formidable "street corner politicians."[29]

LAWS AND POLICE PRACTICES

In addition to determining who should have input into the rule-making process, it is necessary to determine which laws are appropriate for rule making. The laws most appropriate for the rule-making process are those that have the greatest potential for abuse. One source of guidance in this area is Professor James Q. Wilson's model, which classifies police response to law violations. According to Professor Wilson, law enforcement and order maintenance are the two primary functions performed by the police. Law enforcement situations arise when there is a clear violation of law and only guilt needs to be assessed.[30] Order maintenance situations arise when there is not only a violation of the law, but also a need to resolve a dispute, interpret the law, determine standards of proper conduct, and assign blame.[31] Police action in law enforcement and order maintenance situations can be invoked by either the police or citizens. The four possible combinations are: police-invoked law enforcement,[32] citizen-invoked law enforcement,[33] police-invoked order maintenance,[34] and citizen-invoked order maintenance.[35] Professor Wilson found that

> in Cases I [police-invoked law enforcement] and IV [citizen-invoked order maintenance] the patrolman has great discretion, but in the former instance it can be brought under department control and in the latter it cannot. In Case II [citizen-invoked law enforcement] the patrolman has the least discretion except when the suspects are juveniles and then the discretion is substantial and can be affected by general departmental policies and organization. Case III [police-invoked order maintenance] is intermediate in both the degree of discretion and the possibility of department control.[36]

While Wilson's typology of the discretionary situations faced by officers is very useful, it has some flaws. As a practical matter, in almost all situations in which police action is initiated by a citizen, there is likely to be minimal discretion simply because there is active citizen involvement. This would be especially true of citizen-invoked law enforcement situations, the bulk of which tend to be felonies. While Wilson's assumption that this is the category in which the least amount of discretion occurs seems valid, the basis for this conclusion seems erroneous. It is more realistic to assume that less discretion is exercised in this area because, if an offender is identified, there is limited discretion in deciding whether to arrest. The action of the officer will be influenced largely by the fact that most crimes in this category are major crimes, such as felonies, and there is an active complainant.

Likewise, it seems that citizen-invoked order maintenance would in practice be closer to an intermediate area of discretion than an area of great discretion. In citizen-invoked order maintenance situations, the police have been called to the scene, usually by one of the participants in the dispute. The police officer must attempt to settle the dispute and make an arrest or referral. The general tendency of the police in domestic situations, which would seem to constitute a good proportion of citizen-invoked order maintenance situations, has been not to arrest.

> Law enforcement officials offer a variety of explanations for decisions not to arrest in cases of domestic assault. Probably the most frequently cited reason is that the victim does not wish to have [the assailant] arrested. Police officers are accustomed to having the cooperation of the victim of a violent crime, and most want to protect the victim's interests. They are reluctant, therefore, to overrule the victim's desires and arrest her assailant.[37]

Failure to arrest, however, does not mean that the police officer has discretion to do nothing but indicates the officer's decision to take some action other than to arrest.

The frequency and repetition of domestic calls and the existence of a complaint would seem to indicate that, rather than being a situation of wide discretion, citizen-invoked order maintenance is a situation in which there can be substantial administrative control. Certainly, there can be much more control than in the case of police-invoked order maintenance. Professor Wilson maintains that in those situations, which include crimes such as drunkenness and disorderly conduct, a police administrator can exert substantial control by conveying to the officers the administrator's policy preferences, such as "keeping things quiet, making more arrests," or "slowing things down."[38]

As a practical matter, even if such policy is articulated, the directives can control individual encounters of the police only at the margins. Unless the administrator has given specific guidance about when and in what circumstances the law should be invoked and has closely reviewed actions of officers, the third category permits wide-ranging discretion. There are no citizen complainants, administrators are not directly involved, and the individual officer generally acts on his or her own.

The range of policy making, therefore, varies somewhat more than Professor Wilson suggests. Nonetheless, more thinking along the lines he has developed needs to be done to identify the crimes for which rule making is appropriate and those for which it is not, as well as how discretionary problems vary among criminal offenses. Such information would give rule makers much needed guidance.

Another important issue in the enforcement of the criminal laws is the role of the complainant. The role of the complainant in the decision to arrest raises a number of questions that bear on police rule making. First, should the complainant play a significant part in determining whether criminal charges will be filed against a particular defendant? Professor Kenneth Davis found that in many cases in which there was no likelihood of a signed complaint, the police would release the offender.[39] It is within the power of the complainant to decide not to file a complaint,[40] but there seems to be a lack of information about how such power affects the complainant's interaction with the police. Second, to what extent is it permissible to allow police enforcement attitudes toward complainants to vary depending on the socioeconomic status of the neighborhood in which the complainant resides?[41] Do the police push for a complainant to prosecute an offender to the same degree in a lower socioeconomic black community as they do in an upper-class white community? This is a serious concern. Research indicates that the police have, in many cases, decided that a higher level of assault is permissible in lower socioeconomic areas.[42] The question for the rule makers is, how might police rules control such decisions and who should determine the validity of pleas for enforcement of the criminal law? It is doubtful that individual police officers should be allowed to decide on their own.

The extent to which the demeanor of the offender will be allowed to play a part in the arrest decision is another issue. Apparently, many police officers think that verbally abusive conduct by the offender is a violation of the law.[43] Research strongly suggests that non-legal variables, such as the demeanor of the offender and, particularly, disrespect toward the officer, have a significant impact on the arrest decision.[44] It is doubtful that legislatures intended to give officers the authority to arrest a person because the individual "flunked the attitude test."[45] Rule makers need to deal explicitly with this problem.

PUBLIC ACCESS

Professor Arthur Bonfield believes there are valid reasons for exempting agency rules concerning law enforcement policy from public disclosure. According to Professor Bonfield, by permitting public disclosure of some law enforcement rules, the government would provide incentives for technical violations of the law. He believes that complete disclosure of the rules would encourage some citizens to avoid arrest while coming as close as possible to violating the law enforcement policy. Because of these problems, Professor Bonfield thinks that there is a compelling need to maintain confidentiality of enforcement rules.[46]

On the other hand, Professor Kenneth Davis supports public dissemination of police rules. First, he believes that all public agencies should make their policies known. Second, fairness requires that those persons affected have a chance to know enforcement policies. Third, he is of the firm opinion that the public will prefer to know the truth about law enforcement.[47] Because of the sound arguments on both sides of this issue, it is important that the police agencies and government officials explicitly address this problem in the rule-making process.[48] The competing considerations seem to be a concern that some offenders will technically violate the law but not to the degree requiring arrest, thus bringing about inherent disrespect for the law, and a concern that the public should have full knowledge of when laws will be enforced, even if that knowledge may itself cause some disrespect for the law and law enforcement officials. In other words, to what extent does and should mystery about law enforcement motivate and support its deterrent value?

EFFECT OF RULES

A final question that should be addressed is whether the arrest rules should have any legal force and effect beyond the law enforcement agency. For example, what would be the result if a person were arrested by an officer who, while having probable cause to make an arrest, clearly violated agency rules in making the arrest?[49] Can the arrest that is in violation of the enforcement rules be challenged by the arrestee as a violation of due process or equal protection of the laws? In other words, do the rules serve merely as internal guides to assist officers in the enforcement of the laws, or are they rigid standards that must be adhered to lest the courts void the officers' acts?

There is likely to be strong support among the police for restricting rules controlling arrest discretion to the status of internal guides.[50] The problem is, however, that when arrest rules are given only internal effect it might appear to the public that a law enforcement agency can violate its own rules with impunity and escape penalty. Thus, the political legitimacy of acts in violation of arrest rules and, consequently, the rules themselves may be questioned.[51]

In spite of reservations about the political legitimacy of rules having only internal effect, practical considerations and case law seem to support such a position. In *United States v. Caceres*,[52] the Court held that an agency's disobedience of its own regulations is insufficient to overturn agency action when such disobedience does not affect the constitutional or statutory rights of the defendant.[53] By promulgating rules that do not have the force and effect of law, an enforcement agency may be able to avoid creating citizen "rights" that would be prejudiced by non-compliance on the part of an officer.

The view that police rules should not be given external effect in cases in which a citizen seeks to use the rules as a basis for a claim against the police is also supported by some recent state cases. In *Chastain v. Civil Service Board of Orlando*[54] and *City of St. Petersburg v. Reed*,[55] Florida appellate courts concluded that police department regulations limiting the use of deadly force could establish standards for internal disciplinary proceedings but not for civil or criminal actions outside the police departments.[56] However, the one other case that has been decided on this issue reaches a different result. *Peterson v. City of Long Beach* held that administrative regulations concerning the use of force could be used in court proceedings to establish the appropriate standard of conduct for the police.[57] To overcome this problem, legislation has been introduced in both California and Michigan that would amend the rules of evidence in those states so that written policies, procedures, rules, guidelines, orders, or directives of a law enforcement agency concerning the discharge of duties by its officers would not be admissible as evidence of a standard of care or negligence in any civil action other than a disciplinary proceeding.[58]

To be sure, permitting an agency to develop arrest rules that could not be used outside an agency can have significant political ramifications. Nonetheless, it seems that if the overriding desire is to encourage the police to develop and use rules that provide general guidance for the police—and on balance that does seem to be the desired goal—then the search must be for ways to reduce the criticism that is likely to come from permitting the police to periodically violate rules yet not be subject to court challenge.

Conceivably, the involvement of other agencies and officials that are directly accountable to the public in the formulation of police rules would blunt some of the criticism that might come from permitting rules to have only internal effect. Political acceptance of such rules might also be increased if it is made clear that, while the rules may not be used by citizens to contest the legality of their arrests, the rules do establish clear standards of conduct for officers. There must be assurance that law enforcement agencies will discipline officers whose conduct does not conform to the standards.[59] Therefore, the effect of rules promulgated by police agencies would be to establish a means by which officers would gain knowledge of proper police arrest decisions, and every officer who does not comply with the rules must be subject to disciplinary action, including fine, suspension, reduction in rank, or discharge. The assurance of disciplinary action for violation of internal rules would ensure that the public interest would be protected.

The policy issues discussed above are only a few examples of the type of problems likely to be faced when efforts are made to develop rules to control selective enforcement of the criminal law. The problems of rule making will vary from state to state and special needs will need to be taken into consideration. There may be state statutory provisions that provide answers—some possibly not desired—to the questions raised here.[60] In any event, more work needs to be done to determine ways in which to control police discretion and to determine the appropriate administrative framework within which to achieve that objective.

GENERAL PRINCIPLES TO GUIDE DEVELOPMENT OF RULES

After procedural and policy questions have been dealt with there is a need to articulate general principles to guide the development of rules. According to Professor Davis, police rules must be "(a) acceptable to the public, (b) attractive to the police, (c) susceptible of administration by patrolmen, (d) sound substantive policy, and (e) legal."[61] Because Professor Davis does not elaborate on those general requirements, it is appropriate to explore ways to meet them.

Public acceptance of rules is important for both symbolic and practical reasons. If a large proportion of the public is not sympathetic to the enforcement of a law, the law is likely to be violated, especially if the sanction for violation is not severe. Blatant and continuous violations of an unpopular law are likely to produce a spillover effect, debasing the public respect for all law.[62] In the same manner, a needlessly unpopular police rule would be openly violated. For example, if the police in a major university town have a rule requiring the arrest of all persons found drinking at a football stadium, as opposed to a rule that calls for the arrest only of those who are disorderly as well as intoxicated, not only would enforcement in most cases be difficult, but, by the nature of the extensive violation of the offense, arrests necessarily would be arbitrary. There is likely to be continued violation of the rule as well as disrespect for the officers called upon to enforce it.

The most important step in making rules attractive to the police is to give a clear indication that the rules are designed to guide discretion, not to eliminate it. Because of the complexity of the police officer's job and the inability of any person to foresee all the problems that an officer might encounter, police officers must retain broad discretion. The goal for the body formulating police rules is to achieve the appropriate proportion of discretion and guidance to ensure that decisions are based on more than an individual officer's judgment.

Rules might also become more attractive to the police if it is made clear that rules would be helpful in explaining police action to the public. If the police can turn to rules to defend or explain their conduct, then there would be less concern that the police might be abusing their authority. In fact, if police officers can be convinced that it is unfair to them to require them to continue to act with virtually no guidelines, then new rules are likely to be very popular indeed. The replacement of the myth of full enforcement with guidelines and rules would enable the police to show that arrest decisions are not personal decisions but are subject to guidance and control. The rules would place the officer in a straightforward and honest position—one that the public could clearly understand.

Another way in which rules might be made attractive to the police is to include within the rules guidance on choosing alternatives to arrest.[63] Guidance on when it is appropriate to use referral agencies and diversionary programs would assist the police in making discretionary decisions.[64] There has been a recent attempt not only to guide police discretion but to deal with ways to resolve problems confronted by the police in Wisconsin. Legislation was considered that would give officers in cases in which they were considering the issuance of citations in domestic abuse situations the opportunity to require that, as part of the citation process, the offender leave the premises of the violation. If the person did not leave he would be subjected to custodial arrest.[65] This creative way to guide officers' discretion yet respond to the frequently critical need in domestic abuse situations to separate couples, clearly shows great potential for use of departmental rules and guidelines. Such guidelines can clearly be much more than a litany of negative directives.

If the rules focus on common problems faced by the police, they are likely to gain greater support from the officer on the street. Again, it must be recognized that it will be impossible to develop rules controlling the entire range of discretion currently left to the police. The goal should be to concentrate first on developing rules in the area in which the police need the most guidance: the problem areas of enforcement against low-visibility crimes—those frequently recurring crimes that are more susceptible to the formulation of simple and precise rules than are the more complex felonies and major crimes, which, in any event, are likely to be fully enforced. Because low-visibility crimes are committed very frequently, informal enforcement standards probably already exist within most police departments.[66] To review and integrate those informal practices into a system of rules probably would be simpler than to develop rules concerning crimes that occur less frequently and present more complicated factual situations.

Rules must be simple and precise so that they may be easily applied by officers in the field without extensive interpretation and deliberation. If police arrest rules are complex and difficult to implement, there is considerable likelihood that they will not receive widespread support within police departments. This is another argument for developing law enforcement rules for the low-visibility crimes.

The requirement of easy administration goes beyond the application of the rules by officers in the field. The rules also must be susceptible to convenient monitoring by superior officers, who, for the rules to be effective, must exercise regular *control and supervision* of patrol officers. The supervision requirement would mean that there would be more complete reporting of the activities of the police than is presently done.[67] To the extent that records of police/citizen contact have been kept in the past, they generally have permitted very little evaluation of law enforcement activity.

A significant problem has been that in many cities officers make no systematic reports on field encounters that do not result in an arrest.[68] In fact, one study found that in two out of three cities studied, no systematic records were kept of how the officers spent their time, and no information was gathered on what decisions, other than arrest decisions, officers made during police/citizen encounters.[69] Requiring more complete reporting by officers on all citizen contact that arises in the context of possible arrest is essential for adequate supervision. Officers could file written reports or brief field evaluation forms describing the exact nature of the citizen contact and the disposition.[70] Technological advances are such that the forms could be pre-coded and computer analyzed to aid in the determination of whether officers' actions were within departmental enforcement rules.

To ensure that the rules reflect sound substantive policy, it first must be determined whether the rules make sense in terms of the general enforcement goals of the legislature. To make this determination, it must be assumed that the goals of the legislature are to require the police to engage in both law enforcement and order maintenance[71] and that the legislature expects the police to exercise discretion in enforcing laws and ordinances that do not violate significant societal norms.[72] In light of the previous discussion on the objectives of criminal law legislation, such an assumption seems correct.

Order maintenance laws establish general standards of conduct; consequently, their periodic and occasional enforcement does not have a substantial impact on society unless the laws are enforced discriminatorily. Low-visibility crimes constitute a large proportion of the order maintenance category and thus appear to be the type of criminal laws for which rule development would be most desirable.[73]

Sound substantive policy also requires that, in the development of rules, police departments give due consideration to enforcement problems. For example, Professor Wayne LaFave has expressed the concern that legislatures have passed laws that are virtually impossible to enforce and have subjected the police who attempt to enforce them to ridicule and condemnation.[74] Rule makers would be well advised not to make the same mistake by developing highly impractical rules when they draft enforcement policy.

Finally, the rules must be legal. But what does that mean? The basic assumption is that the police cannot criminalize conduct that has not been criminalized by the legislature, but it seems that rules must be "legal" in a much larger sense as well. For example, arrest guidelines that violate constitutional guarantees or permit officers to make arrests based on a citizen's demeanor would be impermissible, as would arrest policies clearly based on racial, sexual, or religious grounds.[75] The public will not accept law enforcement rules if principles against such differential enforcement are not clearly enunciated. The major objective of the guidelines is to decrease disparate treatment, not to institutionalize it. Therefore, it seems important to reinforce the idea that rules must be "legal" in the full sense of the word.

APPLICATION OF GENERAL PRINCIPLES TO SPECIFIC RULES

After general principles have been drafted, it is necessary to use them to develop specific rules for selected crimes. To gain some understanding of how this process might work, it is worthwhile to analyze a possible approach to one minor offense: simple assault. Simple assault is a low-visibility crime, routinely and frequently committed.[76] Simple assault also possesses another important characteristic: there have been numerous allegations that assault laws are not uniformly enforced. More specifically, the allegations are that racial and socioeconomic considerations affect the enforcement of assault laws[77] and that the police improperly consider family relationships when called to the scene of an intrafamily assault.[78]

Most state statutes on assault are cast in specific and unambiguous terms; on their face they require full enforcement. The statutes normally state quite simply that any touching of one person by another against his or her will constitutes an assault.[79] Few assault statutes provide any guidance on when they should be enforced; thus, the police are largely on their own in making enforcement decisions.

The first step in developing enforcement rules is to analyze not only the language of the relevant statute but also the underlying policy objectives likely to have motivated the legislature to enact the specific statute in question. In addition, it is important to attempt to assess how enforcement goals might appropriately fit within these policy objectives. Looking first at the Iowa assault statute one finds that:

A person commits an assault when, without justification, the person does any of the following:

1. Any act which is intended to cause pain or injury to, or which is intended to result in physical contact which will be insulting or offensive to another, coupled with the apparent ability to execute the act.

2. Any act which is intended to place another in fear of immediate physical contact which will be painful, injurious, insulting, or offensive, coupled with the apparent ability to execute the act.

3. Intentionally points any firearm toward another, or displays in a threatening manner any dangerous weapon toward another.

Provided, that where the persons doing any of the above enumerated acts, and such other person, are voluntary participants in a sport, social or other activity, not in itself criminal, and such act is a reasonably foreseeable incident of such sport or activity, and does not create an unreasonable risk of serious injury or breach of the peace, the act shall not be an assault.

. . . .

1. A person who commits an assault, as defined [above], with the intent to inflict a serious injury upon another, shall be guilty of an aggravated misdemeanor.

2. Any other assault is a simple misdemeanor.[80]

One way to understand the policy objectives of the statute is to analyze prior assault sections of the Iowa Code. Remarkably, parts of the Iowa assault statute that was initially enacted in the 1851 Code of Iowa remained unchanged until the recent criminal code revision.[81] The major difference between the older and present provisions was that the 1851 Code did not define what constituted an assault,[82] and until 1978 the Iowa courts applied the common law definition.[83]

In the 1851 Code, the Iowa legislature, to be sure, did express some policy judgments about the crime of assault. In addition to providing specific penalties for acts in which the assault was combined with the effort to commit another crime, such as murder, rape, or arson, the legislature established two levels of assault—simple assault and assault with intent to inflict great bodily injury[84]—without defining these terms. The legislature signaled by virtue of punishment provisions that the crimes were substantially different. For example, for violation of the simple assault provision the penalty was imprisonment for up to six months and/or a fine of $200.[85] Assault with intent to inflict great bodily injury, on the other hand, was punishable by imprisonment for up to one year and/or a fine of $500.[86] The legislature ended its policy statement that the crimes were different simply by establishing the distinction in punishment and apparently deferred to the Iowa Supreme Court for further elaboration on the differences. The court, defining great bodily injury as "an injury to a person of a more grave and serious character than an ordinary battery," concluded that the term could not be more narrowly defined.[87] The factual determination was left to the discretion of the jury.

Present Iowa Code provisions on assault still make a distinction between simple assault and assault that is intended to cause serious injury, and for the first time the Code defines assault. To a limited extent, the new Code provision follows the suggestions of the *Model Penal Code*. The goal of the *Model Penal Code* was to eliminate "the common-law categories and many of the antecedent statutory variations in favor of a single integrated provision.[88] The *Model Penal Code* defines simple assault as follows:

(1) *Simple Assault*. A person is guilty of assault if he:

(a) attempts to cause or purposely, knowingly or recklessly causes bodily injury to another; or

(b) negligently causes bodily injury to another with a deadly weapon; or

> (c) attempts by physical menace to put another in fear of imminent serious bodily injury.
>
> Simple assault is a misdemeanor unless committed in a fight or scuffle entered into by mutual consent, in which case it is a petty misdemeanor.[89]

The *Model Penal Code* punishes attempts to cause bodily injury as well as acts purposely, knowingly, or recklessly causing bodily injury.[90]

On its face, the Iowa assault statute is more inclusive than the *Model Penal Code* and, in its first subsection, purports to proscribe both acts intended to cause pain or injury and acts intended to result in "physical contact which will be insulting or offensive to another."[91] While the Iowa legislature adopted a broad definition of assault, it did not provide any guidance with regard to the enforcement objectives of the statute. Obviously, the legislature does not expect the police to make arrests in all cases in which there is "insulting or offensive" contact, but where do the police draw the line? The legislature did not give any better guidance with regard to the enforcement objectives of the second subsection of the assault statute. That subsection states that an assault also includes "[a]ny act which is intended to place another in fear of immediate physical contact which will be painful, injurious, insulting, or offensive, coupled with the apparent ability to execute the act."[92]

The Iowa assault statute broadens the range of punishable conduct to include action that causes the fear of immediate physical contact which will be painful or injurious. In addition, the first and second subsections require that persons be punished for their intended criminal acts, whether or not the intended victim is aware of the act and even though the intended victim would be unable to recover damages in a tort action in civil court. The Iowa legislature has adopted in essence the somewhat outmoded policy expressed in *McCullers v. State*.[93]

> A criminal assault may be made upon a person even though he had no knowledge of the fact at the time. . . . It should be noted that herein lies the distinction between assault as a crime and assault as a tort. If the intended victim is unaware of the attempt, he has suffered no harm and is not entitled to compensation for the tort committed against him. . . . However, a criminal assault is an offense against the peace and dignity of the state as well as an invasion of private rights.[94]

The Iowa legislature seems to have made a policy decision that a defendant should be punished for assault whether or not that person has the present ability to carry out the assault. By the use of the phrase "apparent ability to execute the act" in both the first and second subsections, the legislature implies that, even if there is no *actual* present ability to inflict harm, there can be an assault as long as there is *apparent* ability to inflict harm.

On balance, the statute expresses the legislature's concern for feelings of personal safety and well being among the citizenry. This may have been the motivation for the legislature taking a stronger position on the punishment of threatening acts than is suggested by the *Model Penal Code*. The legislature adopted the broad approach to assault and included "the concept of not only physical but emotional contact as well."[95]

But what does this Code provision tell the police about enforcement policies? Unfortunately, it reveals very little. The first and second subsections of the Iowa assault statute do not list any specifically proscribed acts. The third subsection, however, requires punishment for the intentional pointing of any firearm or displaying in a threatening manner any dangerous weapon[96] and arguably comes within the ambit of the second subsection's concern about placing a person in fear of immediate physical contact. It is reasonable to assume that there is a great deal of anxiety about the use of weapons to assault citizens. This anxiety is so great that the Iowa legislature eschews the *Model Penal Code*'s suggestion that such acts be punishable only if they can be classified as "attempts by physical menace to put another in fear of imminent serious bodily injury."[97] The *Model Penal Code* provision "reflects the judgment that attempts to place another in fear of any bodily injury, a concept that . . . includes mere physical pain, are too common and too trivial to warrant penal sanctions."[98] But the Iowa assault statute does not limit the proscribed acts to those that place another in fear of imminent serious bodily injury; rather, any act that places another in fear of immediate physical contact, which need only be painful, injurious, insulting, or offensive, comes within the statutory proscription.

In analyzing the policy objectives of the legislature in enacting the assault statute, certain points are important. First, the assault statute seems to present the classic case wherein the provisions primarily are designed more to facilitate convictions when charges are brought than to articulate the circumstances under which enforcement is expected.[99] The provisions are broadly based and implicitly include a multitude of acts, which require discretion by the courts, prosecutors, and police in determining what acts are criminal. Second, the statute is unnecessarily ambiguous; attempts to interpret enforcement goals are complicated because individuals who are assaulted while ''voluntary participants in a sport, social or other activity, not in itself criminal,''[100] are not protected under the statute. Yet there is no enumeration of what might be a relevant ''sport, social or other activity.''[101] This provision suggests that, while the legislature attempted to broadly define the crime of assault, there are definite limitations on when the provisions are to be applied. It must be assumed that the legislature intends the statute to be enforced only when the assault situation is serious and beyond the norm of ordinary activity. The only exception is a major concern with the intentional use of weapons. In those situations, the legislature expects the statute to be applied whether or not the intent was to place the victim in fear of immediate physical contact.[102]

On the basis of the legislative policy objectives that appear to underlie the statute, the following is an example of the type of rule that a police department might consider in guiding enforcement of the assault statute:

> An officer shall file a simple assault charge when the officer has probable cause to believe an individual has engaged in conduct that constitutes an assault, and the victim of the assault suffers significant physical injury or the assault involves the use of a dangerous weapon.
>
> Significant physical injury includes such injuries as temporary physical disfigurement normally visible to members of the general public, including but not limited to a black eye, a large bruise on the body, or a medically diagnosable internal trauma or emotional disturbance. Dangerous weapon means a firearm, knife, or other instrument capable of inflicting serious bodily injury.[103]

After the proposed rule is formulated, it would be appropriate to circulate it among prosecutors, local government officials, and the public.[104] These parties could respond with written comments or statements. The policy then could be modified as appropriate within the extremely broad and non-directive enforcement parameters established by the legislature. It would be better to have enforcement policy decided in such a forum than to leave it solely to the discretion of the officer on the street.

This rule meets the four criteria enumerated by Professor Davis.[105] First, public participation in this effort, while likely to create some initial dissension, would ultimately lead to public acceptance of the rule. Second, the rule likewise would seem to have some attraction for the police as it does give them some discretion to decide when an assault has occurred, and the rule is simple, precise, and easily administered and monitored. Third, the rule reflects sound substantive policy by recognizing that the assault statutes are designed as "order maintenance" offenses. There is a need for rules that have a realistic expectation of enforcement, rather than rigid rules that require the police to make an arrest for "any act . . . which is intended to result in physical contact which will be insulting or offensive to another."[106] Finally, the rule is legal in that it does not punish conduct not criminalized by the legislature but reflects an effort to develop an enforcement policy within the parameters established by the legislature. Of course, the legislature could be much more explicit in saying what acts are permissible, as was done recently in Iowa with respect to gambling.

Gambling is another offense that might be susceptible to rule development. Gambling enforcement in many departments follows informal rules limiting gambling arrests to situations in which there is high visibility of the offense or there is a significant likelihood that the gambling is professional rather than social in nature. Although these informal rules may not be explicitly race based, national crime statistics indicate that approximately 75 percent of the persons arrested for gambling nationwide are black, in spite of the fact that blacks constitute only 11 percent of the total United States population. It is argued that the differential enforcement of the gambling laws is largely due to the fact that the types of gambling participated in by blacks are more visible than those participated in by whites, but, although that could explain the variance in arrest rates, it does not justify it.[107] What such data do show are the problems inherent in developing informal arrest policies without extensive analysis of the possible impact of those decisions.

Enforcement of the gambling laws is a real problem for most police departments and deserves close attention. Gambling is a victimless crime in that external coercion to participate is absent in most cases and there rarely is an active complainant—a factor that makes enforcement difficult.[108] In addition, the laws against gambling are primarily enacted to prohibit the large-scale commercial gambling frequently associated with organized crime; however, the statutes rarely make such distinctions.[109] Most state legislatures have swept with a rather broad brush to alleviate evidentiary difficulties in prosecuting major offenders of the law and have done little to assist police in determining when the gambling laws should be applied against small, informal groups. While participants at very small neighborhood poker games generally have not been charged with violation of gambling laws in the past few years, there has been some concern about how gambling laws are enforced against those activities, as well as against gambling activities conducted by "legitimate" establishments such as churches, schools, and country clubs.[110]

Iowa presents a unique set of circumstances in this regard. During the early 1970s many public officials in Iowa had indicated that it was permissible for churches to conduct bingo games in violation of the state statute. The state attorney general was unwilling to interpret the gambling statute so broadly and thought that, if such activities were to be permitted, the legislature should say so explicitly in the statute. Apparently, to focus public attention on the issue, the attorney general was instrumental in causing a number of raids against churches in Iowa.[111] The effort of the attorney general to change the law was successful; for the first time the legislature undertook to delineate the circumstances under which certain gambling activity is legal in Iowa.[112]

That legislation took particular pains to describe the situations in which both commercial and social gambling are permissible. The statute offers an ideal opportunity for law enforcement agencies to attempt to develop enforcement rules within the policy parameters set by the legislature. The provisions dealing with the type of gambling permitted among individuals constitute a clear policy statement by the legislature.

The types of games that are permitted are limited to the following:

a. Card and parlor games, including but not limited to poker, pinochle, pitch, gin rummy, bridge, euchre, hearts, cribbage, dominoes, checkers, chess, backgammon and darts. However, it shall be unlawful gambling for any person to engage in bookmaking, or to play any punchboard, pushcard, pull-tab or slot machine, or to play craps, chuck-a-luck, roulette, klondike, blackjack, chemin de fer, baccarat, faro, equality, three-card monte or any other game, except poker, which is customarily played in gambling casinos and in which the house customarily provides a banker, dealer or croupier to operate the game, or a specially designed table upon which to play same.

b. Games of skill and games of chance, except those prohibited by paragraph "a" of this subsection.

c. Wagers or bets between two or more individuals who are physically in the presence of each other with respect to a contest specified in section 99B.11, subsection 2, except as provided in subsection 1, paragraph "g", or with respect to any other event or outcome which does not depend upon gambling or the use of a gambling device unlawful in this state.[113]

In fact, the legislation seems to go so far as to allow visitors to houses in which gambling is occurring by not permitting conviction of the visitor unless he or she had knowledge of or reason to know the facts constituting the violation.[114] In a rare example, the legislature has attempted to define which gambling acts are proscribed and which are permitted. Rather than resisting the legislative efforts, it seems incumbent upon the enforcement bodies to follow the policy directives established in the legislation and to develop their own enforcement policy reflecting those legislative policy pronouncements.

CONCLUSION

We must be concerned about the real and perceived unevenness of criminal law enforcement, especially of low-visibility crimes. The critical need at this point is to focus on ways to control the enforcement of such laws. This book has looked to agencies and branches of government that have responsibility for and ability to directly influence the development of law enforcement policy for some leadership on this problem but found none.

In any event it seems clear that there are serious limitations inherent in any plan wherein only one agency or branch of government takes full responsibility for police rule making. The legislature, while possessing ultimate authority for the enactment of criminal statutes, cannot develop a comprehensive plan because of institutional and political problems. The police likewise suffer disabilities if they act alone. First, there exists the problem of attitudes within police departments that still adhere to the full enforcement myth. Second, developing discretionary enforcement rules in light of the obstacle of full enforcement statutes is a problem.[115] Only if the legislatures, courts, prosecutors, and local governments jointly address the issue is there likely to be full public support for efforts to guide police discretion.

A collective effort by all of these agencies would be the best way to solve the problems that this book discusses. An approach that requires local rule making with broad participation and state review would seem to be the best way to proceed; however, such collaboration requires fundamental changes of attitude in many quarters, and it is only realistic to recognize that such changes may not occur. An alternative strategy would be for the police to develop guidelines on their own initiative—a procedure that has considerable *legal* legitimacy—but to do so with the assistance of prosecutors or other local government officials, whose participation would lend *political* legitimacy to the effort. Broader participation would seem to be important because unilateral action by the police would risk evoking a negative reaction from a public suddenly faced with the fact that police make law enforcement policy choices without any outside control.

Although prosecutors have avoided general review of police arrest policies in the past, recent action shows that traditional reasons for inaction may no longer exist. The voluntary involvement of prosecutors and local government officials would provide a degree of legitimacy that currently does not exist in law enforcement policy making. Of course, such action is against the current trend. However, just as too much involvement of politics in law enforcement is undesirable, too little is also undesirable. The involvement of local officials does not require that mayors or other local executives supervise day-to-day arrest policies, but it might require that, when these local executives are passing on police budgets, serious consideration be given to the need to articulate local law enforcement objectives and to consider how resources might be allocated to meet those objectives. Also, it is not politically improper for mayors to require that police chiefs develop explicit law enforcement policies and see that the policies are followed.

The major problem is that none of these alternatives has ever been regarded as viable. How long police rule making will remain a dormant issue is uncertain. But it is clear that the state and local institutions that have responsibility for law enforcement will ultimately have to respond to the problems outlined here. The solutions to the problems will require new thinking and the destruction of some myths about the appropriate role of governmental institutions in guiding law enforcement. Ultimately, however, we do not really have a choice; society's interest in impartial and controlled law enforcement requires serious thinking about police discretion and ways to control it.

Notes

Chapter 1

1. Des Moines Register, May 21, 1981, at C4, col. 1.

2. IOWA ADVISORY COMM. TO THE U.S. COMM'N ON CIVIL RIGHTS, RACE RELATIONS IN TAMA COUNTY 51 (1981).

3. *See* U.S. COMM'N ON CIVIL RIGHTS, CONFRONTING RACIAL ISOLATION IN MIAMI 226–307 (1982); U.S. COMM'N ON CIVIL RIGHTS, POLICE PRACTICES AND THE PRESERVATION OF CIVIL RIGHTS 2–24 (1979).

4. *See* Goldstein, *Police Discretion Not to Invoke the Criminal Process: Low-Visibility Decisions in the Administration of Justice*, 69 YALE L.J. 543, 552–54 (1960).

5. A.J. REISS, THE POLICE AND THE PUBLIC 134 (1971).

6. Amsterdam, *Perspectives on the Fourth Amendment*, 58 MINN. L. REV. 349, 415 (1974).

7. K. DAVIS, DISCRETIONARY JUSTICE: A PRELIMINARY INQUIRY 164–66 (1969).

8. *Id.* at 166.

9. T.K. Moran, Police Decision Making: The Effects of Differential Enforcement Choices on Public Policy 141 (1974) (Ph.D. dissertation, University of Connecticut).

10. Thomas & Fitch, *The Exercise of Discretionary Decision-Making by the Police: An Inquiry into Its Correlates, Consequences, and Control*, 54 N.D.L. REV. 61, 72–81 (1977).

11. A. NIEDERHOFFER, BEHIND THE SHIELD 60 (1967) (emphasis added).

12. Parnas, *The Police Response to the Domestic Disturbance*, WIS. L. REV. 914, 916 (1967).

13. Allen, *The Police and Substantive Rulemaking: Reconciling Principle and Expediency*, 125 U. PA. L. REV. 62, 67, 71 & n.48 (1976); *see* Goldstein, *supra*, note 4 at 543, 586–89.

14. J. EISENSTEIN, POLITICS AND THE LEGAL PROCESS 218 (1973).

15. *See* W. LAFAVE, ARREST: THE DECISION TO TAKE A SUSPECT INTO CUSTODY 111–12 (1965); Banks, *Discretionary Justice and the Black Offender*, in C.E. Owen, ed., BLACKS AND CRIMINAL JUSTICE 37–40 (1977).

16. *See* REPORT OF THE NAT'L ADVISORY COMM'N ON CIVIL DISORDERS 158–60 (1968). Police officers may at times arrest individuals for purposes other than prosecution. Goldstein, *Police Policy Formulation: A Proposal for Improving Police Performance*, 65 MICH. L. REV. 1123, 1126 (1967). For an example of the misuse of discretion directed against homosexuals and bars that they frequent, see Project, *The Consenting Adult Homosexual and the Law: An Empirical Study of Enforcement and Administration in Los Angeles County*, 13 UCLA L. REV. 643, 719–20 (1966).

17. J. SKOLNICK, JUSTICE WITHOUT TRIAL: LAW ENFORCEMENT IN A DEMOCRATIC SOCIETY (2d. ed. rev. 1975).

18. *Id.* at 86.

19. Contemporary Studies Project, *Administrative Control of Police Discretion*, 58 IOWA L. REV. 892, 954 (1973).

20. *See* PRESIDENT'S COMM'N ON LAW ENFORCEMENT AND ADMIN. OF JUSTICE, TASK FORCE REPORT: THE POLICE 13–38 (1967); REPORT OF THE NAT'L ADVISORY COMM'N ON CIVIL DISORDERS 157–68 (1968); NAT'L ADVISORY COMM'N ON CRIMINAL JUSTICE STANDARDS AND GOALS, POLICE 21–27 (1973); STANDARDS FOR CRIMINAL JUSTICE § 1–4.5 (1980).

21. K. DAVIS, *supra*, note 7, at 216 (emphasis omitted).

22. A.B.A., STANDARDS FOR CRIMINAL JUSTICE, 2d ed. 1–6 (1982) (quoting address by Chief Justice Warren E. Burger, FBI National Academy commencement).

23. *See generally* KANSAS ADVISORY COMM. TO THE U.S. COMM'N ON CIVIL RIGHTS, POLICE-COMMUNITY RELATIONS IN THE CITY OF WICHITA AND SEDGWICK COUNTY (1980); OHIO STATE ADVISORY COMM. TO THE U.S. COMM'N ON CIVIL RIGHTS, POLICING IN CINCINNATI, OHIO: OFFICIAL POLICY V. CIVILIAN REALITY (1981); U.S. COMM'N ON CIVIL RIGHTS, POLICE PRACTICES AND THE PRESERVATION OF CIVIL RIGHTS (1979).

24. *See* IOWA ADVISORY COMM. TO THE U.S. COMM'N ON CIVIL RIGHTS, *supra*, note 2, at 51–52.

25. *See* J.Q. Wilson, VARIETIES OF POLICE BEHAVIOR (1968), especially ch. 3 and 4; W. LaFave, *supra*, note 15, ch. 8; and K. Davis, POLICE DISCRETION (1975), ch. 2.

26. "State governments played a minimal role in matters affecting local policing until passage of the Omnibus Crime Control Act of 1968." H. Goldstein, POLICING A FREE SOCIETY 319 (1977).

27. Governors surely have considerable influence on the way policies are made in the states but apparently law enforcement, gambling, and liquor problems are not a high priority among them. W. Francis, LEGISLATIVE ISSUES IN THE FIFTY STATES 77 (1967).

28. Interview with Mark Schantz, solicitor general of Iowa, Iowa City, Iowa, October 1979.

29. *See* K. Davis, *supra*, note 25, at 79; A.B.A. PROJECT ON STANDARDS FOR CRIMINAL JUSTICE, STANDARDS RELATING TO THE URBAN POLICE FUNCTION 114 (1974); NAT'L ADVISORY COMM'N ON CRIMINAL JUSTICE STANDARDS AND GOALS, *supra*, note 20, at 21.

30. *Delaware v. Prouse*, 440 U.S. 648, 99 S.Ct. 139 (1979).

31. *Brown v. Texas*, 443 U.S. 47, 99 S.Ct. 2637 (1979).

32. *Michigan v. DeFillippo*, 443 U.S. 31, 99 S.Ct. 2626 (1979).

33. *United States v. Caceres*, 440 U.S. 741, 99 S.Ct. 1465 (1979).

Chapter 2

1. K. DAVIS, POLICE DISCRETION 168 (1975).

2. Allen, *The Police and Substantive Rulemaking: Reconciling Principle and Expediency*, 125 U. PA. L. REV. 62, 67, 80 (1976).

3. K. DAVIS, *supra*, note 1, at 90.

4. *Id.* at 107–12.

5. *Id.* at 80–81, 131–38. Davis discusses Fourteenth Amendment due process theory, but he does not fully develop the separation of power and delegation problems at the state level nor does he analyze the unique problems one must deal with in considering the police as an administrative agency.

6. Allen, *supra*, note 2, at 62, 75–76.

7. *Id.* at 77–79. While Professor Allen looks at law enforcement policy making by the police in the context of a more rigorous constitutional analysis, he fails to assess the historical role of the police as an institution of government. For example, his classic separation of power analysis is limited by an assumption that the police are an executive agency exercising only the power

of the executive branch. Furthermore, he fails to address the due process or equal protection problems.

8. *See infra* note 62.

9. *See infra* notes 60–117 and accompanying text.

10. *See* K. DAVIS, DISCRETIONARY JUSTICE: A PRELIMINARY INQUIRY (1969). Davis conducted an extensive number of interviews with members of the Chicago Police Department and was apparently concerned with the lack of control maintained over the arrest decisions of patrol officers. K. Davis, *supra*, note 1, at 167–71.

11. Allen, *supra*, note 2, at 70, quoting J. Goldstein, *Police Discretion Not to Invoke the Criminal Process: Low-Visibility Decisions in the Administration of Justice*, 69 Yale L.J. 543, 554 (1960). Professor Davis simply asserted that police departments operate as administrative agencies and should be viewed as such. Allen, aided by Davis' limited development of the administrative agency analogy, easily rejected it and proceeded to develop powerful arguments against discretionary enforcement policy making.

Because of Davis' failure to develop his theory of the police as an administrative agency, Allen was able to engage in a discussion of the separation of powers doctrine without articulating how the police have fitted into that doctrine.

12. Allen, *supra*, note 2, at 97.

13. IND. CONST. art. VI, §§ 2–11 lists sheriffs as administrative agencies.

14. *See infra* note 31.

15. "It is important to emphasize that the institutional segregation of the police from the judiciary is a relatively recent phenomenon and that it is particularly characteristic of the English and American models of law enforcement. Under the common law, the Justice of the Peace was the magistrate and the chief police officer in his jurisdiction." E. BITTNER, THE FUNCTIONS OF THE POLICE IN MODERN SOCIETY: A REVIEW OF BACKGROUND FACTORS, CURRENT PRACTICES AND POSSIBLE ROLE MODELS 31 (1975). *See also* B. SMITH, POLICE SYSTEMS IN THE UNITED STATES 80–81 (1940); and W. C. Webster, *Comparative Study of State Constitutions of the American Revolution*, ANNALS OF THE AMERICAN ACADEMY OF POLITICAL AND SOCIAL SCIENCE, Supp.

16. B. Smith, *supra*, note 15, at 80.

17. *Id.*

18. B. SMITH, RURAL CRIME CONTROL 39 (1933). *See also* J.P. HALL, THE HISTORY AND PHILOSOPHY OF LAW ENFORCEMENT (1975). "Originally a very powerful man on the local law enforcement scene; by the end of the 1200s the Crown had cause to resent and suspect some of the abuses of power that were being perpetrated by the local sheriff. During

the following century steps were taken to curtail his power somewhat.'' *Id.* at 47.

19. J.P. Hall, *supra*, note 18, at 41.

20. W. LEE, A HISTORY OF POLICE IN ENGLAND 46 (1901).

21. B. Smith, *supra*, note 15, at 82–83.

22. In fact, one writer observed, ''It is impossible . . . to divorce the functions of the justice from the constable. W. Lee, *supra*, note 20, at 43.

23. *Id.* at 54.

24. C.H. KARRAKER, THE SEVENTEENTH-CENTURY SHERIFF 21 (1930). ''In still other matters of county administration the sheriff frequently acted as an associate of the justices of the peace.'' The privy council was equally dependent on the sheriff and the justices for the capture of criminals and for the suppression and investigation of disorders in various parts of the county. J. BACKUS, 2 A DIGEST OF LAWS RELATING TO THE OFFICES AND DUTIES OF SHERIFF, CORONER AND CONSTABLE 82 (1812).

25. F. MAITLAND, THE CONSTITUTIONAL HISTORY OF ENGLAND 39, 233–34, 485–90 (1931).

26. Sir Robert Peel, Home Secretary in the Duke of Wellington's administration issued the order creating the ''New System of Police,'' in September 1829, in London, England. Most law enforcement scholars trace the origin of the modern force to this event. D. BAYLEY, POLICE AND SOCIETY 73 (1977). *See also* F. Maitland, *supra*, note 25, at 487.

27. B. Smith, *supra*, note 18, at 42–43.

28. *Id.* at 45.

29. B. Smith, *supra*, note 15, at 81–86.

30. Although in some states the governor had the power to remove the sheriff from office. *Id.* at 85.

31. One state legislature selected the sheriffs for the state and, while one might try to argue that made sheriffs legislative officials, such selection was clearly not the case nationally. J. DEALEY, GROWTH OF AMERICAN STATE CONSTITUTIONS 248 (1915). The Mississippi constitution speaks of the sheriff as a county officer, although he has constitutional status, §§ 135, 138.

32. For example, the state of Maryland attempted to eliminate the office of sheriff from its constitution in a draft revision; however, this attempt failed. *See* CONSTITUTIONAL CONVENTION COMM'N, REPORT OF THE CONSTITUTIONAL CONVENTION COMM'N 366 (1967).

33. W. JACKSON, THE OFFICE OF SHERIFF IN IOWA 14–43 (1924) (Ph.D. dissertation, Department of Political Science, University of Iowa).

34. In fact, sheriffs have been called the ''central administrative post in a community.'' B. Smith, *supra*, note 18, at 46–54.

35. F. GREEN, CONSTITUTIONAL DEVELOPMENT IN THE SOUTH ATLANTIC STATES 1776–1860 at 83–84 (1930).

36. Allen, *supra*, note 2, at 62–70; K. Davis, *supra*, note 1, at iii.

37. R. FOSDICK, AMERICAN POLICE SYSTEMS 58–117 (1920, reprint 1969).

38. B. Smith, *supra*, note 15, at 4.

39. It is significant that while there were numerous battles for control of the police, rarely was there any effort to limit their powers. R. FOSDICK, *supra*, note 37, at 211–13 (1920).

40. *Id.* at 58–117.

41. *Id.* at 78–80.

42. *Id.* at 84.

43. *Id.* at 85.

44. *Id.* at 89.

45. *Id.* at 109–10.

46. *Id.* at 111.

47. *Id.* at 90–96.

48. Iowa Code § 1225.09 (1939).

49. R. FOGELSON, BIG CITY POLICE 9–11 (1977).

50. S. WALKER, POPULAR JUSTICE: A HISTORY OF AMERICAN CRIMINAL JUSTICE 137–38 (1980).

51. *Id.*

52. *Id.* at 134–35.

53. S. WALKER, CRITICAL HISTORY OF POLICE REFORM 71 (1977).

54. S. WALKER, *supra*, note 50, at 140.

55. Allen, *supra*, note 2, at 71.

56. Actually, usage of the term "full enforcement" to describe the statutes may itself be a misnomer, as the "full enforcement" provisions of the so-called full enforcement statutes are in actuality a very minor part of that legislation. In fact, at least one court has referred to the legislation as the "peace statute" which in actuality may be a more accurate reflection of what the statute was intended to do. *See Emmetsburg v. Gunn*, 249 Iowa 297, 86 N.W.2d 829 (1958) at 834. There is little help from the scholars in interpreting the full enforcement statutes. Not only has there been a failure to develop an understanding of the historical background of the statutes, the language of the statutes has been subjected to only very cursory examination. The general approach has been to remark on the similarity of the statutes and to analyze only selected segments before drawing conclusions about their purpose and application. Allen, *supra*, note 2, at 71; W. LaFave, Arrest: The Decision to Take a Subject into Custody 76–78 (1965).

Also, there has been some confusion over the exact number of such statutes. Professor Joseph Goldstein, the first person to attempt to list the full enforcement statutes, found twenty statutes in 1960. Goldstein, *supra*, note 11, at 543, 557 n.26.

Professor Wayne LaFave found twelve "pure" full enforcement statutes (applying to all state law enforcement officers); eight statutes that specifically mandated that state sheriffs exercise full enforcement; seven statutes that required local police to exercise full enforcement; three statutes that required peace officers to arrest "all felons"; and four statutes that required the arrest of all persons committing an offense in an officer's presence. W. LaFave, *supra*.

Professor Allen found twenty-three states to have statutes "mandating either that the law enforcement agencies arrest all who violate the criminal law or that the agencies enforce all the criminal laws." Allen also found two other statutes requiring peace officers to arrest all persons committing offenses in their presence and two statutes directing the police to arrest all felons. Allen, *supra*, note 2, at 71 n.48.

The figures used by Allen and Goldstein are misleading because they include, as pure full enforcement statutes, statutes that are specifically directed either to local police or sheriffs. Approximately thirty-four states within the past twenty years have had some type of "full enforcement" legislation.

57. 1883 Cal. Stat., ch. 75, § 93; 1891 N.D. Sess. Laws, ch. 55, § 3; 1891 Wash. Laws, ch. 45, § 1; 1895 Mich. Pub. Acts, No. 215, ch. 12, § 4; 1890 Utah Laws, ch. 131, § 76; 1901 Ariz. Sess. Laws; 1901 Neb. Laws, ch. 18, § 30; 1902 Ohio Laws, ch. 96; 1905 Ind. Acts, ch. 129, § 161; 1908 Colo. Sess. Laws, § 497; 1908 Va. Acts, ch. 157, § 61; Mass. Ann. Laws, ch. 591, § 24 (Michie/Law. Co-op. 1920); 1921 N.M. Laws, ch. 170, § 1; Del. Laws, ch. 84, § 4 (1925). The present full enforcement statutes are as follows: Alaska Stat. § 18.65.080 (1969); Ariz. Rev. Stat. Ann. § 11.441 (1956); Ark. Stat. Ann. § 17–3601(5) (1947, 1980); Cal. Gov't Code § 26601 (West 1968); Colo. Rev. Stat. § 30–10–516 (1973); Conn. Gen. Stat. § 6–49 (1966); Del. Code Ann. tit. 11, § 8302 (1974); Fla. Stat. Ann. § 30.15 (West 1974); Hawaii Rev. Stat. § 6–52–67 (1968); Idaho Code § 19–4804 (Supp. 1975); Ind. Code § 36–2–13–5 (1982); La. Rev. Stat. Ann. § 15.575 (West 1967); Me. Rev. Stat. Ann. tit. 15, § 704 (1964); Mass. Ann. Laws ch. 41, § 98 (Michie/Law. Co-op. 1973); Mich. Stat. Ann. § 5–1752 (Callaghan 1949); Neb. Rev. Stat. § 16–323 (1974); N.M. Stat. Ann. § 4–41–2 (1978); N.D. Cent. Code § 11–15–03 (1960); Ohio Rev. Code Ann. § 737.11 (Page 1976); Utah Code Ann. §§ 10–6–66, 17–22–2 (1953); Va. Code § 15–1–138 (1973); Wash. Rev. Code Ann. § 36.28.010 (Supp. 1975); W. Va. Code § 8–14–3 (1976). Statutes requiring officers to arrest all persons committing crimes in their presence include: Ill. Ann. Stat. ch. 125, § 82 (Smith-Hurd 1976); Ind. Code Ann. § 36–2–13–5 (1982). Statutes requiring officers to arrest all felons include: Minn. Stat. Ann. § 387.03 (West 1968); Mo. Ann. Stat. § 57–100 (Vernon 1966).

58. R. Fosdick, *supra*, note 39, at 97.

59. While the language was not always the same, it generally followed the format of the character of the town of Flatbush.

> Subsection 13. It is hereby made the duty of said police force at all time of the day or night, within the said district, and the members of said force are accordingly thereunto empowered, *especially to preserve the public peace, prevent crimes, detect and arrest offenders, suppress riots and insurrections, protect the rights of persons and property, guard the public health, preserve order at every primary and public election, report nuisances in streets and roadways, restrain disorderly houses and houses of ill-fame, observe and inspect all places having excise or other licenses to carry on business, arrest beggars, protect property at fires, assist travelers, and enforce all laws relating to the suppression and punishment of crimes and disorder and all violation of the excise law*. [1888 N.Y. Laws, ch. 556, § 13 (emphasis added)]

60. Alaska Stat. § 18.65.080 (1969); Ariz. Rev. Stat. Ann. § 11–441 (1956); Ark. Stat. Ann. §§ 12–1110 (1947), 19–1705 (Supp. 1960); Cal. Gov't Code § 26601 (West 1968); Colo. Rev. Stat. Ann. § 31–3–105 (1973); Del. Code Ann. tit. 11, § 8302 (1974); Fla. Stat. Ann. § 30.15 (West 1974); Hawaii Rev. Stat. § 6–52–67 (1968); Ind. Code § 48–6107 (West 1950); Ky. Rev. Stat. Ann. § 70.570 (Bobbs-Merrill 1970); Mass. Ann. Laws ch. 41, § 98 (Michie/Law. Co-op. 1973); Md. Rev. Stat. § 85.060 (1952); Mich. Stat. Ann. § 5–1752 (Callaghan 1949); Neb. Rev. Stat. § 16–323 (1974); N.D. Cent. Code § 11–15–03 (1960); Ohio Rev. Code Ann. § 737.11 (Page 1976); Utah Code Ann. §§ 10–6–66, 17–22–2 (1953); Va. Code Ann. § 15.1–138 (1973); Wash. Rev. Code Ann. § 36.28.010 (Supp. 1975); W. Va. Code Ann. § 8–14–3 (1976).

61. *See* Conn. Gen. Stat. § 6–49 (1966); Ill. Ann. Stat. ch. 125, § 82 (Smith-Hurd 1976); Iowa Code § 748.6 (1976); La. Rev. Stat. § 15.575 (West 1967); Me. Rev. Stat. Ann. tit. 15, § 704 (1964); Wyo. Stat. § 7–12 155 (1959).

62. 249 Iowa 297, 86 N.W.2d 829 (1958). *Emmetsburg* addressed the question of whether the state or a locality was responsible for payment of police officers' medical expenses resulting from injuries two officers incurred while on duty. The state would only be responsible if the officers were acting in their official duties as law enforcement officers; in other words, actually enforcing the laws of the state. One of the officers had been injured when he slipped while checking parking meters. The other had tripped off a curb while inspecting locked doors. The court found that an officers' duty of law enforcement consists of every aspect or duty in the category of his work, whether hazardous or routine. Because the full enforcement statute required an officer to prevent breaches of the peace, the court reasoned that the officer was on call at all times to enforce this duty. *Id.* at 834.

63. In 1911 the Iowa attorney general stated that it was within the powers

of the sheriff to make arrests for gambling in the cities as well as the counties and that municipal officers had no discretion to prevent the sheriff from carrying out his statutory duty. Op. Attn'y Gen. 408–9 (1911).

64. *See infra* note 72.

65. 197 Cal. App. 2d 479, 483 (1961).

66. For another example of a case in which a law enforcement officer was removed from office for violating community norms regarding acceptable levels of public behavior see *Larue v. David*, 8 Cal. App. 750 (1908) where removal of a town constable was upheld because rather than intervene to stop a street fight he simply let the participants continue to fight.

67. 32 Cal. App. Rptr, 2d 165, 167 (1939).

68. 157 Mich. 443, 122 N.W. 286 (1909).

69. *Id.* at 295.

70. 1895 Mich. Pub. Acts 215.

71. 157 Mich. 443, 122 N.W. 286, 295 (1909).

72. 226 Ark. 309, 289 S.W.2d 679 (1956), *cert. denied* 352 U.S. 894 (1956).

73. 289 S.W.2d 681.

74. *Id.*

75. 407 Pa. 129, 179 A.2d 439, 441 (1962).

76. *Id.* at 442.

77. *See* Allen, *supra*, note 2, at 62, 112.

78. *See* LaFave, *The Police and Non-enforcement of the Law, Part I*, Wis. L. Rev. 104, 130 (1962).

79. 99 N.W.2d 829 (Wis. 1959).

80. *Id.* at 829.

81. *Id.* at 831–32.

82. 396 N.Y.S.2d 974, 976 (1977).

83. 407 N.Y.S.2d 165 (1978).

84. 396 N.Y.S.2d 974 (1977).

85. *Bruno v. Codd*, consent decree between (1) plaintiffs and (2) defendants Robert McGuire, Harold Schryber, Carl Ravens, James Corridan, James T. Sullivan, Devitt and George Peters, index #21946/76, June 26, 1978.

86. N.Y.S.2d 165, 167 (1978).

87. L. Radzinowicz, 2 *A History of English Criminal Law and its Administration from 1750: The Clash Between Private Initiative and Public Interest in the Enforcement of the Law* 162–63 (1948).

88. Iowa Code § 748.4 (1975) (emphasis added).

89. Iowa Code § 170 (1851) originally applied only to sheriffs and their deputies. The section was in effect until 1927, although the section number was changed frequently. Code Revision Sec. 383 (1860); Code Sec. 337 (1873); McClain's Code Sec. 472 (1888); Code Sec. 499 (1897); Code Supp. Sec. 499

(1913); and Code Sec. 5181 (1924). In 1927, the forty-second general assembly amended the statute (Acts 1927, ch. 122) to include all peace officers and their deputies in addition to sheriffs and their deputies. The statute was repealed effective January 1, 1978 when the new Criminal Code was enacted in 1976 by the sixty-sixth general assembly (Acts 1976, ch. 1245, ch. 4, sec. 526).

90. Since the word "criminal" is not defined in the code, one must make an assumption as to its meaning. A legitimate argument could be made that only the courts have the authority to determine who is a criminal and that until the courts have made that determination by virtue of a preliminary hearing and issued a warrant, peace officers are not required to "apprehend and arrest." However, it is likely that the choice of the word "criminal" was simply inappropriate and that the legislature intended for the police to arrest anyone they had probable cause to believe had committed a crime.

91. J. DILLON, 1 COMMENTARIES ON THE LAW OF MUNICIPAL CORPORATIONS 295 (1890).

92. *Id.* at 294–95.

93. The "Dillon" rule on the interpretation of local government power is a "severe standard" and "even resolves reasonable doubts against the local government." R. LINEBERRY & I. SHARKANSKY, URBAN POLITICS AND PUBLIC POLICY 106 (1974).

94. At least one court explicitly recognized statutory inconsistency in requiring officers to execute the laws as well as to suppress crime and conserve the peace and concluded that the conflicting terminology must be construed as allowing police officers to exercise discretion. *Gowan v. Smith*, 157 Mich. 443, 122 N.W. 286, 297 (1909).

95. W. Jackson, *supra*, note 33, at 26–27. *See supra* note 89.

96. Allen, *supra*, note 2, at 114–15.

97. Ariz. Rev. Stat. Ann. § 11–441 (1956); Ark. Stat. Ann. § 19–1750 (Supp. 1960); Cal. Gov't Code § 26602 (West 1968); Colo. Rev. Stat. Ann. § 31–4–112 (1973); Del. Code Ann. tit. 11, § 8302 (1974); Fla. Stat. Ann. § 30115 (West 1979); Idaho Code § 11–15–03 (Supp. 1975); Mass. Ann. Laws ch. 41, § 898 (Michie/Law. Co-op. 1973); Mich. Stat. Ann. 85–1752 (Callaghan 1949); N.D. Cent. Code § 11–15–03 (1960); Wash. Rev. Code Ann. § 36.28.010 (Supp. 1975).

98. Allen, *supra*, note 2, at 75.

99. Des Moines Register, Aug. 23, 1981, at A1.

100.

(1) Execute writs of attachment.

The sheriff shall in all cases attach the amount of property directed, if sufficient property not exempt from execution is found in his county, giving that in which the defendant has a legal and questionable title a preference over that in which the title is doubtful or only equitable.

(2) Conduct sheriff's sale.

(3) Keep the jail.

(4) Collect delinquent taxes by distress and sale.

(5) Select jury in condemnation cases and receive and administer money payments.

W. Jackson, *supra*, note 33, at 19–36.

101. Iowa Code, ch. 4, § 4.6 (1981).

102. R. Fosdick, *supra*, note 39, at 53–54. In the states of Arizona, California, Delaware, Florida, Idaho, Indiana, Kentucky, North Dakota, Ohio, and Utah, "preserve the peace" is listed as the first law enforcement duty of peace officers. *See also supra*, note 57.

103. W. Jackson, *supra*, note 33, at 27.

104. B. SMITH, THE STATE POLICE: ORGANIZATION AND ADMINISTRATION 16–19 (1925).

105. Ohio Rev. Code Ann. § 2833 (Page 1976).

106. R. HEIGES, THE OFFICE OF SHERIFF IN THE RURAL COUNTIES OF OHIO 15 (1933) (Ph.D. dissertation, Department of Political Science, Columbia University).

107. B. Smith, *supra*, note 104, at 16–19, 26–27.

108. *E.g.*, Iowa Code 80B (1981).

109. *See supra* note 57 for listing of state statutes that describe duties of state and local law enforcement officers.

110. *E.g.*, Iowa Code 372 (1981).

111. Allen, *supra*, note 2, at 75–76.

112. *Id.* at 76 n.65.

113. Iowa Const. art. 3, § 1.

114. Allen, *supra*, note 2, at 76–77.

115. *Id.* at 98; Goldstein, *supra*, note 11, at 586–87.

116. THE FEDERALIST no. 47 325–26 (J. Madison) (J. Cooke ed. 1961) expresses the practical view of the separation of powers doctrine. The political philosophers Locke and Montesquieu, who contributed greatly to the theoretical development of the concept of separation of powers, however, were not overly concerned with its practical effect. Unfortunately, this was a concern the constitutional convention would not avoid. For the philosophical view, *see* B. DE MONTESQUIEU, THE SPIRIT OF THE LAW 151–62 (1949 ed.); J. LOCKE, OF CIVIL GOVERNMENT 124–34 (1962 ed.); W. BONDY, THE SEPARATION OF GOVERNMENTAL POWERS 12–14 (1967).

117. U.S. CONST. art. II, § 2, cl. 1.

118. *Id.* cl. 2.

119. *Id.* § 3.

120. *Id.* § 2, cl. 2.

121. U.S. CONST. art. I, §§ 2, 3.

122. *Id.* § 7, cl. 2.

123. R.E. CUSHMAN & R.F. CUSHMAN, CASES IN CONSTITUTIONAL LAW 57 (1958).

124. J. Madison, *supra*, note 116, at 325.

125. *Id.* at 325–26.

126. *Springer v. Philippine Islands*, 277 U.S. 189, 209–11 (1928).

127. 343 U.S. 579, 635 (1952). *See generally Hampton v. U.S.*, 276 U.S. 394, 406 (1928); *United States v. Nixon*, 418 U.S. 683, 707 (1974); *Buckley v. Valeo*, 424 U.S. 1, 120–22 (1976); *Nixon v. Adm'r. of Gen. Services*, 433 U.S. 425, 441–44 (1977); *United States v. American Tel. & Tel.*, 567 F.2d 121, 127–28 (D.C. Cir. 1977); *Olegario v. United States*, 629 F.2d 204, 226–27 (2d Cir. 1980); *Chadha v. Immigration & Naturalization Service*, 634 F.2d 408, 424–25 (9th Cir. 1980) (defining a "standard" for determining violations of the separation of powers doctrine); *United States v. Mississippi Power & Light Co.*, 638 F.2d 899, 906 n.12 (5th Cir. 1981); F. FRANKFURTER, THE PUBLIC AND ITS GOVERNMENT, 77–79 (1930); *see generally* J. Madison, *supra*, note 116.

128. F. Green, *supra*, note 35, at 83.

129. J. Dealey, *supra*, note 32, at 8 n.1, 243.

130. *People v. Chase*, 165 Ill. 527 (1897), *discussed in* F. GOODNOW, SELECTED CASES ON GOVERNMENT AND ADMINISTRATION 25 (1906).

131. F. Green, *supra*, note 35, at 91; J. Dealey, *supra*, note 32 at 160.

132. F. Green, *supra*, note 35, at 83.

133. *Id.* at 102–03, 162; J. Dealey, *supra*, note 32, at 160.

134. R. HIGHSAW, THE GOVERNMENT AND ADMINISTRATION OF MISSISSIPPI 5 (1954); C. RANSONE, THE OFFICE OF GOVERNOR IN THE UNITED STATES 160 (1970).

135. F. COOPER, STATE ADMINISTRATIVE LAW 15 (1965).

136. THE FEDERALIST no. 48 (J. Madison) (J. Cooke ed. 1961).

137. K. DAVIS, ADMINISTRATIVE LAW TEXT 36–41 (1973).

138. K. Davis, *supra*, note 1, at 107–12, 121–25, 131–38.

139. Allen, *supra*, note 2, at 86–88.

140. Note, *Safeguards, Standards and Necessity: Permissible Parameters for Legislative Delegations in Iowa*, 58 Iowa L. Rev. 974, 976–77 (1973).

141. 10 Wheat. 1 (1825).

142. 220 U.S. 506 (1911).

143. Act of Mar. 3, 1891, ch. 566, 26 Stat. 1103.

144. 220 U.S. 506, 522–23. *Grimaud* has not been overruled. *See Singer v. United States*, 323 U.S. 338, 345–46 (1945); *United States v. Cassiagnol*, 420 F.2d 868, 875–77 (4th Cir. 1978), *cert. denied*, 439 U.S. 1051 (1978).

145. K. DAVIS, *supra*, note 137, at 26–28.

146. L. JAFFE, JUDICIAL CONTROL OF ADMINISTRATIVE ACTION 35 (1965).

147. K. Davis, *supra*, note 1, at 103–12.

148. *Skidmore v. Swift*, 323 U.S. 134 (1944).

149. 29 U.S.C. (1938) §§ 203, 207.

150. *Skidmore v. Swift*, 323 U.S. 134 (1944).

151. *Id.* at 139–40.

152. K. Davis, *supra*, note 1, at 108–10.

153. *Id.* at 137–38. Following *Skidmore*, courts have shown exceptional deference to the construction of a statute by the administrative agency charged with enforcing the statute, *NLRB v. Boeing*, 412 U.S. 67, 75 (1973); *United States v. Consumer Life Ins. Co.*, 430 U.S. 725, 751–52 (1977); *Good Samaritan Hospital, Corvallis v. Matthews*, 609 F.2d 949, 954, 955 (9th Cir. 1979); *Eirhart v. Libbey-Owens Ford Co.*, 616 F.2d 278, 281–82 (7th Cir. 1980) and cases cited; and to an agency's interpretation of its own administrative regulation, *Udall v. Tallman*, 380 U.S. 1, 16–17 (1965), citing *Bowles v. Seminole Rock Co.*, 325 U.S. 410, 413–14 (1945); *Montana Power Co. v. Environmental Protection Agency*, 608 F.2d 334, 344, 348 & n.27 (9th Cir. 1979).

154. *Moog Industries v. FTC*, 355 U.S. 411 (1958).

155. *Id.* at 412.

156. *Id.* at 413.

157. Allen, *supra*, note 2, at 112–14.

158. *Moog Industries v. FTC*, 355 U.S. 411, 413 (1958).

159. 387 U.S. 244, 246–49 (1967).

160. *Id.* at 251.

161. 411 U.S. 182, 183 (1973).

162. *Glover Livestock Commission Co. v. Hardin*, 454 F.2d 109, 115 (8th Cir. 1972).

163. *Phelps Dodge Corp. v. Labor Board*, 313 U.S. 177, 194 (1941), *cited in American Power Co. v. SEC*, 329 U.S. 90, 112 (1946), *cited in Butz v. Glover Livestock Commission Co.*, 411 U.S. 182, 185–86 (1973).

164. *Butz v. Glover Livestock Commission Co.*, 411 U.S. 182, 185–89 (1973). There are other cases at the federal level that continue to follow the rationale of *Moog*. In *Jewell Company v. FTC*, 432 F.2d 1155 (7th Cir. 1970), the Federal Trade Commission conducted proceedings pursuant to a complaint alleging violations of the Robinson-Pattman Act. The court held the district court had no jurisdiction to determine whether a commissioner had misconstrued his statutory obligation by assuming that he had no discretion to consider whether issuance of the complaint was in the public interest since that was a legal, not a factual termination. *Moog* was cited for the proposition that

the courts have no jurisdiction to interfere with the discretion of the commissioner in issuing its complaints. In *L.G. Balfour v. FTC*, 442 F.2d 1 (7th Cir. 1971), an FTC order against the plaintiff for unfair method of competition was upheld. Both *Moog*'s holding that a cease and desist order against only one firm in a context of industry-wide abuse is valid, and *Moog*'s approach concerning an agency's expertise and need for latitude to form orders that best serve its congressionally appointed function were cited with approval. In *Glover Livestock Commission Co. v. Hardin* 454 F.2d 109 (8th Cir. 1972), the secretary of agriculture issued a cease and desist order for violation of Packers and Stockyards Act and suspended registration. *Moog* was cited for its dictum concerning the province of an agency to act within the area of its expertise. However, the court refused to allow the suspension of registration ruling to stand, claiming that such a suspension would serve no reasonable purpose and that the cease and desist order plus the publicity surrounding the case are punishment enough. This is the only case in which we see a limitation on allowing the agency to determine and implement its enforcement policy.

In *Hanley v. Kleindienst*, 471 F.2d 823 (2d Cir. 1972), the court addressed the situation in which there was an agency requirement under the statute to determine the impact of a proposed agency action on surrounding environment. *Moog* was cited in dictum for its language concerning agency expertise and congressional intention. The court reiterated the standard established in *NLRB v. Hearst Publications*, 322 U.S. 111, 131 (1944) for review of mixed question of fact and law. That standard established a rational basis test in which the agency's decision will be accepted where it is warranted in the record and has a reasonable basis in law. Yet the court interestingly enough opted for a less stringent arbitrary and capricious standard as embodied in the Administrative Procedures Act, thus giving even stronger support for the principle of agency discretion established in *Moog*.

In *Sirbo Holdings Inc. v. CIR*, 476 F.2d 981 (2d Cir. 1973), the court of appeals addressed the question of whether the payment of $125,000 by a tenant to a landlord to restore premises would be considered an involuntary conversion of landlord's property for tax purposes. In asking the district court to reconsider the effect of the precedent on all houses with the present case, the court argued that the IRS commissioner could not rule one way in one case and the other in a case with the identical facts and cited *Moog*'s holding that "rulings of an agency can be traditionally overturned when a patent abuse of discretion is shown as support." This, of course, shows a limitation on enforcement policy; specifically, that enforcement policy cannot violate equal protection provisions.

In *GER-RO-MAR Inc. v. FTC*, 518 F.2d 33 (2d Cir. 1975), an underwear manufacturer sought review of a cease and desist order that also did not name its competitors. *Moog* was cited for the proposition that the FTC need not move against all violators.

In *Cross v. Board of Supervisors of San Mateo County*, 326 F.Supp. 634 (D. Ct. N.D. Cal. 1968), *aff'd.* 442 F.2d 362 (9th Cir. 1971) plaintiff sought to base a private federal civil rights complaint on violations of the FTC act. A motion to dismiss for failure to state a claim on which relief can be granted was upheld. The court found that the FTC was better equipped to prosecute these violations and cited *Moog* for its dictum that the FTC was the best judge and the only legal judge to shape its enforcement policy. In *Winn-Dixie Stores Inc. v. FTC*, 377 F.Supp. 773 (D. Ct. M.D. Fla. 1974), the district court held that a cease and desist order was less restrictive against a second grocery chain and the FTC refused to modify this order. *Moog* was cited for the proposition that similarly situated firms are not necessarily entitled to quick treatment by the FTC but the court appeared to reject that proposition in the *Winn-Dixie* case because of the presence of a favored nation trading clause in the consent decree.

Further, courts have recognized that an agency must have freedom to develop its own enforcement policy. The need for wide agency authority was also discussed in the context of the discretion of the administrator of the Environmental Protection Agency in *Beltone Electronics Corporation v. FTC*, 402 F.Supp. 590 (D. Ct. N.D. Ill. 1975).

In that case, the FTC ordered affirmative disclosures of negative aspects of plaintiff's product, the absence of which, according to the FTC made the plaintiff's advertising misleading. The plaintiff claimed the omissions were industry-wide and that the agency's ruling was unlawful. *Moog* was cited for its holding that whether an agency moves against only one firm or an entire industry is a matter purely within the discretion of the agency. *Johnson Products Co. v. FTC*, 549 F.2d 35 (7th Cir. 1977) is another case in which the courts recognize that the FTC has the discretion to enforce an order against one firm that is practicing an industry-wide illegal trade practice without simultaneously proceeding against all firms in the industry, and that the FTC discretionary determinations may be overturned only for a patent abuse of discretion.

At the federal level, there continues to be further recognition of the broad authority of the agency to set up its own enforcement policy. In the case of *Pendleton v. Transportation Union Systems Corp.*, 430 F.Supp. 95 (D. Ct. E.D. Penn. 1977), the plaintiffs filed class actions enjoining the FTC and claiming violations of the Consumer Credit Protection Act by the lender and the failure of the Federal Trade Commission to enforce provisions of the act. Plaintiffs sought a mandamus against the FTC. The court first found that the act did not create a clear-cut duty on the part of the FTC that can be the proper subject of a mandamus. It specifically found that the statute involved only gives the FTC the power to enforce it and it doesn't create a duty; thereby the court treated the powers of enforcement as being broadly discretionary and invoked *Moog*'s holding that the FTC is alone empowered to determine its enforcement policy including discretion to allocate its funds and personnel as it sees fit.

This idea of deference to administrative agencies is summed up in a statement of the court, "because enforcement is essentially discretionary courts repeatedly have refused to require prosecutors or agencies to investigate particular alleged violations or institute proceedings against certain persons." See *Inmates of Attica Correctional Facility v. Rockefeller*, 477 F.2d 375, 397 (2d Cir. 1973).

The United States Supreme Court and the federal courts of appeal have continued to rule, consistent with *Moog*, that administrative officials possess wide discretion in formulating enforcement policy. *Marshall v. Jerrico, Inc.*, 446 U.S. 238, 248–49 (1980); *United States v. Leggett & Platt, Inc.*, 542 F.2d 655, 658 (6th Cir. 1976); *Noell v. Bensinger*, 586 F.2d 554, 558 (5th Cir. 1978); *Encyclopedia Britannica, Inc. v. FTC*, 605 F.2d 964, 973–74 (7th Cir. 1979).

165. 402 U.S. 183, 275 (1971).

166. 415 U.S. 199, 204–05 (1974).

167. *Id.* at 231.

168. *Id.* at 236.

169. 440 U.S. 741, 754–55 (1979).

170. *Id.* at 752–53.

171. *Ogala Sioux Tribe of Indians v. Andrus*, 603 F.2d 707, 713, 721 (8th Cir. 1979) (*citing Caceres*); *Alamo Express, Inc. v. United States*, 613 F.2d 96, 98 (5th Cir. 1980).

172. 415 U.S. 199, 231 (1974).

173. Allen, *supra*, note 1, at 87.

174. *Id.*

175. *Id.* at 90 quoting Schwenk, *The Administrative Crime, Its Creation and Punishment by Administrative Agencies*, 42 Mich. L. Rev. 51, 61 (1943).

176. 300 S.2d 774 (Miss. 1974).

177. Miss. Code Ann. §§ 41–29–101—183 (1972).

178. 300 So.2d 774, 781 (Miss. 1974).

179. H. PACKER, THE LIMITS OF THE CRIMINAL SANCTION 142 (1968).

180. *Id.* at 139–45.

181. *See infra* notes 246–288 and accompanying text.

182. *U.S. v. Cox*, 342 F.2d 167 (5th Cir. 1965).

183. *United States v. Dougherty*, 473 F.2d 1113, 1136 (D.C. Cir. 1972).

184. *Howell v. Mississippi*, 300 So.2d 774, 781 (Miss. 1974).

185. Allen, *supra*, note 2, at 90.

186. *People v. Avery*, 367 N.E.2d 79 (Ill. 1979), is illustrative of the proposition that delegation of power to reschedule controlled substances is considered an acceptable delegation of power at the state level. *See also Strong v. Bostick*, 420 So.2d 1356 (Miss. 1982), and *Ex Parte McCurley*, 390 So.2d (Ark. 1980).

187. *See infra* notes 238–44 and accompanying text.

188. Allen, *supra*, note 2, at 90.

189. *Michigan v. Nelson*, 255 N.W.2d 788 (Mich. Ct. App. 1977); *Missouri v. Lovelace*, 585 S.W.2d 507 (Mo. Ct. App. 1979); *contra Matter of Powell*, 602 P.2d 711 (Wash. 1979); *Utah v. Gallion*, 572 P.2d 683 (1977). For federal cases that also support this point, see *United States v. Pastor*, 419 F.Supp. 1318 (D. N.Y. 1975); *United States v. Gordon*, 580 F.2d 827 (5th Cir. 1978).

190. Allen, *supra*, note 2, at 92, 94.

191. *Id.* at 95.

192. Training of police personnel is a relatively new phenomenon. The importance of training to upgrade the abilities of the police officer was not recognized until World War II. Police and Fire Services of the City of Meriden, Conn. 110 (1962). It seems that the primary reason for the slow development of training for police officers was general resistance from within the police departments. This was also reflected in the prevailing public opinion that training of officers was superfluous since a police officer best learned his job by performing it.

The Wickersham Report of 1931 stated that of 383 cities surveyed, only 20 percent conducted any training of their police officers, and in smaller cities there was not even a pretense of training. Nat'l Comm'n on Law Observation and Enforcement Report on the Police 70 (1931). Most of the training given was of the military type, which included instruction on military drills, firearms, U.S. Army calisthenics, first aid, etc.

In a very few years, considerable change has been made in the extent of police training. A 1965 survey conducted by the International City Managers Association showed that of 1,352 cities surveyed, 1,135 conducted some training for their officers. Int'l City Managers Ass'n, Municipal Yearbook, 1966, at 435 (1966). The amount of initial training varies extensively, from less than a week to the nine-month course of the Chicago Police Department. More and more frequently the Task Force Reports on the police recommendations of 400 to 600 hours of classroom work are being met.

193. Officers at the Iowa Law Enforcement Academy are also required to take at least two courses that focus on the exercise of discretion by the police. Interview with John Callaghan, director, Iowa Law Enforcement Academy, Camp Dodge, Iowa, March 1980.

194. Allen, *supra*, note 2, at 113–14.

195. *Id.* at 95.

196. *Id.* at 95 n.144, citing WECHSLER, THE CHALLENGE OF A MODEL PENAL CODE, 65 Harv. L. Rev. 1097, 1098 (1952).

197. The different levels of penalties provided for misdemeanors and felonies convey the priorities established by the state legislatures, and the distinctions should be reflected in law enforcement policy. Felonies are clearly

more important and should receive a higher enforcement priority. To get a better grasp of the felony-misdemeanor dichotomy, it is beneficial to look at the *malum prohibitum* and *malum en se* distinction. *Malum prohibitum* crimes are frequently misdemeanors because these crimes do not violate significant moral principles of society, but legislative bodies have determined that such crimes are socially disruptive and must be regulated. Thus, while crimes like disorderly conduct, public intoxication, gambling, and simple assault are not as great a threat to personal security as are crimes like murder, armed robbery, kidnapping, and burglary, they are nonetheless outlawed in the interest of social stability. In establishing priorities, it would certainly seem more appropriate for legislatures to spend the time they have available on matters connected with *malum en se* crimes rather than *malum prohibitum* crimes. BLACK'S LAW DICTIONARY 865 (rev. 5th ed. 1979). *See People v. Pavlic*, 227 Mich. 562, 199 N.W. 373, 374 (1924), 35 A.L.R. 741; *State v. Shedoudy*, 45 N.M. 516, 118 P.2d 280, 287 (1941).

198. K. Davis, *supra*, note 1, at 64.

199. *Id.* at 119.

200. Allen, *supra*, note 2 at 92, n.138.

201. J.Q. Wilson, *Varieties of Police Behavior* 17–18 (1968).

202. Allen, *supra*, note 2, at 94–96.

203. *Id.* at 92 n.138.

204. *Id.*

205. *Id.*

206. *See supra* notes 179–87 and accompanying text.

207. Allen, *supra*, note 2, at 90 n.126.

208. South Carolina and Iowa. *Id.* at 96 n.150.

209. Note, *supra*, note 140, at 976.

210. *Id.* at 976 n.20 quoting K. DAVIS, *supra*, note 137, at 26–27.

211. 148 Iowa 36, 126 N.W. 914 (1910). 217 Iowa 98, 251 N.W. 39 (1933).

212. 148 Iowa 36, 43–45, 126 N.W. 914, 917 (1930). "All hotels shall be kept and maintained in a clean and sanitary condition and free from any effluvia, gas or offensive odors arising from any sewer, drain, privy or any other source whatever within the control of the owner manager, agent or person in charge thereof." Chapter 168, Acts 33d Gen. Assem. (1909).

213. 217 Iowa 98, 100, 25 N.W. 39, 40 (1933).

214. *Id.* To support his position that, in states where delegation of rule-making authority has been upheld, it has been limited to "subject matter [that] required particular skills or attributes that could not reasonably be demanded of a legislature," he cites eighteen such cases from fourteen states. Allen, *supra*, note 2 at 91–94. If one assumes that Professor Allen is accurate in his assessment of the position of the states, six states clearly prohibit the delegation of rule-making authority to agencies and fourteen permit such delegation

in narrowly prescribed circumstances. As suggested by Professor Allen, at most only twenty-two state courts had addressed the issue in *Howell*. This leaves twenty-eight states that have no settled law on the issue of whether the state legislature may delegate crime-defining power to an administrative agency.

215. Note, *supra*, note 209.

216. 220 Iowa 525, 529, 259 N.W. 213, 216 (1935).

217. *Id.* at 532, 259 N.W. 217.

218. *Id.* at 532–33, 259 N.W. 217.

219. Note, *supra*, note 140, at 982.

220. While the Iowa Supreme Court found that it was necessary "to vest unguided discretion in supervising and directing the disposition and transfer of funds" (*State v. Manning*, 220 Iowa 525, 534, 259 N.W. 213, 218 (1935)), the court also found that "the Budget Act, properly interpreted, contains ample provisions for guidance and direction of the budget director in making his decisions." *Id.* at 535–36, 259 N.W. 219.

221. 224 Iowa 504, 275 N.W. 569 (1937).

222. *Id.* at 507, 509, 275 N.W. 571–72.

223. *Id.* at 504, 505, 275 N.W. 570.

224. *Id.* at 509, 275 N.W. 572.

225. *Id.* at 507, 508, 275 N.W. 571.

226. *Miller v. Schuster*, 227 Iowa 1005, 289 N.W. 702 (1940).

227. 234 N.W.2d 894, 900–01 (Iowa 1976).

228. *Spurbeck v. Stratton*, 252 Iowa 279, 290, 106 N.W.2d 660, 666 (1960), *cited in Warren County v. Judges of the Fifth Judicial District*, 234 N.W.2d 894, 899 (Iowa 1976). *See also Danner v. Hass*, 257 Iowa 654, 134 N.W.2d 534, 540 (1965).

229. *State v. Rivera*, 260 Iowa 320, 325, 149 N.W.2d 127, 131 (1967), *cited in Warren County v. Judges of the Fifth Judicial District*, 234 N.W.2d 894, 899–900 (Iowa 1976).

230. *Iron Workers Local No. 67 v. Hart*, 191 N.W.2d 758, 772 (Iowa 1971), *cited in Warren County v. Judges of the Fifth Judicial District*, 234 N.W.2d 894, 900 (Iowa 1976). *See also Elk Run Telephone Co. v. General Telephone Co.*, 160 N.W.2d 311, 317 (Iowa 1968).

231. *Warren County v. Judges of the Fifth Judicial District*, 234 N.W.2d 894, 901 (Iowa 1976) (emphasis added).

232. *State v. Van Trump*, 224 Iowa 504, 506, 275 N.W. 569, 570 (1937).

233. *Id.*

234. 260 Iowa 320, 325, 149 N.W.2d 127, 131 (1967). The court in *Rivera* stated: "The legislature recognized as we do, that statutes cannot always detail motor vehicle safety regulations under all highway conditions. It therefore has, in certain areas, given the State Highway Commission authority to carry out the purposes of its statutes." *Id.* Earlier courts have recognized the

same proposition: It is manifest that the Legislature in seeking to control . . . businesses subject to its control . . . cannot always anticipate and foresee all the conditions that may arise affecting the conduct of the business. . . . It, therefore, may delegate to the ministerial officers certain powers, somewhat independent in their nature, the exercise of which is essential to the proper and effectual carrying out of the purpose and objective of the law itself. [*Danner v. Hass*, 257 Iowa 654, 663, 134 N.W.2d 534, 540 (1965), citing *Noble v. English*, 183 Iowa 893, 895, 167 N.W. 629 (1918)]

235. 252 Iowa 279, 106 N.W.2d 660 (1960).

236. In a number of cases, the Iowa courts recognized the need for more administrative discretion in the area of public safety. In *Sueppel v. Eads*, 156 N.W.2d 115, 118 (1968), the trial court had set aside a habitual violator conviction saying that "habitual violator" was not defined and too indefinite. The Supreme Court disagreed. It cited a Minnesota case *Anderson v. Commissioner of Highways*, 267 Minn. 308, 126 N.W.2d 778 (1964), dealing with a habitual offender and upholding such a statute that said, "While the privilege [of driving] is a valuable one, and may not be unreasonably or arbitrarily taken away, its enjoyment depends upon compliance with conditions prescribed by law and is always subject to such regulation and control as public authorities may see fit to impose under the police power in the interest of public safety and welfare." The Court found this rationalization applicable and persuasive in upholding the statute as not too broad. *Id.* at 118. In *Richard v. Holliday*, 153 N.W.2d 473 (Iowa 1967), the plaintiff claimed that the department of transportation was required to have definite standards for serious violation. The Supreme Court followed *Danner*, 257 Iowa 654, 661–64, 134 N.W.2d 534, 539–41 (1965) and said, "the statutory language—a serious violation—is a sufficient standard to permit the department to use its discretion and judgment." *Id.* at 479. Plaintiff had her license revoked.

237. 260 Iowa 320, 149 N.W.2d 127 (1967).

238. 186 N.W.2d 611, 613 (Iowa 1971).

239. *Id.* at 616.

240. *Id.* citing *Elk Run Telephone Co. v. General Telephone Co.*, 160 N.W.2d 311, 317 (Iowa 1968).

241. *See supra*, note 179.

242. In *City of Des Moines v. Reiter*, 251 Iowa 1206, 102 N.W.2d 363 (1960), the Iowa Supreme Court noted that "the fact that a municipal ordinance enlarges on the provisions of a statute by requiring more than the state statute requires creates no conflict therewith." The court in *Reiter* also held that "unless restrained by a statute a municipality may, in its discretion, determine for itself the methods of exercising the powers conferred on it."

243. Another example of an approach different from Professor Allen's is evident in a Washington case decided on February 21, 1980. in *State v. Bryan*,

93 Wash.2d 177, 606 P.2d, 1228 (1980), the Washington court upheld a delegation to the Department of Social and Health Services to establish sentencing regulations governing juvenile offenders (27 CrL20114, Apr. 2, 1980). A trial judge called upon to pass sentence upon a juvenile offender believed that the application of the standards would result in very little punishment for the juvenile. The trial court judge declared the sentencing guidelines provided by the Juvenile Justice Act of 1977 and administrative regulations promulgated pursuant to it unconstitutional and committed the juvenile.

While the Washington Supreme Court held that the determination of crimes and punishment has traditionally been a legislative prerogative, it stated that the legislature can constitutionally delegate its power to define sentences. The concern of the Washington Supreme Court was that constitutional requirements be met; primarily, that the legislature provide standards defining generally what is to be done and what body is to accomplish it, and procedural safeguards must be established to control arbitrary action. In this case, the state conceded the adequacy of standards so they were not an issue. RCW 13.40.030(1), (5), (6), (7) provide an explicit set of standards governing the period of confinement or other supervision based on the offense committed and a wide range of other listed factors. The court found the standards to be at least as complete as those considered in *State v. Mulcare*, 189 Wash. 625, 66 P.2d 360 (1937), in which the indeterminate sentence act establishing the prison and parole board to set sentences within legislatively prescribed maximums was upheld. The Washington rules provide that the sentencing standards must be established "on the basis of a youth's age, the instant offense, and the history and seriousness of previous offenses, but in no case shall the period of confinement and supervision exceed that to which an adult may be subjected for the same offense[s]." The section further requires that standards for sentencing "serious offenders" shall not be less than thirty days, and provides explicit restrictions on the possible length of time and sentencing alternatives that may be proposed. RCW 13.40.030(6), (7) also set out the permissible ranges of confinement. In addition to standards, the court found that the legislature had included safeguards in the authorizing legislation. As part of the Juvenile Justice Act, the legislation reserved the right to review, adopt, or require modification of the proposed standards. RCW 13.40.030(2), (3). The court further found that the legislature built into the statute provisions to facilitate constant monitoring of the administrative agency. Specifically, the proposed guidelines will always be before the legislature in a year in which a legislative session is mandated. Wash. Const. art. 2, 12. The end result was that the Washington Supreme Court found the standards adequate and there were sufficient safeguards to ensure that the statutory scheme proposed does not unconstitutionally delegate legislative functions to an administrative agency.

The meaning of *Bryan* is clear to the extent that if *Howell* ever truly expressed the attitude of the states toward delegation of substantive rule making in the area of criminal law, that day is now at an end.

244. *See supra* note 226 and accompanying text.

245. *Id.*

246. G.H. Williams, Legal and Political Problems of Police Discretion (Ph.D. dissertation, George Washington University, 1982) at 19, n.53.

247. *Supra* note 4.

248. K. Davis, *supra*, note 1, at 84–88.

249. *Id.* at 138.

250. Allen, *supra*, note 2 at 81–86.

251. *Id.* at 81.

252. Bonfield, *The Abrogation of Penal Statutes by Nonenforcement*, 49 Iowa L. Rev. 389, 429 (1964).

253. Allen, *supra*, note 2, at 82.

254. *Id.* at 85–86.

255. Bonfield, *supra*, note 252.

256. *Id.* at 439.

257. *Id.* at 410, 412.

258. *Id.* at 416.

259. 118 U.S. 356 (1885).

260. *Id.* at 373–74.

261. *Id.*

262. Abernathy, *Police Discretion and Equal Protection*, 14 S.C. L. Rev. 472, 473 (1962).

263. *See supra* note 251.

264. See *United States v. O'Neill*, 619 F.2d 222 (3d Cir. 1980), *reported in* 27 Crim. L. Rptr. (BNA) 2079 (Apr. 23, 1980) for an example of the difficulty of securing documents from police departments.

265. W. LaFave, *The Police and Non-Enforcement of the Law, Part I*, Wis. L. Rev. 104, 135 (1962).

266. 19 N.Y.2d 283, 279 N.Y.S.2d 161, 225 N.E.2d 871 (1967).

267. *Id.* at 19 N.Y.2d 289.

268. *Id.* at 19 N.Y.2d 291.

269. 461 F.2d 1148, 1150–51 (9th Cir. 1972).

270. 182 Cal. App.2d Supp. 827, 5 Cal. Rptr. 852 (1960).

271. *Id.* at 839.

272. *Id.*

273. 182 Cal. App.2d Supp. at 842, 5 Cal. Rptr. at 855–56; *Ah Sin v. Wittman*, 198 U.S. 500, 508 (1905).

274. *See* discussion of *United States v. Steele supra* notes 301–06 and accompanying text.

275. *See* K. Davis, *Administrative Law of the Seventies* 629 (1976), *dis-*

cussing Smith v. Goguen, 415 U.S. 566, 94 S.Ct. 1242, 39 L.Ed.2d 605 (1974).

276. 405 U.S. 156 (1972).

277. *Id.* at 162, *citing United States v. Harris*, 347 U.S. 612, 617 (1954), and *Thornhill v. Alabama*, 310 U.S. 88 (1940).

278. The argument should be made that while police rule making is constitutional, it may not be able to save a statute like that in *Papachristou* from constitutional attack.

279. 306 U.S. 451, 453 (1939). In *Lanzetta*, the Court invalidated a New Jersey statute making it a felony to be a "gangster." The statute defined a "gangster" as "any person not engaged in any lawful occupation, known to be a member of a gang consisting of two or more persons, who has been convicted at least three times of being a disorderly person."

280. 326 F.2d 605, 612 (5th Cir. 1964).

281. *Infra* notes 317–26 and accompanying text.

282. 398 F.2d 262, 264 (2d Cir. 1968).

283. *Id.* at 264–65.

284. *Id.* at 265.

285. *Id. citing Hornsby v. Allen*, 326 F.2d 605, 612 (5th Cir. 1964); *see Baker-Chaput v. Gammet*, 406 F.Supp. 1134, 1140 (D.N.H. 1976).

286. 439 F.2d 584, 596 (D.C. Cir. 1971).

287. *Id.* at 598.

288. This factor was of importance in *Hornsby v. Allen*, 326 F.2d 605 (5th Cir. 1964); *Holmes v. New York Housing Authority*, 398 F.2d 262 (2d Cir. 1968); and *Baker-Chaput v. Gammet*, 406 F.Supp. 1134, 1140 (D.N.H. 1976). The basic significance of public trust in administrative action was underscored in *Baker-Chaput v. Gammet*, 406 F.Supp. 1134, 1140 (D.N.H. 1976). In holding that "the establishment of written, objective, and ascertainable standards is an elementary and intrinsic part of due process," the court reasoned that "the absence of standards creates a void in which malice, vindictiveness, intolerance, or prejudice can fester. Plaintiff had a paramount interest in receiving those benefits for which she statutorily qualifies. In addition, as a member of our society she has an interest not only in being treated fairly by the administrative agency, but, just as important, in believing that she had been treated fairly. A standardless method of administration negates these interests." 406 F.Supp. at 1140.

289. *See* President's Comm'n on Law Enforcement and Administration of Justice, Task Force Report: The Police, 94 (1967), *cited* at n.81 in Amsterdam, *The Supreme Court and the Rights of Suspects in Criminal Cases*, 45 N.Y.U. L. Rev. 785, 814 (1970); and Amsterdam, *Perspectives on the Fourth Amendment*, 58 Minn. L. Rev. 349, 416 (1974).

290. K. Davis, *supra*, note 1, at 112–20.

291. Allen, *supra*, note 2, at 85–86 n.106.

292. Allen, *supra*, note 2, at 62–71.
293. *Id.* at 85–86 n.106.
294. *Id.* at 67, 76 *et seq.*
295. *Id.* at 104–05.
296. *Id.*
297. K. Davis, *supra*, note 1, at 110.
298. 323 U.S. 134, 140 (1944). This position has been reaffirmed in *Morton v. Ruiz*, which held that the power of an administrative agency to administer a congressionally created and funded program necessarily requires the formulation of policy and the making of rules to fill any gap left implicitly or explicitly by Congress. 415 U.S. 199, 231 (1974).
299. 115 N.W.2d 161, 163–64 (Iowa 1970).
300. 177 N.W.2d 1, 4 (Iowa 1970).
301. 277 N.W.2d 921, 923 (Iowa 1979).
302. *Id.* at 925.
303. *Id.*
304. 517 P.2d 289, 293 (Or. App. 1973).
305. Iowa Code, ch. 17A §§ 2, 7 (1981).
306. Allen, *supra*, note 2, at 113–14 n.216.
307. *Hagedorn v. Schrum*, 283 N.W. 876 (1939). The law of Iowa is well settled that a law-enforcing officer, whose office is created by state statute and whose duties are prescribed by statute, is an agent of the public in general and is not the agent of the municipality, *even though he is chosen by the municipality and is paid by it*. *Id.* at 877. *See also* Iowa Code § 364.1 (1981), §§ 372.4, 372.5, 372.14.
308. Iowa Code § 80B.2–.14 (1981). See *Ex Parte Corliss*, 114 N.W. 962 (1907) at 975 for a listing of those states in which the local police were considered state officers.
309. *Maquoketa Valley Comm. School Dist. v. Maquoketa Valley Ed. Ass'n.*, 279 N.W.2d 510 (Iowa 1979). Also, the case of *Hagedorn v. Schrum*, 283 N.W. 876 (1939) at 877 makes it clear that local police in Iowa are state officers, while that opinion was modified in some respect by *Strong v. Town of Lensing*, 179 N.W.2d 365 (Iowa 1970). *Hagedorn* was not overruled.
310. Iowa Code, ch. 17A §§ 2, 7 (1981).

Chapter 3

1. Remington & Rosenblum, *The Criminal Law and the Legislative Process*, U. Ill. L.F. 481 n.2 (1960).
2. T. Dye, *Understanding Public Policy* 18, 19 (1975).
3. W. LAFAVE, MODERN CRIMINAL LAW 41 (1978).
4. *See* K. DAVIS, POLICE DISCRETION 81 (1975).

5. Interview with Norman Jesse, former chairman of the judiciary committee of the Iowa House of Representatives, in Des Moines, Iowa, December 1981. A number of interviews were conducted with various persons working in the criminal justice system in Iowa. The results of those interviews are on file in the author's office. While it is recognized that the limited number of interviews does not permit strong empirical statements to be made, the interviews do provide some concrete perceptions of the criminal justice system by those primarily responsible for the operation of various aspects of that system in one state.

6. *See* Goldstein, *Police Discretion Not to Invoke the Criminal Process: Low-Visibility Decisions in the Administration of Justice*, 69 YALE L.J. 543, 557 n.26 (1960) (listing of state full enforcement statutes and regulations). Full enforcement can be defined as follows:

> [*F*]*ull enforcement*, so far as the police are concerned, means (1) the investigation of every disturbing event which is reported to or observed by them and which they have reason to suspect may be a violation of the criminal law; (2) following a determination that some crime has been committed, an effort to discover its perpetrators; and (3) the presentation of all information collected by them to the prosecutor for his determination of the appropriateness of further invoking the criminal process.

Id. at 559–60.

7. Allen, *The Police and Substantive Rulemaking: Reconciling Principle and Expediency*, 125 U. PA. L. REV. 62, 71 (1976).

8. *See* chapter 2 notes 59–61 and accompanying text.

9. *See, e.g.*, ARIZ. REV. STAT. ANN. ¶ 13 (1978); IDAHO CODE ¶ 18 (1979); MINN. STAT. ¶ 609 (1980).

10. Three states that substantially completed their criminal code revisions prior to 1970 were selected: Illinois (1962), Minnesota (1969), and Kentucky (1970). Four states that have taken action since the mid–1970s were selected: Arkansas (1976), Arizona (1977), Iowa (1978), and Missouri (1979). It is important to stress that this analysis is not solely limited to action taken during the time of each state's criminal code reform, but that time does serve as a primary focus.

11. *See* chapter 1 note 20 *supra*.

12. *See* Act of Mar. 27, 1824, § 2, ILL. REV. STAT. ch. 125, § 82 (1981); MINN. STAT. ¶ 387.03 (1980); MO. REV. STAT. ¶ 57.100 (1978).

13. *See, e.g.*, Act of Feb. 22, 1927, ch. 122, § 1, 1927 Iowa Acts 115 (repealed 1978); Act of 1942, ch. 115, § 1, 1942 Ky. Acts 548, 551–52 (repealed 1978). In Iowa, there was an indication that the repeal of the full enforcement legislation was almost totally inadvertent rather than directed at addressing problems of police discretion. Interview with Serge Garrison, director of Iowa Legislative Service Bureau, in Des Moines, Iowa, October 1978.

14. Israel, *The Process of Penal Law Reform—A Look at the Proposed*

Michigan Revised Criminal Code, 14 WAYNE L. REV. 772, 813–14 (1968).

15. *Id.* at 818–19. Although the recommendations of the joint committee of the Michigan state legislature were not enacted into law, their approach is typical of many other states and thus worthy of discussion.

16. *Id.* at 814.

17. *See* Note, *Disorderly Conduct and Loitering—A Modern Approach to Traditional Legislation*, 30 ARK. L. REV. 186, 203–04 (1976); Note, *Public Disorder Statutes in Iowa: An Evaluation of Existing Statutes and the Proposed Revision*, 57 IOWA L. REV. 862, 881–83 (1972).

18. Schantz, *Objectives of Criminal Code Revision: Guidelines to Evaluation*, 60 IOWA L. REV. 430, 448 (1975).

19. In 1975, the Minnesota legislature decriminalized various forms of sexual conduct engaged in by adults cohabitating in an ongoing voluntary relationship. *See* MINN. STAT. § 609.349 (1980).

20. *See* MISSOURI COMM. TO DRAFT A MODERN CRIMINAL CODE, THE PROPOSED CRIMINAL CODE FOR THE STATE OF MISSOURI 148–49 (1973).

21. *See* Iowa Code ch. 99B (1981); *see also* chapter 4, note 107 *infra*.

22. One Iowa newspaper reported:

> A public standoff exists on the issue of gambling, the Iowa attorney general says, and there appears to be little popular support to prosecute or change the law.
>
> . . . .
>
> The attorney general said the public and the Legislature need to decide what they want to prohibit in terms of gambling and what they want as a priority in law enforcement.
>
> . . . .
>
> Interviews with legislators last week found no evidence of strong concern about changes in the law.
>
> "You're the first person who's asked about it," Senator Carl Hultman, . . . the Senate majority leader, told a reporter.
>
> . . . . .
>
> Social gambling law amendments "are not high on my priority list" for legislative attention in the upcoming session, Hultman said.

Des Moines Register, December 9, 1979, at B6, cols. 1–2.

23. Ala. Code Crim. P. 815–18–5 (Supp. 1973); Alaska Stat. tit. 12, § 12.25.180 (1980); Ariz. Crim. Code § 13–3903 (1982); Ark. R. Crim. P. rule 5.2 (1980); Cal. Penal Code § 853.6 (West Cum. Supp. 1978); Colo. Rev. Stat. § 16–3–105 (1973); Conn. Gen. Stat. Ann. § 54–1(h) (West 1982); Del. Code tit. 11, § 1905 (1974); D.C. Stat. § 23–1110 (1980); Fla. R. Crim. P. rule 3.125(b) (West 1975); Ga. Code Ann. § 17–4–23 (1975); Hawaii Rev. Stat. § 803–6(b) (1975); Ill. Ann. Stat. ch. 38, § 107.12 (Smith-Hurd 1973); Iowa Code Ann. § 805.1 (West 1976); Kan. Stat. § 22–2–406 (1980); Ky. Rev. Stat. Ann. § 431–015 (Baldwin 1975); La. Code Crim. Proc. tit. 5, art. 211 (1980); Me. Crim. Code tit. 17–A, § 15 (1982); Md. Ann. Code art. 27, § 594B (Supp. 1982); Mich. Code Crim. P. § 780.581 (1977); Minn. R. Crim. P. rule 6.01(1) (1980); Miss. Code Ann. § 99–3–18 (1980); Mont. Rev. Code Ann. § 95–614 (1969) and Mont. R. Crim. P. § 46–6–404 (1982); Neb. R. Crim. P. § 29–422 (1980); Nev. Rev. Stat. §§ 171.177–1771 (1975); N.H. Rev. Stat. Ann. § 594:14 (Supp. 1977); N.J. Rules of Court § 3:3–1 (1983); N.M. Stat. Ann. § 31–1–6 (Supp. 1982); N.Y. Crim. Proc. Law § 150.20 (Supp. 1982); N.C. Gen. Stat. § 15A–301 (Supp. 1975); Ohio Rev. Stat. § 2935.26 (1980); Okla. Stat. Ann. tit. 22, § 207 (West 1969); Or. Rev. Stat. §§ 133.005–140 (1975); Pa. R. Crim. P. rule 6002 (Purdon Supp. 1983); R.I. Gen. Laws § 12–7–11 (1970 & Cum. Supp. 1977); Tenn. Code Ann. § 40–7–118 (1973); Utah Code Crim. P. § 77–7–18 (1980); Vt. R. Crim. P. 3 (1980); Va. Code § 19.2–74 (1980); Wash. J. Ct. Crim. R. 2.04 (West 1980); W. Va. Code § 62–1–5a (Supp. 1983).

24. A.B.A. STANDARDS FOR CRIMINAL JUSTICE, 2d ed., Standard 10–2.1 (1982).

25. *Id.* at 10.24.

26. *Id.* at 10.25.

27. *See id.* Arkansas attempts to address the second problem by providing a list of criteria to consider before issuing the citation, but gives no direction on what crimes are citable. *Id.* The Iowa citation statute gives no direction on who should be cited but does give limited direction on what crimes are citable. *See* IOWA CODE §§ 805.6, 805.8 (1981). Neither the Arkansas nor the Iowa statute follows the suggestion of the American Law Institute to require the police to issue administrative regulations to control the issuance of citations. Also, neither statute makes the issuance of citations mandatory for certain crimes, such as simple misdemeanors. American Law Institute, MODEL CODE OF PRE-ARRAIGNMENT PROCEDURE § 120.2 (1972).

28. Informal meeting with police chiefs and sheriffs from twenty largest Iowa communities, Iowa City, Iowa, August 23, 1983.

29. Kirkpatrick, *Arrest, Citation and Summons—The Supreme Court Takes a Giant Step Forward*, 30 ARK. L. REV. 137, 146–48 (1976).

30. ARK. R. CRIM. P. rule 5.2 (1980).

31. U.S. COMM'N ON CIVIL RIGHTS, WHO IS GUARDING THE GUARDIANS? A REPORT ON POLICE PRACTICES 149 (1981).

32. *Id.* at 149–50; *see also* KANSAS ADVISORY COMM. TO THE U.S. COMM'N ON CIVIL RIGHTS, POLICE-COMMUNITY RELATIONS IN THE CITY OF WICHITA AND SEDGWICK COUNTY 13–18 (1980).

33. American Law Institute, MODEL PENAL CODE § 3.07(2)(b) (proposed official draft 1962).

34. *See* MISSOURI COMM. TO DRAFT A MODERN CRIMINAL CODE, *supra*, note 20, at 102–4.

35. MO. REV. STAT. § 563.046(3)(2) (1978).

36. *See, e.g.*, ARIZ. REV. STAT. ANN. § 13–410 (1956); Crim. Code of 1967, § 7–5, ILL. REV. STAT. ch. 38, ¶ 7–5 (1981); IOWA CODE § 804.8 (1981).

37. J. KRESS, PRESCRIPTION FOR JUSTICE: THE THEORY AND PRACTICE OF SENTENCING GUIDELINES 3 (1980); MASSACHUSETTS CRIMINAL LAW REVISIONS COMM'N, PROPOSED CRIMINAL CODE OF MASSACHUSETTS ch. 264 (1972); PRESIDENT'S COMM'N ON LAW ENFORCEMENT AND ADMINISTRATION OF JUSTICE, TASK FORCE REPORT: THE COURTS 14–25 (1967).

38. Gerber, *Arizona's New Criminal Code: An Overview and Critique*, ARIZ. ST. L.J. 483, 502–06 (1977).

39. *See* ARIZ. REV. STAT. ANN. § 13–701 (1978).

40. Gerber, *supra*, note 38, at 483, 503.

41. *See* ARIZ. REV. STAT. ANN. § 13–702 (1978).

42. *See State v. Bly*, 127 Ariz. 370, 371–73, 621 P.2d 279, 280–82 (1980); *State v. Jenson*, 123 Ariz. 72, 73–74, 597 P.2d 554, 555–56 (Ct. App. 1979).

43. W. FRANCIS, LEGISLATIVE ISSUES IN THE FIFTY STATES: A COMPARATIVE ANALYSIS 12–14 (1967).

44. Francis used his model to measure the importance to state legislative bodies of twenty policy areas. *Id.* at 10–11. Of the twenty policy areas considered by Professor Francis, three arguably include concerns about police discretion within their scope. The closest to police discretion would be what he characterizes as "courts-penal-crime." Among his other policy areas, gambling and liquor probably include some concerns about police discretion. Liquor legislation normally requires the legislature to decide what is acceptable drinking behavior, and the legislation has significant enforcement implications for the police. While the situation has changed to some degree, the statement of the Missouri crime survey that "[t]here is scarcely any other field of law enforcement in the United States about which there is at present so varied a state of public opinion as that of the enforcement of those laws, state and federal, which are designed to prevent the sale and use of alcoholic beverages"

still has a strong element of truth today. MISSOURI ASS'N FOR CRIMINAL JUSTICE SURVEY COMM., THE MISSOURI CRIME SURVEY 302 (1926). Gambling legislation, unless it legalizes all forms of gambling, requires the legislature to make some decisions about how the gambling laws are to be enforced and what type of gambling behavior is and is not acceptable.

45. Packer, *The Case for Revision of the Penal Code*, 13 STAN. L. REV. 252, 263 (1961); Heinz, Gettleman & Seekin, *Legislative Politics and Criminal Law*, 64 N.W. U. L. REV. 280 (1969).

46. Packer, *supra*, note 45.

47. In Iowa no significant interest in police discretion was found among the executive agencies, legislators, or citizens interviewed. Interest among the news media and pressure groups was only marginal, but it was increasing; however, it could hardly be characterized as significant. The level of interest certainly did not seem sufficient to raise the issue to one of major legislative concern.

48. H. GOLDSTEIN, POLICING A FREE SOCIETY 136–55 (1977); *see also* G. BERKLEY, THE DEMOCRATIC POLICEMAN 154 (1969).

49. W. FRANCIS, *supra*, note 43, at 29. However, it seems unwise to argue that the low level of interest and conflict is perfectly reflective of low community, as well as low legislative, priority. Police discretion studies have found that the police prefer to work within the consensus of public opinion as they perceive it. Laws that are supported by local custom are enforced rigorously. Laws that the police view as having weak support from community leaders are enforced less frequently. For example, if the police think that there is little community concern with social, as opposed to commercial, gambling, the police will condone some fairly open violations of gambling laws, at least among those groups who could motivate change. D. Peterson, Police Discretion and the Decision to Arrest 158–59 (1968) (Ph.D. dissertation, University of Kentucky).

50. W. FRANCIS, *supra*, note 43, at 13–14. The legislation would have the most direct effect on the operation of local police agencies and would involve state government only marginally. Likewise, the legislation would not establish binding commitments for all levels of government because the state legislature, as the primary repository of power to enact criminal law legislation, would have the constitutional authority and capability to change such legislation.

51. Interviews with Norman Jesse, Iowa state representative, in Des Moines, Iowa, December 1981; John Patchett, Iowa state representative, in Iowa City, Iowa, May 1979; and Arthur Small, Iowa state senator, in Iowa City, Iowa, August 1980.

52. M. HOWE, 2 ed., HOLMES-POLLOCK LETTERS 59 (1941).

53. Remington & Rosenblum, *supra*, note 2, at 481.

54. In LaFave, *Penal Code Revision: Considering the Problems and Practices of the Police*, 45 TEX. L. REV. 434, 439–41 (1967).

55. Goldstein, *supra*, note 6, at 543, 573.

56. *Id.* at 488–89.

57. *See generally* Schiller, *More Light on a Low Visibility Function: The Selective Enforcement of Laws, Part I*, POLICE L.Q. 6 (Summer 1972); Schiller, *More Light on a Low Visibility Function: The Selective Enforcement of Laws, Part 2*, POLICE L.Q. 20 (Fall 1972); Schiller, *More Light on a Low Visibility Function: The Selective Enforcement of Laws, Part 3*, POLICE L.Q. 17 (Winter 1973); Schiller, *More Light on a Low Visibility Function: The Selective Enforcement of Laws, Part 4, POLICE L.Q. 35 (Spring 1973).*

58. *See generally* Schmidt, *A Proposal for a Statewide Law Enforcement Administrative Law Council*, 2 J. POLICE SCI. & AD. 330 (1974).

59. F. WILEMAN, MODEL POLICY MANUAL FOR POLICE AGENCIES (1976).

60. J. KENNEY & J. WILLIAMS, POLICE OPERATIONS: POLICE AND PROCEDURES—400 FIELD SITUATIONS WITH SOLUTIONS 18–19 (2d ed. 1968).

61. F. VANDALL, POLICE TRAINING FOR TOUGH CALLS: DISCRETIONARY SITUATIONS (1976).

62. *See* W. FRANCIS, *supra*, note 43, at 16–17 (important legislative matters will have a direct impact on a large number of people, attract publicity in the mass media, attract gubernatorial interest, and involve a large amount of money); notes 43–50 *supra* and accompanying text.

63. *See* notes 159–80 *infra* and accompanying text.

64. H. GLICK & K. VINES, STATE COURT SYSTEMS 89-91 (1973).

65. 392 U.S. 1, 12 (1968).

66. *See* G. SCHUBERT, JUDICIAL POLICY MAKING—THE POLITICAL ROLE OF THE COURTS, rev. ed. 10, 198–213 (1974).

67. Amsterdam, *The Supreme Court and the Rights of Suspects in Criminal Cases*, 45 N.Y.U. L. REV. 785, 786–93 (1970).

68. *Foley v. Connelie*, 435 U.S. 291 (1978) *citing Sugarman v. McDougall*, 413 U.S. 634, 647 (1973).

69. *Id.* at 298–99.

70. 440 U.S. 648, 650 (1979).

71. *Id.* at 651.

72. 392 U.S. 1 (1968).

73. 422 U.S. 884.

74. 440 U.S. 663.

75. *Id.* at 661.

76. *Id.*

77. 443 U.S. 47, 49–51 (1979).

78. 440 U.S. 661 (1979).

79. *Thompson v. City of Louisville*, 362 U.S. 199 (1960), may be an early example of Supreme Court concern about police discretion and an implicit policy decision to curtail that discretion. *See id.* at 205–6. However, that aspect of the *Thompson* case was never refined or subjected to further analysis. In fact, *Jackson v. Virginia*, 443 U.S. 307 (1979), makes *Thompson* appear more like a doctrinal sufficiency-of-evidence case than an effort to place controls on police discretion. *See id.* at 314–15.

80. 440 U.S. 661.

81. *Id.* at 663.

82. 443 U.S. 31 (1979). *De Fillippo* is another example of ambiguity of the courts' decisions concerning how to control police investigative discretion. In *DeFillippo*, the defendant was arrested under a Detroit ordinance that provides:

> When a police officer has reasonable cause to believe that the behavior of an individual warrants further investigation for criminal activity, the officer may stop and question such person. It shall be unlawful for any person stopped pursuant to this section to refuse to identify himself, and to produce verifiable documents or other evidence of such identification.

Id. at 33 n.1. DeFillippo was arrested for failure to produce identification and subsequently was searched. *Id.* at 34. Marijuana was found during the search. The defendant was not charged with violating the identification ordinance, but was convicted for possession of marijuana. The constitutionality of the stop under the identification ordinance was challenged, and the Michigan Court of Appeals held the ordinance unconstitutional. On appeal, the Supreme Court of the United States assumed the ordinance was unconstitutional but refused to invalidate the arrest. *Id.* at 37.

The unanswered question in *DeFillippo* is how far the Supreme Court is willing to go to limit the discretion of officers to stop "suspicious" persons on the street. *DeFillippo* can be distinguished from *Brown* because in *DeFillippo* reasonable suspicion existed as a basis for stopping the defendant, whereas such suspicion did not exist in *Brown*. However, in both cases the failure to declare the ordinances unconstitutional raises the possibility that communities may be able to give local officers extensive discretion to investigate suspicious activity. In fact, the dissent in *DeFillippo* argued that the Court, in permitting the arrest to stand, would allow many communities to use "suspicious persons" ordinances to give police broad discretion to do what might not otherwise be permitted under the Fourth Amendment. *Id.* at 45–46 (Brennan, J., dissenting). Local communities could pass such ordinances, and, according to the *Brown* and *DeFillippo* dicta, as long as law enforcement officers had a minimum level of suspicion to believe that the ordinances were violated, the arrest would be upheld. Of course, the ordinances would not pass constitutional muster if challenged, but until challenged they would give the police another tool to use in their work.

The concern expressed by the dissenting and concurring justices in *De-Fillippo* shows a clear recognition of the practical realities of police work. *See id.* at 41 (Blackmun, J., concurring); *id.* at 45–46 (Brennan, J., dissenting). There is a real danger that a large proportion of these "low-visibility offenses" will be used simply as investigative tools and that the validity of arrests under these ordinances rarely will be reviewed by courts at any level. At least one member of the Court was concerned about this and stated in a concurring opinion that there was no evidence that the ordinance in this case had been used as a pretext to make a stop. *Id.* at 41 (Blackmun, J., concurring). This concurring opinion implies that, if such evidence did exist, Justice Blackmun would have been much more likely to vote for invalidating the ordinance as well as the arrest.

83. *Cf.* C. PRITCHETT, THE AMERICAN CONSTITUTION 136–38 (3d ed. 1977) (Supreme Court will avoid passing on constitutional questions when possible).

84. 443 U.S. 37 (1979).

85. *Id.* at 31.

86. *Id.* at 47.

87. 103 S.Ct. 1855 (1983).

88. *Id.* at 1856.

89. *Id.* at 1858, 1859 quoting *Smith v. Goguen* 415 U.S. 566, 575 (1974).

90. *Id.* at 1859.

91. *See* McGowan, *Rulemaking and the Police*, 70 MICH. L. REV. 659, 676–94 (1972).

92. See *United States v. Perry*, 449 F.2d 1026 (D.C. Cir. 1971).

93. *United States v. Wade*, 408 F.2d 1230 (D.C. Cir. 1968).

94. See *United States v. Bryant*, 439 F.2d 642 (D.C. Cir. 1971).

95. 449 F.2d 1026, 1037 (D.C. Cir. 1971).

96. 338 U.S. 218, 87 S.Ct. 1926 (1967).

97. 408 F.2d 1230, 1237 (D.C. Cir. 1968).

98. 395 F.2d. 636, 638–39 (D.C. Cir. 1968).

99. 385 F.Supp. 193 (E.D. Wis. 1974).

100. 342 U.S. 167, 72 S.Ct. 205 (1952).

101. 385 F.Supp. 193, 200–201 (E.D. Wis. 1974).

102. Iowa *Code* 804.30 (1983).

103. *Id.* at 804.30(5).

104. 514 F.2d. 294 (2d Cir. 1975).

105. 439 F.2d 642, 652 (D.C. Cir. 1971).

106. *Id.* at 652 n.22.

107. 400 F.Supp. 186, 217 (D.C. Cir. 1975).

108. 357 F.Supp. 1289, 1322 (E.D. Pa. 1973).

109. 506 F.2d 542 (3d Cir. 1974).

110. 432 U.S. 362, 377–80, 96 S.Ct. 598 (1976).

111. Justice Stevens, having recently been appointed to the Supreme Court, did not take part in the consideration or decision of the case 423 U.S. 362, 364. Justice O'Connor was not then a member of the Court.

112. *United States v. City of Philadelphia*, filed October 7, 1979; *see* 25 Crim. L. Rep. (BNA) 2537 (1979).

113. *United States v. City of Philadelphia*, 482 F.Supp. 1248, 1274 (E.D. Pa. 1979) and 644 F.2d 187 (3d Cir. 1980) aff'd.

114. *People v. Gissendanner*, 46 N.Y.2d 543, 399 N.E.2d 924 (1979); *People v. Walker* 610 P.2d 496 (Colo. 1980); *Lucas v. U.S.*, 411 F.2d 360 (D.C. Cir. 1980); *Martinelli v. District Court*, 612 P.2d 1083 (Colo. 1980); *People v. Zamora* 167 Cal. Rptr. 573, 615 P.2d 1361 (1980).

115. 440 U.S. 741, 755, 99 S.Ct. 1465 (1979).

116. 405 U.S. 156 (1972).

117. 103 S.Ct. 1660 (1983).

118. 440 U.S. at 661.

119. at 757.

120. 103 S.Ct. 1859 (1983).

121. 157 Mich. 443, 122 N.W. 286 (1909).

122. *Id.* at 444–73.

123. 407 Pa. 129, 131, 179 A.2d 439, 441 (1962).

124. *Cf.* LaFave, *The Police and Non-enforcement of the Law, Part I*, WIS. L. REV. 104, 134–37 (1962) (recognizing that many courts would find a constitutional violation when arrest decisions are based on "race, religion, color or the like").

125. 90 Misc.2d 1047, 396 N.Y.S.2d 974 (S.Ct. 1977), *rev'd*, 64 A.D.2d 582, 407 N.Y.S.2d 165 (1978).

126. *Id.* at 1049–51, 396 N.Y.S.2d 976, 977.

127. *Bruno v. Codd*, consent decree between (1) plaintiffs and (2) defendants Robert McGuire, Harold Schryber, Carl Ravens, James Corridan, James T. Sullivan, Devitt and George Peters, index 21946/76, June 1978.

128. *Id.* at 583, 407 N.Y.S.2d 167.

129. 64 A.D.2d 582, 407 N.Y.S.2d 165 (1978).

130. 443 U.S. 47 (1979).

131. *See* G. FELKENES, THE CRIMINAL JUSTICE SYSTEM: ITS FUNCTIONS AND PERSONNEL 145–50 (1973).

132. Interviews with Iowa prosecutors on file in author's office.

133. *See* G. FELKENES, *supra*, note 131, at 150.

134. J. JACOBY, THE AMERICAN PROSECUTOR: A SEARCH FOR

IDENTITY 108–16 (1980). "The evolution of the American criminal justice system has separated the responsibilities of the police from the prosecutor and has moved toward clearer divisions of responsibility." *Id.* at 109.

135. *See* H. JACOB, JUSTICE IN AMERICA: COURTS, LAWYERS AND THE JUDICIAL PROCESS 161 (1965) (discretionary decision making by prosecutor done in privacy of prosecutor's office).

136. J. JACOBY, *supra*, note 134, at 30. However, there are recent cases that continue to test the parameters of prosecutorial powers to select cases for prosecution. *United States v. Wayte*, 549 F.Supp. 1376 (C.D. Cal. 1982); *see also United States v. Wayte* 82–1699 (9th Cir. decided July 10, 1983).

137. CALIFORNIA DISTRICT ATTORNEYS ASS'N, UNIFORM CRIME CHARGING STANDARDS 27–49 (1974).

138. U.S. Department of Justice, *Materials Relating to Prosecutorial Discretion*, 24 CRIM. L. REP. (BNA) 3001 (Nov. 22, 1978).

139. *Id.*

140. G.H. Williams, Maryland State's Attorneys 69 (1969) (M.A. thesis, University of Maryland); *see also* F. REMINGTON, D. NEWMAN, E. KIMBALL, H. GOLDSTEIN & W. DICKEY, CRIMINAL JUSTICE ADMINISTRATION: CASES AND MATERIALS 410 (rev. ed. 1982); Jacoby, *The Charging Policies of Prosecutors*, in THE PROSECUTOR 75, 81–86 (W. McDonald, ed. 1979); Vorenberg, *Narrowing the Discretion of Criminal Justice Officials*, DUKE L.J. 651, 678–83 (1976). *See generally* Kuh, *Plea Bargaining: Guidelines for the Manhattan District Attorney's Office*, 11 CRIM. L. BULL. 48 (1975) (example of efforts to control plea bargaining decisions in prosecutorial offices).

141. *See* chapter 4 note 24 *infra* and accompanying text.

142. Interview with Norman Jesse, assistant county attorney, Polk County, Des Moines, Iowa, December 1981.

143. *See* text accompanying note 144 *infra*.

144. Des Moines, Iowa, Police Department Regulations: Article VII—Issuance of Citations ¶ A (1979) (emphasis added).

145. *See* KANSAS ADVISORY COMM. TO THE U.S. COMM'N ON CIVIL RIGHTS, *supra*, note 37, at 67–68 (1980); OHIO STATE ADVISORY COMM. TO THE U.S. COMM'N ON CIVIL RIGHTS, POLICING IN CINCINNATI, OHIO: OFFICIAL POLICY V. CIVILIAN REALITY 68–70 (1981); G. BERKLEY, *supra*, note 56.

146. UNITED STATES COMM'N ON CIVIL RIGHTS, POLICE PRACTICES AND THE PRESERVATION OF CIVIL RIGHTS 2 (1979).

147. H. GOLDSTEIN, *supra*, note 48, at 134–35.

148. Interviews on file in author's office.

149. *See* note 48 *supra*.

150. *See* notes 152–55 *infra* and accompanying text.

151. *See* notes 156–58 *infra* and accompanying text.

152. *See* R. FOGELSON, BIG-CITY POLICE 13–15 (1977).

153. *See generally id.* at 93–116.

154. Contemporary Studies Project, *Administrative Control of Police Discretion*, 58 IOWA L. REV. 893, 912–13 (1973).

155. Interviews on file in author's office.

156. Wilson, *Politics and Police*, in CRIMINAL JUSTICE: LAW AND POLITICS 138, 144–45 (G. Cole, ed., 3d ed. 1972).

157. *See* Hudson, *Police Review Boards and Police Accountability*, 36 LAW & CONTEMP. PROBS. 515, 521 (1971).

158. M. BROWN, WORKING THE STREET: POLICE DISCRETION AND THE DILEMMAS OF REFORM 89, 294–95 (1981).

159. See *Britt v. Ocala*, 65 So.2d 753 (Fla. 1953) (city immune from liability for alleged negligent failure to provide medical care at time of arrest); *Hoggard v. City of Richmond*, 172 Va. 145, 147–78, 200 S.E. 610, 611 (1939) (municipality has immunity in performance of governmental function but not in performance of proprietary function).

160. K. DAVIS, ADMINISTRATIVE LAW TEXT § 25.01 (3d ed. 1972).

161. *Id.* There does seem to be some change at the state level as there is a distinct trend toward the abolition of sovereign immunity in the states. *See* K. DAVIS, ADMINISTRATIVE LAW OF THE SEVENTIES § 25.00, 551 (1976).

162. *See* K. DAVIS, *supra*, note 161, at § 26.00, 573; T. EISENBERG, CIVIL RIGHTS LEGISLATION: CASES AND MATERIALS 74 (1981).

163. 365 U.S. 167, 191 & n.50 (1961).

164. 436 U.S. 658 (1978).

165. *Id.* at 700–01.

166. *Id.* at 690.

167. *Id.* at 690–95.

168. *Id.* at 694.

169. 42 U.S.C. § 1983 (Supp. IV 1980).

170. 436 U.S. 701 (1978).

171. 445 U.S. 622 (1980).

172. *Id.* at 651.

173. *Id.* at 652 (emphasis added).

174. *Id.* at 652 n.36.

175. *See Leite v. City of Providence*, 463 F.Supp. 585, 588 (D.C.R. I. 1978); *cf. McClelland v. Facteau*, 610 F.2d 693, 697 (10th Cir. 1979); *Smith v. Hill*, 510 F.Supp. 767, 773 (D.C. Utah 1981); *Garris V. Rowland*, 678 F.2d 1264 (1982).

176. 689 F.2d 1220, 1225–27 (5th Cir. 1982).

177. *Id.* at 1227.

178. 451 U.S. 527, 544 (1981).

179. *Smith v. Wade*, 103 S.Ct. 1625 (1983).

180. One notable exception and clearly a positive step in law enforcement discovered during this research was the work of the Police Department of Cedar Falls, Iowa. The mission and goals of the department were briefly capsulized in budget requests submitted to the Cedar Falls city council in 1978, 1979, 1980, and 1981. However, although prevention and detection of crime and apprehension of offenders were the first and second goals of each year's request, there was no explicit mention of enforcement priorities for specific crimes. While it would seem highly desirable to include further explanation of these goals, this is the direction in which it seems appropriate to proceed. Interview with Paul Hoffey, chief of police of Cedar Falls, Iowa, in Des Moines, Iowa, December 1981.

Chapter 4

1. *See* IOWA CODE § 80B. 13 (1981).

2. *Id.* at § 80C.1.

3. *See id.* at §§ 13.1, 13.2.

4. *See id.* at §§ 80B.2, 80B.4.

5. For an example of mandatory hiring requirements, see IOWA ADMIN. CODE § 550–1.1(80B) (1981).

6. Contemporary Studies Project, *Administrative Control of Police Discretion*, 58 IOWA L. REV. 892, 965 (1973).

7. *Id.* at 964–65; *see also* IOWA CODE §§ 80C.3, 80C.5 (1981) (describing the Iowa crime commission's fund-allocation functions); KANSAS ADVISORY COMM. TO THE U.S. COMM'N ON CIVIL RIGHTS, POLICE-COMMUNITY RELATIONS IN THE CITY OF WICHITA AND SEDGWICK COUNTY 61 (1980) (describing fund-allocation functions of Kansas governor's committee on criminal administration).

8. H. JACOB, JUSTICE IN AMERICA: COURTS, LAWYERS AND THE JUDICIAL PROCESS 82, 84 (2d ed. 1972).

9. American Law Institute, MODEL CODE OF PRE-ARRAIGNMENT PROCEDURE § 10.3 (proposed official draft no. 1, 1972).

10. H. JACOB, *supra*, note 8, at 84.

11. Obviously, the attorney general and the state legislature can, should they desire to do so, influence local law enforcement, but in the main, that is a local function in which they rarely intervene. *See* chapter 3, notes 113–22 *supra* and accompanying text. Governors have considerable influence on the manner in which policies are made in the state, but law enforcement apparently is not a high priority among them. *See* W. FRANCIS, LEGISLATIVE ISSUES IN THE FIFTY STATES: A COMPARATIVE ANALYSIS 77 (1967).

During this study several state legislatures indicated that the tradition of local control would be a major obstacle to state agency formulation of police rules. Interviews with Lee Holt, Iowa state representative, in Des Moines, Iowa, December 1981; John Patchett, Iowa state representative, in Iowa City, Iowa, October 1979; and Arthur Small, Iowa state senator, in Iowa City, Iowa, August 1980.

12. Interviews with John Patchett, Iowa state representative, in Iowa City, Iowa, October 1979 and Arthur Small, Iowa state senator, in Iowa City, Iowa, August 1980. Resistance to the implementation of police rules at the state level also comes from state legislators, who traditionally have protected local agency control of law enforcement. As an example of this resistance by state legislators, consider that it was not until 1968 that the Iowa general assembly required local law enforcement officers to meet minimum education and training standards established by the state. Interview with John Callaghan, director of the Iowa Law Enforcement Academy, in Camp Dodge, Iowa, March 1980. Recently, the Iowa general assembly's concern about state control over law enforcement agencies was evidenced by the passage of reserve-law-enforcement-officer legislation. *See* Act of May 24, 1980, ch. 1191, 1980 Iowa Acts 605 (current version at IOWA CODE § 80D.1 (1981)). That legislation, in addition to authorizing the existence of local reserve-law-enforcement officers, IOWA CODE § 80D (1981) exempts the reserves from the minimum training standards established by the Iowa Law Enforcement Academy. *See id.* § 80D.3 (training standards to be established by local officials).

13. It is worth noting that courts are willing to limit rather than expand the power of "central" agencies to control "lower" levels of government. See *National League of Cities v. Usery*, 426 U.S. 833, 851–52 (1976) (power of Labor Department limited because Congress cannot displace state's freedom to operate in areas of traditional governmental functions). It seems that the same philosophy is equally, and even more passionately, applicable to the question of state agency control over local police agencies.

14. *See* Schiller, *More Light on a Low Visibility Function: The Selective Enforcement of Laws, Part 4*, POLICE L.Q. 35, 39–40 (Spring 1973). *See generally* K. DAVIS, POLICE DISCRETION 99–103 (1975); Caplan, *The Case for Rulemaking by Law Enforcement Agencies*, 36 LAW & CONTEMP. PROBS. 500 (1971); McGowan, *Rulemaking and the Police*, 70 MICH. L. REV. 659 (1972).

15. These boards would be created by local police departments and the chief of police would chair each board. Schiller, *supra*, note 14, at 35, 39.

16. *See* chapter 3 notes 144–47 *supra* and accompanying text.

17. *See* K. DAVIS, *supra*, note 14, at 98–120; McGowan, *supra*, note 14, at 659, 676–82.

18. *See* Goldstein, *Police Discretion Not to Invoke the Criminal Process: Low-Visibility Decisions in the Administration of Justice*, 69 YALE L.J. 543, 552–54 (1960).

19. Schmidt, *A Proposal for a Statewide Law Enforcement Administrative Law Council*, 2 J. POLICE SCI. & AD. 330, 331–32 (1974).

20. The proposed plan is basically a compromise. In implementing such a compromise, the legislature, mindful of the need to allow police departments some flexibility, might find it necessary to permit or even to encourage each city to collaborate with cities of similar size in the development of rules applicable to common problems. If law enforcement problems vary substantially throughout a state, such collaboration could occur on a regional basis, thus facilitating the development of rules that would reflect the variation of problems from region to region.

21. Conn. *Stat.* § 14–2839 (1983).

22. Iowa *Code* § 805.1 (Supp. 1983).

23. *Id.* at 805.1(3)(a).

24. Interview with Billie B. Wallace, chief of police of Des Moines, Iowa, in Des Moines, Iowa, June 1981.

25. Wilson develops what he refers to as three "styles of policing": watchman, legalistic, and service. *See* J. WILSON, VARIETIES OF POLICE BEHAVIOR 140–226 (1968). The watchman style is primarily concerned with the maintenance of order. Arrests are made only when an incident threatens to become uncontrollable. *Id.* at 141–42. In the legalistic style, if the police are called and the behavior violates the criminal code, the police intervene with an arrest. Police in the legalistic mode are concerned with law enforcement. *Id.* at 172–73. The service style falls between the two extremes. Police in the service style are generally concerned with maintaining good public relations. *Id.* at 202–3. There is a need to recognize the type of enforcement in a community, determine the style desired, and develop rules accordingly.

26. D. Peterson, Police Discretion and the Decision to Arrest 158–69 (1968) (Ph.D. dissertation, University of Kentucky).

27. Professor Davis contends that the appropriate rule-making process should have four steps, one of which is the circulation of tentative drafts of police rules outside the police department. K. DAVIS, *supra*, note 14, at 105–06. In addition to circulation of such drafts to judges, prosecutors, and other local government officials, Davis thinks that the drafts should be available for public inspection to permit the citizenry some formal input into the process. *Id.* at 77, 106. *See also* K. DAVIS, DISCRETIONARY JUSTICE: A PRELIMINARY INQUIRY 111 (1969). ("One valuable weapon in the fight against arbitrary exercise of discretion is openness. . . . What is needed . . . is increased openness of informal processes and the resulting records.") McGowan, *supra*, note 14, at 659, 680. ("There is something about the very

process of having to write down on paper detailed guidelines for one's conduct which summons rationality and elevates principle. This is especially true if the process is highly visible and if the rule-maker is held accountable for the results. . . . ") Contemporary Studies Project, *supra*, note 6, at 892, 966 (recommending open rule making as a deterrent to potential abuse of discretion).

28. Interview with Herman Goldstein, professor of law, University of Wisconsin, in Madison, Wisconsin, October 1979; *see also* K. DAVIS, *supra*, note 27, at 94–95 ("police will usually prefer to retain their broad discretionary power to make ad hoc decisions about arrests in individual cases").

29. W. MUIR, POLICE: STREETCORNER POLITICIANS 258–59 (1977).

30. J. WILSON, *supra*, note 25, at 84–85.

31. *Id.*; *see also id.* at 31–34.

32. Police-invoked law enforcement is the result of investigative work by the police, normally acting on their own initiative. The criminal activity focused on is primarily the "victimless" crimes such as gambling, prostitution, and traffic offenses. *Id.* at 85–86. Police action in this category would seem to be most susceptible to rule development and control by police officials in that specific resources can be allocated to the enforcement of these laws, and enforcement goals can be established.

33. Citizen-invoked law enforcement includes crimes with victims, the vast majority of which are property crimes such as larceny, auto theft, and burglary. *Id.* at 86. Because there is a citizen complaint, there is little discretion about whether to intervene in these situations. *Id.* Also, according to Wilson, because most property crimes are not solved by arrest, police have little opportunity to exercise arrest discretion. *See id.* at 87.

34. Police-invoked order maintenance occurs when the police, "on their own authority and initiative, intervene in situations of actual or potential disorder." *Id.* at 88. Because most "low-visibility" crimes such as drunkenness, disorderly conduct, and breach of the peace fall into this category, there is some opportunity for limited supervisory control over an officer's decision. Wilson suggests that the police administrator can tell the police officers to keep things quiet and take it easy or to be more vigorous. *Id.* But the administrator cannot control specific situations unless there is a general mandate to treat crimes like public intoxication more as law enforcement crimes than as order maintenance crimes.

35. Citizen-invoked order maintenance occurs when citizens call for police assistance in settling public or private disorders. *Id.* at 88–89. Discretion to intervene and discretion to act vary a great deal in the different situations. In citizen-invoked order maintenance situations Wilson thinks that the police administrator has less influence over the discretion of the patrolman than in any of the other three situations. He thinks that few rules can be prescribed in advance for handling disorderly situations. *Id.* at 128. Wilson also concludes

that different police in different cities do not differ greatly in the handling of order maintenance situations in which citizens have summoned the police. *Id.* at 138.

36. *Id.* at 89.

37. UNITED STATES COMM'N ON CIVIL RIGHTS, UNDER THE RULE OF THUMB: BATTERED WOMEN AND ADMINISTRATION OF JUSTICE 15 (1982).

38. J. WILSON, *supra*, note 25, at 88.

39. K. DAVIS, *supra*, note 14, at 3.

40. Of course, the prosecutor could still file charges, but would it be worth it?

41. *See* W. LAFAVE, ARREST: THE DECISION TO TAKE A SUSPECT INTO CUSTODY 110–14 (1965).

42. *Id. See also* Bank, *Discretionary Justice and the Black Offender*, in BLACKS AND CRIMINAL JUSTICE 37, 37–40 (C. Owens, J. Bell, eds. 1977).

43. See *Diehl v. State*, 451 A.2d 115, 120 (1982) (rejecting police officer's contention that he had a right to arrest defendant when defendant said "fuck you" to police officer).

44. *See* D. Peterson, *supra*, note 26, at 23–24.

45. Interview with Norman Jesse, assistant county attorney for Polk County, Iowa, in Des Moines, Iowa, December 1981.

46. *See* Bonfield, *The Iowa Administrative Procedure Act: Background, Construction, Applicability, Public Access to Agency Law—The Rulemaking Process*, 60 IOWA L. REV. 731, 787–89 (1975).

47. K. DAVIS, *supra*, note 14, at 71–78.

48. A related concern is that the rules give the public notice of what conduct will give rise to criminal culpability. The notice is provided, at least in a theoretical sense, by the criminal statutes. Questions may be raised, however, about whether the statutes will provide the required notice, particularly when statutes are not fully enforced under police rules. It is a fundamental proposition of the criminal that statutes must provide notice to the public of what conduct is proscribed; see *Papachristou v. City of Jacksonville*, 405 U.S. 156, 162 (1972), permitting the citizenry the chance to bring their acts into conformity with the law. The public might not receive adequate notice if law enforcement rules are not available for public review.

49. The following hypothetical situation illustrates how problems might occur. Officer *A*, a twenty-year veteran of the Police Department of River City, Iowa, arrested *B*, a prominent River City citizen, on the charge of simple assault in violation of IOWA CODE § 708.1 (1983). The River City Police Department has established certain guidelines to control arrest policy on charges of simple assault. The policy is as follows:

A law enforcement officer shall arrest a person for simple assault only when the officer has personally observed or has probable cause to believe that such person has engaged in conduct which he reasonably believes constitutes an assault, and the victim of the assault sustains significant physical injury or the assault involves the use of a dangerous weapon. Significant physical injury includes temporary physical disfigurement normally visible to members of the general public, including but not limited to a "black eye," a large bruise on the body, or a medically diagnosable internal trauma or emotional disturbance.

B complained to the chief of the River City Police Department that his arrest violated departmental policy. *B* stated that his arrest was due to the fact that when Officer *A* told him to cease his conduct, *B* replied, "I know the rules and you can't arrest me." Officer *A* maintains that he arrested *B* because he saw *B* slap a panhandler in a downtown River City park where a number of people were present. Officer *A* thought that failure to act in this case would bring ridicule and shame to the River City Police Department. After a review of the arrest, the chief found that Officer *A* had violated departmental policy in the arrest of *B* and suspended Officer *A* for five days without pay. Officer *A* then contacted a local attorney and filed suit. The suit sought damages and injunctive relief and claimed that the River City Police Department, in adopting the regulations on arrests for simple assault, exceeded its authority under state law and violated state and federal constitutional principles.

50. A member of the American Bar Association committee that analyzed the urban police function indicated that concern about the applicability of such rules outside the agency is a major cause of police resistance to such rules. Interview with Keith Mossman, member of the American Bar Association committee on urban police function, in Iowa City, Iowa, October 1979.

51. *See* Berger, *Do Regulations Really Bind Regulators?* 62 NW. U.L. REV. 137, 178 (1967); Note, *Violations by Agencies of Their Own Regulations*, 87 HARV. L. REV. 629, 630 (1974). The counter, and more compelling, argument would be that it is not inappropriate for rules to be used only in the situations for which they were explicitly intended. In this case, the rules would be used to guide police action and to provide a standard against which to measure their conduct, and departments would apply internal sanction if such standards were not followed.

52. 440 U.S. 741 (1979).

53. *Id.* at 749–52. Although *Caceres* allows guidelines to be violated, *Vander Linden v. United States*, 502 F.Supp. 693 (S.D. Iowa 1980), limits *Caceres*. The *Vander Linden* court held that documents given the IRS by a suspect without his valid consent could not be used to support a civil tax assessment against the suspect and his wife. The court reasoned that suppression of the evidence would advance the deterrence purpose of the exclusionary rule. *Id.* at 697.

54. 327 So.2d 230 (Fla. Dist. Ct. App. 1976).

55. 330 So.2d 256 (Fla. Dist. Ct. App. 1976).

56. *Reed*, 330 So.2d at 258; *Chastain*, 327 S.2d at 232 (*dictum*).

57. *Peterson v. City of Long Beach*, 24 Cal.3d 238, 245, 594 P.2d 477, 480–81, 155 Cal. Rptr. 360, 363–64 (1979).

58. H. GOLDSTEIN, POLICING A FREE SOCIETY 182 (1977).

59. W. CHAMBLISS & R. SEIDMAN, LAW, ORDER, AND POWER 389 (1971). Of course, the standards of performance must be clear. An officer is entitled to know in advance the specific definition of conduct that will subject him to discipline. *See Bence v. Breier*, 501 F.2d 1185, 1190 (7th Cir. 1974); *Perea v. Fales*, 39 Cal. App.3d 939, 942, 114 Cal. Rptr. 808, 810 (1975); H. GOLDSTEIN, *supra*, note 58, at 162.

60. For example, if the local police in Iowa are designated as the primary rule-making body, particular state statutes would probably answer some of the questions that have been raised. In Iowa local police would be presented with a special problem because there is no specific procedure governing local administrative agencies. While the Iowa Code "is intended to provide a minimum procedural code for the operation of all state agencies," IOWA CODE § 17A.1 (1981), "agency" does not mean "a political subdivision of the state or its offices and units." *Id.* at § 17A.2(1).

If there were a desire to limit public participation in formulation of enforcement criteria, local police could take refuge in the Iowa "open meetings" law. *Id.* at §§ 28A.1–8. That law provides that a governmental body may hold a closed session "[t]o avoid disclosure of specific law enforcement matters, such as allowable tolerances or criteria for the selection, prosecution or settlement of cases, which if disclosed would facilitate disregard of requirements imposed by law." *Id.* at § 28A.5(h). Thus, under the Iowa open-meetings law, a local police agency would have the power to exclude the public from rule-making sessions. There is some doubt, however, about whether the results of such meetings would be exempt from public disclosure under the Iowa "public record" as described in the Iowa Code. The state provides: "Wherever used in this chapter, public records includes all records and documents of or belonging to this state or any county, city, township, school corporation, political subdivision, or tax-supported district in this state, or any branch, department, board, bureau, commission, council, or committee of any of the foregoing." *Id.* at § 68A.1. Only two exemptions in the "public records" law are related to law enforcement. One section provides confidentiality for "[p]eace officers' investigative reports, except where disclosure is authorized elsewhere in [the] Code," *id.* at § 68A.7(5), and another provides for confidentiality of criminal identification files of law enforcement agencies, *id.* at § 68A.7(9). It is likely, therefore, that, while police rules could be developed in closed sessions, the rules would be accessible to the public once formulated.

The only way in which a police agency could prohibit access to police arrest policies would be by seeking an injunction in a state court. The agency would bear the burden of proving that the disclosure of the rules "would clearly not be in the public interest." *Id.* at § 68A.8. Although the Iowa Administrative Procedure Act (IAPA) provision for exempting enforcement rules from disclosure does not directly apply to local agencies, *see* Bonfield, *supra*, note 46, at 731, 762. The policy from which this provision arises might be offered on behalf of an injunction petition.

The language of the IAPA implies that disclosure of police rules would not be in the public interest. The argument could also be made that it is doubtful that the Iowa general assembly intended to permit agencies to develop enforcement rules in secret, yet require disclosure of the rules once formulated. In summary, in Iowa there is one state statute providing for the opening of public records on enforcement strategies and another permitting state agencies to formulate enforcement strategies in closed sessions. The primary purpose for holding a meeting in a closed session is to guarantee that the enforcement strategies are not available to the public. Adherence to the public records law violates the spirit of the open meeting law's exemptions.

61. K. DAVIS, ADMINISTRATIVE LAW AND GOVERNMENT 278 (2d ed. 1975).

62. *Cf.* LaFave, *Penal Code Revision: Considering the Problems and Practices of the Police*, 45 TEX. L. REV. 434, 437–38 (1967) (discussing police discretion in enforcing an overbroad statute).

63. *See* Goldstein, *Improving Policing: A Problem-Oriented Approach*, 25 CRIME & DELINQ. 236, 250–51 (1979). For one case concerned with the need to provide yet control discretion, see *People v. Coutard*, 32 Crim. L. Rep. (BNA) 2166 (December 1, 1982).

64. Professor Goldstein thinks it would be a major advance if a police administrator clarified the objectives for handling minor disputes. If the prime objective is to solve the dispute, a number of alternatives and techniques might be developed for the officer. H. GOLDSTEIN, *supra*, note 58, at 112.

65. Assembly Bill 169, 1979 Wis. § 14.

66. *See* Contemporary Studies Project, *supra* note 6, at 892, 917–38.

67. *Id.* at 954–58.

68. W. LAFAVE, *supra*, note 41, at 153–55.

69. Contemporary Studies Project, *supra*, note 6, at 892, 954.

70. Reporting is one way to fulfill the need recognized by the American Bar Association for structure and control of police operation. *See* A.B.A., A.B.A. STANDARDS FOR CRIMINAL JUSTICE, 2d ed. § 1–4.2 (1982).

71. *See* notes 30–55 *supra* and accompanying text.

72. *See generally* chapter 3 notes 6–62 *supra* and accompanying text.

73. *See* notes 30–55 *supra* and accompanying text.

74. *See* LaFave, *supra*, note 62, at 434, 438.

75. *See* LaFave, *The Police and Non-enforcement of the Law, Part I*, WIS. L. REV. 104, 134–37 (1962).

76. In a compilation of number and rate of arrests for the ten most frequent offenses nationwide in 1965, simple assault was fifth in rank with a total of 207,615 arrests. PRESIDENT'S COMM'N ON LAW ENFORCEMENT AND ADMINISTRATION OF JUSTICE, CHALLENGE OF CRIME IN A FREE SOCIETY 20 (1967).

77. *See* chapter 1 notes 15–16 *supra* and accompanying text.

78. *See* notes 41–42 *supra* and accompanying text.

79. *See, e.g.*, CAL. PENAL CODE § 242 (West 1971); IOWA CODE § 708.1 (1981); N.Y. PENAL LAW § 120.00 (McKinney 1975). The term "assault," as used in this section, will include both of the common law misdemeanors: assault and battery. For a discussion of these common law definitions, *see* W. LAFAVE & A. SCOTT, HANDBOOK ON CRIMINAL LAW § 80, 602–03 (1972).

80. IOWA CODE § 708.1–.2 (1981).

81. *See* IOWA CODE §§ 2593, 2594, 2595, 2597 (1851). Although the § 2597 assault standard remained the same, the penalty was reduced. *See* note 97 *infra* and accompanying text.

82. *See* IOWA CODE §§ 2593, 2594, 2595, 2597 (1851).

83. *See State v. Twogood*, 7 Iowa 252, 253–54 (1858). The legislature, until the recent criminal code revision, apparently was willing to defer to the common law interpretation of the Iowa courts for the actual meaning of assault.

84. *See* IOWA CODE §§ 2594, 2597 (1851).

85. *Id.* at 2597. In 1860 the penalty was reduced to thirty days and/or a $100 fine. IOWA CODE § 4220 (1860).

86. IOWA CODE § 2594 (1851).

87. *See State v. Gillette*, 56 Iowa 459, 460, 9 N.W. 362, 362 (1881).

88. American Law Institute, MODEL PENAL CODE § 211.1 commentary, 183 (1962).

89. *Id.* at § 211.1(1).

90. *Id.* at § 211.1(1)(a).

91. IOWA CODE § 708.1 (1981).

92. *Id.* at § 708.1(2).

93. 206 S.2d 30 (Fla. 1968), *discussed in* J. HALL, B.J. GEORGE & R. FORCE, CRIMINAL LAW AND PROCEDURE 198 (3d ed. 1976).

94. *Id.* at 33, *accord Nelson v. State*, 157 S.2d 96, 98 (Fla. 1963); *Clark v. State*, 318 So.2d 487, 487–89 (Fla. Dist. Ct. App. 1975); *Battle v. State*, 292 So.2d 594, 595–96 (Fla. Dist. Ct. App. 1974); *contra State v. White*, 324 So.2d 630, 631 (Fla. 1975).

95. J. ROEHRICK, THE NEW IOWA CRIMINAL CODE: A COMPARISON 66 (1978).

96. IOWA CODE § 708.1(3) (1981).

97. American Law Institute, *supra*, note 88 at § 211.1(1)(c).

98. *Id.* at § 211.1 commentary, 192.

99. The distinction between the two types of statute is explained in LaFave, *supra*, note 62, at 434, 436–42.

100. IOWA CODE § 708.1(3) (1981).

101. *See id.* at § 708.1.

102. *See id.* at § 708.1(3).

103. This is just one example of the type of approach that might be taken by a legislative body attempting to address the problem. It is one of several developed in a project at the University of Iowa College of Law on ways to control police discretion.

104. *See* notes 19–20 *supra* and accompanying text.

105. *See* notes 61–75 *supra* and accompanying text.

106. IOWA CODE § 708.1(1) (1981).

107. *See* U.S. COMM'N ON THE REVIEW OF THE NATIONAL POLICY TOWARD GAMBLING, GAMBLING IN AMERICA 37–38 (1976).

108. *Id.* at 39.

109. LaFave, *supra*, note 62, at 434, 436–37.

110. Interview with Billie B. Wallace, chief of police in Des Moines, Iowa, in Des Moines, Iowa, June 1981.

111. *See* Des Moines Register, June 21, 1972, at A1, col. 2; Des Moines Register, June 13, 1972, at A1, col. 7; Des Moines Register, June 12, 1972, at A1, col. 1.

112. *See* Des Moines Register, Dec. 9, 1979, at B6, cols. 1–2; *see also* IOWA CODE ch. 99B (1981).

113. IOWA CODE 899B.12(2) (1981).

114. *Id.* at 899B.12(3).

115. Because police do engage in selective enforcement, what inhibits formal rule making? The most important reason is perhaps the "myth of full enforcement." That is, the police have imbued themselves and the public with the idea that the criminal laws are impartially enforced and no choices are made in determining if or against whom the laws will be enforced. In other words, the general tendency has been to consider the police in their law enforcement capacity as an organization performing ministerial, and not discretionary, functions. Schiller cites a major reason why police administrators refuse to acknowledge selective enforcement policies: to do so would require the chief of police to state the policies the department follows and to defend those policies. Schiller, *supra*, note 14, at 35, 36–37.

Bibliography

BOOKS

American Bar Association. *Standards for Criminal Justice*, 2d ed., vol. 1. Boston: Little, Brown, 1982.

American Bar Association Project on Standards for Criminal Justice. *Standards Relating to the Urban Police Function*. Boston: Little, Brown, 1974.

American Law Institute. *Model Code of Pre-arraignment Procedure*. Philadelphia: American Law Institute, 1972.

———. *Model Penal Code*. Philadelphia: American Law Institute, 1962.

American Political Science Association. *Political Science and State and Local Government*. Washington, D.C.: American Political Science Association, 1973.

Arnold, Thurman. *The Symbols of Government*. New Haven, Conn.: Yale University Press, 1935.

Backus, Joseph. *A Digest of Laws Relating to the Offices and Duties of Sheriff, Coroner and Constable*. Vol. 2. New York: W.A. Davis, 1812.

Bayley, David H. *Police and Society*. Beverly Hills, Calif.: Sage Publications, 1977.

Berkley, George E. *The Democratic Policeman*. Boston: Beacon Press, 1969.

Beyle, Thad L., and J. Oliver Williams, eds. *The American Governor in Behavioral Perspective*. New York: Harper and Row, 1972.

Bittner, Egon. *The Function of the Police in Modern Society: A Review of Background, Current Practices and Possible Role Models*. Rockville, Md.: National Institute of Mental Health Center for Studies of Crime and Delinquency, 1975.

Bondy, William. *The Separation of Governmental Powers*. New York: AMS Press, 1967.

Brown, Michael K. *Working the Street: Police Discretion and the Dilemmas of Reform*. New York: Russell Sage Foundation, 1981.

California District Attorneys Association. *Uniform Crime Charging Standards*. Sacramento, Calif.: California District Attorneys Association, 1974.

Chambliss, William J., and Robert J. Seidman. *Law, Order, and Power*. Reading, Mass.: Addison-Wesley, 1971.

Chevigny, Paul. *Police Power*. New York: Pantheon Books, 1969.

Citizens Conference on State Legislatures. *The Sometimes Governments, A Critical Study of the 50 American Legislatures*. Kansas City: Citizens Conference on State Legislatures, 1973.

Cole, George F., ed. *Criminal Justice: Law and Politics*. 3d ed. Belmont, Calif.: Wadsworth, 1972.

Cooper, Frank. *State Administrative Law*. Vol. 1. New York: Bobbs-Merrill, 1965.

Crenson, Matthew A. *The Un-Politics of Air Pollution: A Study of Non-decisionmaking in the Cities*. Baltimore: Johns Hopkins University Press, 1971.

Cushman, Robert E., and Robert F. Cushman. *Cases in Constitutional Law*. New York: Appleton-Century-Crofts, 1958.

Davis, Kenneth Culp. *Administrative Law and Government*. 2d ed. St. Paul, Minn.: West, 1975.

———. *Administrative Law of the Seventies*. Rochester, N.Y.: Lawyers Co-operative Publishing Company, 1976.

———. *Administrative Law Text*. 3d ed. St. Paul, Minn.: West, 1972.

———. *Discretionary Justice: A Preliminary Inquiry*. Baton Rouge: Louisiana State University Press, 1969.

———. *Police Discretion*. St. Paul, Minn.: West, 1975.

Dealey, James Quayle. *Growth of American State Constitutions*. Boston: Athenaeum Press, 1915.

de Montesquieu, Baron. *The Spirit of the Law*. Trans. Thomas Nugent. New York: Macmillan, 1949.

Dillon, John F. *Commentaries on the Law of Municipal Corporations*. Boston: Little, Brown, 1890.

Dye, Thomas R. *Understanding Public Policy*. 2d ed. Englewood Cliffs, N.J.: Prentice-Hall, 1975.

Eisenberg, Theodore. *Civil Rights Legislation: Cases and Materials*. Indianapolis, New York, Charlottesville, Va.: Michie/Bobbs-Merrill, 1981.

Eisenstein, James. *Politics and the Legal Process*. New York: Harper and Row, 1973.

Felkenes, George T. *The Criminal Justice System: Its Functions and Personnel*. Englewood Cliffs, N.J.: Prentice-Hall, 1973.

Fogelson, Robert M. *Big City Police*. Cambridge, Mass.: Harvard University Press, 1977.

Fosdick, Raymond B. *American Police Systems*. New York: Century Company, 1920; reprint, Patterson Smith, 1968.

Francis, Wayne. *Legislative Issues in the Fifty States: A Comparative Analysis*. Chicago: Rand, McNally, 1967.

Glick, Henry Robert, and Kenneth R. Vines. *State Court Systems*. Englewood Cliffs, N.J.: Prentice-Hall, 1973.

Goldstein, Herman. *Policing a Free Society*. Cambridge, Mass.: Ballinger, 1977.

Goodnow, Frank J. *Municipal Government*. New York: Century Company, 1925.

Gottfredson, Michael R. and Don M. Gottfredson. *Decisionmaking in Criminal Justice: Toward the Rational Exercise of Discretion*. Cambridge, Mass.: Ballinger, 1980.

Green, Fletcher M. *Constitutional Development in the South Atlantic States 1776–1860*. Chapel Hill: University of North Carolina Press, 1930.

Hall, James P. *The History and Philosophy of Law Enforcement*. Dubuque, Ia.: Kendall/Hunt, 1975.

Hall, Jerome, B.J. George, Jr., and Robert Force. *Criminal Law and Procedure*. 3d ed. Indianapolis: Bobbs-Merrill, 1976.

Highsaw, Robert. *The Government and Administration of Mississippi*. New York: Thomas Y. Crowell Company, 1954.

Howe, M., ed. *Holmes-Pollock Letters*. Cambridge, Mass.: Harvard University Press, 1941.

Inbau, Fred E., James R. Thompson, and Andre A. Moenssens. *Criminal Law*. Mineola, N.Y.: Foundation Press, 1979.

Jacob, Herbert. *Justice in America: Courts, Lawyers and the Judicial Process*. Boston: Little, Brown, 1965; 2d ed. 1972.

Jacoby, Joan. *The American Prosecutor: A Search for Identity*. Lexington, Mass.: D.C. Heath, 1980).

Jaffe, Louis. *Judicial Control of Administrative Action*. Boston: Little, Brown, 1965.

Kamisar, Yale, W. LaFave, and J. Israel. *Modern Criminal Procedure 1980 Supplement*. St. Paul, Minn.: West, 1980.

Karraker, Cyrus Harreld. *The Seventeenth-Century Sheriff*. Chapel Hill: University of North Carolina Press, 1930.

Kenney, John P., and John B. Williams. *Police Operations: Police and Procedures—400 Field Situations with Solutions*. 2d ed. Springfield, Ill.: Charles C. Thomas, 1968.

Kress, Jack. *Prescription for Justice: The Theory and Practice of Sentencing Guidelines*. Cambridge, Mass.: Ballinger, 1980.

LaFave, Wayne. *Arrest: The Decision to Take a Suspect into Custody*. Boston: Little, Brown, 1965.

———. *Modern Criminal Law*. St. Paul, Minn.: West, 1978.

———, and Austin Scott. *Handbook on Criminal Law*. St. Paul, Minn.: West, 1972.

Lee, W.L. Melville. *A History of Police in England*. London: Methuen, 1901.

Lineberry, Robert L., and Ira Sharkansky. *Urban Politics and Public Policy*. New York: Harper and Row, 1974.

Locke, John. *On Civil Government*. ed. Russell Kirk. London, 1689. Chicago: Henry Regnery Company, 1955.

McDonald, William F., ed. *The Prosecutor*. Beverly Hills, Calif.: Sage Publications, 1979.

[Madison, James]. *The Federalist*. ed. J. Cooke, Middletown, Conn.: Wesleyan University Press, 1961.

Maitland, Frederick William. *The Constitutional History of England*. Cambridge: Cambridge University Press, 1931.

Muir, William K. *Police: Streetcorner Politicians*. Chicago: University of Chicago Press, 1977.

Niederhoffer, Arthur. *Behind the Shield*. Garden City, N.Y.: Doubleday, 1967.

Owens, Charles E., and Jimmy Bell, eds. *Blacks and Criminal Justice*. Lexington, Mass.: D.C. Heath, 1977.

Packer, Herbert L. *The Limits of the Criminal Sanction*. Stanford, Calif.: Stanford University Press, 1968.

Pepinsky, Harold E. *Crime and Conflict*. London: Martin Robertson, 1976.

Pritchett, C. Herman. *The American Constitution*. 3d ed. New York: McGraw-Hill, 1977.

Radzinowicz, Leon. *A History of English Criminal Law and its Administration from 1750. Vol. 2, The Clash Between Private Initiative and Public Interest in the Enforcement of the Law*. London: Stevens, 1948.

Ransone, Coleman. *The Office of Governor in the United States*. Freeport, N.Y.: Books for Libraries Press, 1970.

Reiss, Albert J., Jr. *The Police and the Public*. New Haven, Conn.: Yale University Press, 1971.

Remington, Frank J., Donald J. Newman, Edward L. Kimball, Herman Goldstein, and Walter J. Dickey. *Criminal Justice Administration: Cases and Materials*. Rev. ed. Charlottesville, Va.: Michie/Bobbs-Merrill, 1982.

Roehrick, John P. *The New Iowa Criminal Code: A Comparison*. Des Moines: Association of Trial Lawyers of Iowa, 1975.

Schubert, Glendon A. *Judicial Policy Making—The Political Role of the Courts*. Rev. ed. Glenview, Ill.: Scott, Foresman, 1975.

Sigler, Jay A., and Benjamin R. Beede. *The Legal Sources of Public Policy*. Lexington, Mass.: D.C. Heath, 1977.

Skolnick, Jerome. *Justice without Trial: Law Enforcement in a Democratic Society*. 2d ed. rev. New York: John Wiley and Sons, 1975.

Smith, Bruce. *Police Systems in the United States*. New York: Harper and Brothers, 1940.

———. *Rural Crime Control*. Portland, Me.: Southworth Press, 1933.

———. *The State Police: Organization and Administration*. New York: Macmillan, 1925.

Vandall, Frank J. *Police Training for Tough Calls: Discretionary Situations*. Atlanta: Emory University for Research in Social Change, 1976.

Walker, Samuel. *A Critical History of Police Reform*. Lexington, Mass.: D.C. Heath, 1977.

———. *Popular Justice: A History of American Criminal Justice*. New York: Oxford University Press, 1980.

Wilson, James Q. *Varieties of Police Behavior*. Cambridge, Mass.: Harvard University Press, 1968.

ARTICLES

Aaronson, David E., C. Thomas Dienes, and Michael C. Musheno. "Improving Police Discretion Rationality in Handling Public Inebriates, Parts I and II." *Administrative Law Review* 29 (Fall 1977):447–85; 30 (Winter 1978):93–132.

Abernathy, M. Glenn. "Police Discretion and Equal Protection." *South Carolina Law Quarterly* 14 (Summer 1962):472–86.

"Administrative Control of Police Discretion." *Iowa Law Review* 58 (1973):892–973.

Allen, Ronald J. "The Police and Substantive Rulemaking: A Brief Rejoiner." *University of Pennsylvania Law Review* 125 (June 1977):1172–81.

———. "The Police and Substantive Rulemaking: Reconciling Principle and Expediency." *University of Pennsylvania Law Review* 125 (November 1976):62–118.

American Bar Association Criminal Justice Section. "Report on 1980 Annual Meeting, Honolulu, Hawaii." *Criminal Law Reporter* (September 17, 1980):2548–50.

Amsterdam, Anthony. "Perspectives on the Fourth Amendment." *Minnesota Law Review* 58 (January 1974):349–477.

———. "The Supreme Court and the Rights of Suspects in Criminal Cases." *New York University Law Review* 45 (October 1970):785–815.

Ancel, Marc, and Jacques Verin. "The Politics of Criminal Law Reform: France." *American Journal of Comparative Law* 21 (Spring 1973):263–68.

Bachrach, Peter, and Morton S. Baratz. "The Two Faces of Power." *American Political Science Review* 56 (December 1962):947–52.

Bell, Jeffrey. "Legislative Notes: Disorderly Conduct and Loitering—A Modern Approach to Traditional Legislation." *Arkansas Law Review* 30 (Summer 1976):186–208.

Berger, Mark. "Law Enforcement Control: Checks and Balances for the Police System." *Connecticut Law Review* 4 (Winter 1972):467–507.

Berger, Raoul. "Do Regulations Really Bind Regulators?" *Northwestern University Law Review* 62 (May–June 1967):137–80.

Bonfield, Arthur. "The Abrogation of Penal Statutes by Nonenforcement." *Iowa Law Review* 49 (Winter 1964):389–440.

———. "The Iowa Administrative Procedure Act: Background, Construction, Applicability, Public Access to Agency Law—The Rulemaking Process." *Iowa Law Review* 60 (1975):731–936.

Buxton, R.J. "The Politics of Criminal Law Reform: England." *American Journal of Comparative Law* 21 (Spring 1973):230–44.

Caplan, Gerald. "The Case for Rulemaking by Law Enforcement Agencies." *Law and Contemporary Problems* 36 (Autumn 1971):500–14.

Coleman, Clive A., and A. Keith Bottomley. "Police Conceptions of Crime and 'No Crime.' " *The Criminal Law Review* (June 1976):344–60.

"The Consenting Adult Homosexual and the Law: An Empirical Study of Enforcement and Administration in Los Angeles County." *University of California Los Angeles Law Review* 13 (1966):643–832.

"Criminal Law—The Controlled Use of Police Discretion to Avert Civil Disorder." *Wisconsin Law Review* (1970):907–14.

Davis, Kenneth Culp. "Approach to Legal Control of the Police." *Texas Law Review* 52 (April 1974):703–25.

———. "Dialogue on Police Rulemaking." *University of Pennsylvania Law Review* 125 (June 1977):1167–81.

"Disorderly Conduct and Loitering—A Modern Approach to Traditional Legislation." *Arkansas Law Review* 30 (1976):186–208.

Eser, Albin. "The Politics of Criminal Law Reform: Germany." *American Journal of Comparative Law* 21 (Spring 1973):245–62.

Finckenhauer, J.O. "Some Factors in Police Discretion and Decisionmaking." *Journal of Criminal Justice* 4 (Spring 1976):29–46.

Gerber, R.J. "Arizona's New Criminal Code: An Overview and Critique." *Arizona State Law Journal* (1977):483–533.

Goldstein, Herman. "Administrative Problems in Controlling the Exercise of Police Authority." *Journal of Criminal Law, Criminology and Police Science* 58 (June 1967):160–72.

———. "Improving Policing: A Problem-Oriented Approach." *Crime and Delinquency* 25 (April 1979):236–58.

———. "Police Policy Formulation: A Proposal for Improving Police Performance." *Michigan Law Review* 65 (April 1967):1123–46.

Goldstein, Joseph. "Police Discretion Not to Invoke the Criminal Process: Low-Visibility Decisions in the Administration of Justice." *Yale Law Journal* 69 (March 1960):543–94.

Hall, Jerome. "Police and Law in a Democratic Society." *Indiana Law Journal* 28 (Winter 1953):133–77.

Heinz, John P., Robert W. Gettleman, and Morris A. Seekin. "Legislative Politics and Criminal Law." *Northwestern University Law Review* 64 (July-August 1969):273–358.

Hudson, James R. "Police Review Boards and Police Accountability." *Law and Contemporary Problems* 36 (1971):515–38.

Israel, Jerold H. "The Process of Penal Law Reform—A Look at the Proposed Michigan Revised Criminal Code." *Wayne Law Review* 14 (1968):772–830.

Kirkpatrick, Terry R. "Arrest, Citation and Summons—The Supreme Court Takes a Giant Step Forward." *Arkansas Law Review* 30 (Summer 1976):137–59.

Kuh, Richard H. "Plea Bargaining: Guidelines for the Manhattan District Attorney's Office." *Criminal Law Bulletin* 11 (1975):48–61.

LaFave, Wayne. "Penal Code Revision: Considering the Problems and Practices of the Police." *Texas Law Review* 45 (February 1967):434–54.

———. "The Police and Non-enforcement of the Law, Part I." *Wisconsin Law Review* (January 1962):104–76.

McClellan, John L. "Codification, Reform and Revision: The Challenge of a Modern Federal Criminal Code." *Duke Law Journal* (September 1971):663–713.

McGowan, Carl. "Rulemaking and the Police." *Michigan Law Review* 70 (March 1972):659–94.

Nelson, Alvar. "The Politics of Criminal Law Reform." *American Journal of Comparative Law* 21 (Spring 1973):269–86.

Packer, Herbert L. "The Case for Revision of the Penal Code." *Stanford Law Review* 13 (March 1961):252–63.

Parnas, Raymond. "The Police Response to the Domestic Disturbance." *Wisconsin Law Review* (1967):914–60.

Platz, William A. "The Criminal Code." *Wisconsin Law Review* (1956):350–84.

"Procedural Due Process in the Context of Informal Administrative Action: The Requirements for Notice, Hearing and Prospective Standards Relating to Police Selective Enforcement Practice." *Boston University Law Review* 53 (November 1973):1033–70.

"Public Disorder Statutes in Iowa: An Evaluation of Existing Statutes and the Proposed Revision." *Iowa Law Review* 57 (February 1972):862–88.

Quinn, John. "The Effect of Police Rulemaking on the Scope of Fourth Amendment Rights." *Journal of Urban Law* 52 (August 1974):25–43.

Reiss, Albert J., Jr. "Discretionary Justice in the United States." *International Journal of Criminology and Penology* 2 (1974):181–205.

Remington, Frank J., and Victor G. Rosenblum. "The Criminal Law and the Legislative Process." *University of Illinois Law Forum* (Winter 1960):481–99.

"The Right to Nondiscriminatory Enforcement of State Penal Laws." *Columbia Law Review* 61 (June 1961):1103–41.

"Safeguards, Standards and Necessity: Permissible Parameters for Legislative Delegations in Iowa." *Iowa Law Review* 58 (1973):974–99.

Schantz, Mark E. "Objectives of Criminal Code Revision: Guidelines to Evaluation." *Iowa Law Review* 60 (February 1975):430–61.

Schiller, Stephen A. "More Light on a Low Visibility Function: The Selective Enforcement of Laws, Parts 1–4." *Police Law Quarterly* (Summer 1972):6–11; (Fall 1972):20–32; (Winter 1973):17–20; (Spring 1973):35–44.

Schmidt, Wayne A. "A Proposal for a Statewide Law Enforcement Administrative Law Council." *Journal of Police Science and Administration* 2 (September 1974):330–38.

Schroder, Friedrick-Christian. "The Politics of Criminal Law Reform: Eastern Europe." *American Journal of Comparative Law* 21 (Spring 1973):304–17.

Schwenk, Edmund H. "The Administrative Crime, Its Creation and Punishment by Administrative Agencies." *Michigan Law Review* 42 (1943):51–86.

Sherry, Arthur H. "The Politics of Criminal Law Reform: The United States." *American Journal of Comparative Law* 21 (Spring 1973):201–29.

"Socio-Legal Aspects of Racially Motivated Police Misconduct." *Duke Law Journal* (September 1971):751–83.

Suzuki, Yoshio. "The Politics of Criminal Law Reform." *American Journal of Comparative Law* 21 (Spring 1973):287–303.

Thomas, Charles W., and W. Anthony Fitch. "The Exercise of Discretionary

Decision-Making by the Police: An Inquiry into Its Correlates, Consequences, and Control." *North Dakota Law Review* 54 (1977):61–95.
Tieger, Joseph H. "Police Discretion and Discriminatory Enforcement." *Duke Law Journal* (September 1971):717–43.
United States Department of Justice. "Materials Relating to Prosecutorial Discretion." *Criminal Law Reporter* (BNA) 24 (1978):3001–08.
Vanagunas, Stanley. "Toward Checks and Balances." *Marquette Law Journal* 57 (1974):505–14.
"Violations by Agencies of Their Own Regulations." *Harvard Law Review* 87 (January 1974):629–55.
Vorenberg, James. "Narrowing the Discretion of Criminal Justice Officials." *Duke Law Journal* (1976):651–97.
Webster, W. C. "Comparative Study of State Constitutions of the American Revolution." *Annals of the American Academy Supp.* (1897):380–420.
Wechsler, Herbert. "The Challenge of a Modern Penal Code." *Harvard Law Review* 65 (1952):1097–133.
Williams, Gregory H."Police Discretion: The Institutional Dilemma—Who Is in Charge?" *Iowa Law Review* 68, no. 3 (March 1983):431–93.
———. "Police Rulemaking Revisited: Some New Thoughts on an Old Problem." *Law and Contemporary Problems* 48, no. 2 (Spring 1985):in press.
———. "The Politics of Police Discretion," in Carl F. Pinkele and William C. Louthan, eds. *Discretion, Justice, and Democracy: A Public Policy Perspective*. Ames, Ia.: Iowa State University Press (1984):in press.
Wilson, Jerry V., and Geoffrey M. Alprin. "Controlling Police Conduct: Alternatives to the Exclusionary Rule." *Law and Contemporary Problems* 36, no. 4 (Autumn 1971):488–99.
Wright, J. Skelly. "Beyond Discretionary Justice." *Yale Law Journal* 81 (January 1972):575–97.

CASES

Ah Sin v. Wittman, 198 U.S. 500 (1905).
Alamo Express, Inc. v. United States, 613 F.2d 96 (5th Cir. 1980).
American Power Co. v. SEC, 329 U.S. 90 (1946).
Anderson v. Commissioner of Highways, 267 Minn. 308, 126 N.W.2d 778 (1964).
Anthony v. State, 349 So.2d 1066 (1977).
Baker-Chaput v. Gammet, 406 F.Supp. 1134 (D.N.H. 1976).
Bargain City U.S.A. v. Dilworth, 179 A.2d 439 (Pa. 1962).
Battle v. State, 292 So.2d 594 (Fla. Dist. Ct. App. 1974).

Beltone Electronics Corporation v. FTC, 402 F.Supp. 590 (D. Ct. N.D. Ill.) (1975).
Bence v. Breier, 501 F.2d 1185 (7th Cir. 1974).
Bowles v. Seminole Rock Co., 325 U.S. 410 (1945).
Britt v. Ocala, 65 S.2d 753 (Fla. 1953).
Brown v. Texas, 443 U.S. 47, 99 S.Ct. 2637 (1979).
Bruno v. Codd, 396 N.Y.S.2d 974 (1977), 407 N.Y.S.2d 165 (1978).
Buckley v. Valeo, 424 U.S. 1 (1976).
Buttrick v. Lowell, Allen 172, 83 Mass. 172 (1861).
Butz v. Glover Livestock Commission Co., 411 U.S. 182 (1973).
Chadha v. Immigration & Naturalization Service, 634 F.2d 408 (9th Cir. 1980).
Chastain v. Civil Service Board of Orlando, 327 So.2d 230 (Fla. 4th Dist. Ct. App. 1976).
Citizens, etc. v. Pottawattamie County Board of Adjustment, 277 N.W.2d 921 (Iowa 1979).
City of Des Moines v. Reiter, 251 Iowa 1206, 102 N.W.2d 363 (1960).
City of St. Petersburg v. Reed, 330 So.2d 256 (Fla. 2d Dist. Ct. App. 1976).
Clark v. State, 318 So.2d 487 (Fla. Dist. Ct. App. 1975).
Clemons v. United States, 408 F.2d 1230 (D.C. Cir. 1968).
Council of Organizations on Philadelphia Police Accountability and Responsibility v. Rizzo, 357 F.Supp. 1289 (E.D. Pa. 1973).
Cross v. Board of Supervisors of San Mateo County, 326 F.Supp. 634 (D. Ct. N.D. Cal. 1968), *aff'd.* 442 F.2d 362 (9th Cir. 1971).
Culver v. Streator, 130 Ill. 238 (1889).
Dancy v. United States, 395 F.2d 636 (D.C. Cir. 1968).
Danner v. Hass, 257 Iowa 654, 134 N.W.2d 534 (1965).
Delaware v. Prouse, 440 U.S. 648, 99 S.Ct. 139 (1979).
Diehl v. State, 451 A.2d 115, 120 (1982).
Echols v. Strickland, 28 *Criminal Law Reporter* 2092 (U.S. Dist. Ct. S.Tex, 1980).
Eirhart v. Libbey-Owens Ford Co., 616 F.2d 278 (7th Cir. 1980).
Elk Run Telephone Co. v. General Telephone Co., 160 N.W.2d 311 (Iowa 1968).
Emmetsburg v. Gunn, 249 Iowa 297, 86 N.W.2d 829 (1958).
Encyclopedia Britannica, Inc. v. FTC, 605 F.2d 964 (7th Cir. 1979).
Environmental Defense Fund Inc. v. Ruckelhaus, 439 F.2d 584 (D.C. Cir. 1971).
Ex Parte Corliss, 114 N.W. 962 (1907).
Ex Parte McCurley, 390 So.2d 25 (Ark. 1980).
Field v. Clark, 143 U.S. 649 (1882).
Foley v. Connelie, 435 U.S. 291 (1978).
FTC v. Universal-Rundle Commission, 387 U.S. 244 (1967).
Garris v. Rowland, 678 F.2d 1264 (1982).

GER-RO-MAR Inc. v. FTC, 518 F.2d 33 (2d Cir. 1975).
Glover Livestock Commission Co. v. Hardin, 454 F.2d 109 (8th Cir. 1972).
Goode v. Rizzo, 506 F.2d 542 (3rd Cir. 1974).
Good Samaritan Hospital, Corvallis v. Mathews, 609 F.2d 949 (9th Cir. 1979).
Gowan v. Smith, 157 Mich. 443, 122 N.W. 286 (1909).
Grant v. Fritz, 201 N.W.2d 188 (Iowa 1972).
Hagedorn v. Schrum, 283 N.W. 876 (1939).
Hampton v. U.S., 276 U.S. 394 (1928).
Hanley v. Kleindienst, 471 F.2d 823 (2d Cir. 1972).
Hoggard v. City of Richmond, 172 Va. 145, 200 S.E. 610 (1939).
Holland v. State, 115 N.W.2d 1 (Iowa 1970).
Holmes v. New York City Housing Authority, 398 F.2d 262 (2d Cir. 1968).
Hornsby v. Allen, 326 F.2d 605 (5th Cir. 1964).
Howell v. Mississippi, 300 So.2d 774 (Miss. 1974).
Inmates of Attica Correctional Facility v. Rockefeller, 477 F.2d 375 (2d Cir. 1973).
Iron Worker's Local No. 67 v. Hart, 191 N.W.2d 758 (Iowa 1971).
Jackson v. Virginia, 443 U.S. 307 (1979).
Jewell Company v. FTC, 432 F.2d 1155 (7th Cir. 1970).
Johnson Products Co. v. FTC, 549 F.2d 35 (7th Cir. 1977).
Kolender v. Lawson, 103 S.Ct. 1855 (1983).
Lanzetta v. New Jersey, 306 U.S. 451 (1939).
Larue v. David, 8 Cal. App. 750 (1908).
Leite v. City of Providence, 463 F.Supp. 585 (D.C. R.I. 1978).
L.G. Balfour v. FTC, 442 F.2d 1 (7th Cir. 1971).
Lucas v. United States, 411 F.2d 360 (D.C. Cir. 1980).
Lyons v. Los Angeles, 103 S.Ct. 1660 (1983).
McClelland v. Facteau, 610 F.2d 693 (10th Cir. 1979).
McCullers v. State, 206 So.2d 30 (Fla. App. 1968).
McGautha v. California, 402 U.S. 183 (1971).
McNamara v. Moody, 606 F.2d 621 (5th Cir. 1979).
Maquoketa Valley Comm. School Dist. v. Maquoketa Valley Ed. Ass'n., 279 N.W.2d 510 (Iowa 1979).
Marshall v. Jerrico, Inc., 466 U.S. 238 (1980).
Martinelli v. District Court, 612 P.2d 1083 (Colo. 1980).
Matter of Di Maggio v. Brown, 19 N.Y.2d 283, 279 N.Y.S.2d 161, 225 N.E.2d 871 (1967).
Matter of Powell, 602 P.2d 711 (Wash. 1979).
Michigan v. DeFillippo, 443 U.S. 31, 99 S.Ct. 2626 (1979).
Michigan v. Nelson, 255 N.W.2d 788 (Mich. Ct. App. 1977).
Miller v. Schuster, 227 Iowa 1005, 289 N.W. 702 (1940).
Missouri v. Lovelace, 585 S.W.2d 507 (Mo. Ct. App. 1979).

Moog Industries v. FTC, 355 U.S. 411 (1958).
Monell v. New York City Department of Social Services, 437 U.S. 411 (1958).
Monroe v. Pape, 365 U.S. 167 (1961).
Montana Power Co. v. Environmental Protection Agency, 608 F.2d 334 (9th Cir. 1979).
Morton v. Ruiz, 415 U.S. 199 (1974).
National League of Cities v. Usery, 426 U.S. 833 (1976).
Nelson v. State, 157 So.2d 96 (Fla. 1963).
Nixon v. Adm'r. of Gen. Services, 433 U.S. 425 (1977).
NLRB v. Boeing, 412 U.S. 67 (1973).
NLRB v. Hearst Publications, 322 U.S. 111 (1944).
Noble v. English, 183 Iowa 893, 167 N.W. 629 (Iowa 1918).
Noell v. Bensinger, 586 F.2d 554 (5th Cir. 1978).
Ogala Sioux Tribe of Indians v. Andrus, 603 F.2d 707 (8th Cir. 1979).
Olegario v. United States, 629 F.2d 204 (2d Cir. 1980).
Owen v. City of Independence, 445 U.S. 622 (1980).
Papachristou v. City of Jacksonville, 405 U.S. 156 (1972).
Parris Adult Theatre v. Slaton, 413 U.S. 49 (1973).
Parratt v. Taylor, 451 U.S. 527 (1981).
Pendleton v. Transportation Union Systems Corp., 430 F.Supp. 95 (D. Ct. E.D. Penn. 1977).
People v. Avery, 367 N.E.2d 79 (Ill. 1979).
People v. Coutard, 32 Criminal Law Reporter 2166 (December 1, 1982).
People v. Gissendanner, 48 N.Y.2d 543, 399 N.E.2d 924 (1979).
People v. Harris, 182 Cal. App.2d Supp. 827, 5 Cal. Rptr. 852 (1960).
People v. Mullin, 197 Cal. App.2d 479 (1961).
People v. Pavlic, 227 Mich. 562, 199 N.W. 373, (1924).
People v. Spear, 32 Cal. App. Rptr. 2d 165 (1939).
People v. Walker, 610 P.2d 496 (Colo. 1980).
People v. Zamora, 167 Cal. Rptr. 573, 615 P.2d 1361 (1980).
Perea v. Fales, 39 Cal. App.3d 939, 114 Cal. Rptr. 808 (1975).
The Permian Basin Area Rate Cases, 390 U.S. 747 (1978).
Peterson v. City of Long Beach, 594 P.2d 477 (Cal. 1979).
Phelps Dodge Corp. v. Labor Board, 313 U.S. 177 (1941).
Prather v. Lexington, 13 B. Monroe 559, 51 Ky. R. 449 (1852).
Richard v. Holliday, 153 N.W.2d 473 (Iowa 1967).
Rizzo v. Goode, 423 U.S. 362, 96 S.Ct. 598 (1976).
Rochin v. California, 342 U.S. 167, 72 S.Ct. 205 (1952).
San Antonio Independent School District v. Rodriguez, 411 U.S. 1 (1972).
Singer v. United States, 323 U.S. 338 (1945).
Sirbo Holdings Inc. v. CIR, 476 F.2d 981 (2d Cir. 1973).
Skidmore v. Swift, 323 U.S. 134 (1944).

Smith v. Goguen, 415 U.S. 566, 94 S.Ct. 1242, 39 L.Ed.2d 605 (1974).
Smith v. Hill, 510 F.Supp. 767 (D.C. Utah 1981).
Smith v. Wade, 103 S.Ct. 1625 (1983).
Springer v. Philippine Islands, 227 U.S. 189 (1928).
Spurbeck v. Stratton, 252 Iowa 279, 106 N.W.2d 660 (1960).
State v. Bly, 127 Ariz. 370, 621 P.2d 279 (1980).
State v. Bryan, 93 Wash.2d 177, 606 P.2d 1228 (1980).
State v. Gillette, 56 Iowa 459, 9 N.W. 362 (1881).
State v. Jenson, 123 Ariz. 72, 597 P.2d 554 (Ct. App. 1979).
State v. Lombardi, 99 N.W.2d 829 (Wis. 1959).
State v. Manning, 220 Iowa 525, 259 N.W. 213 (1935).
State v. Mulcare, 189 Wash. 625, 66 P.2d 360 (1937).
State v. Rivera, 260 Iowa 320, 149 N.W.2d 127 (1967).
State v. Shedoudy, 45 N.M. 516, 118 P.2d 280 (1941).
State v. Twogood, 7 Iowa 252 (1858).
State v. Van Trump, 224 Iowa 504, 275 N.W. 569 (1937).
State v. Watts, 186 N.W.2d 611 (Iowa 1971).
State v. White, 324 So.2d 630 (Fla. 1975).
Strong v. Bostick, 420 So.2d 1356 (Miss. 1982).
Strong v. Town of Lansing, 179 N.W.2d 365 (Iowa 1970).
Sueppel v. Eads, 156 N.W.2d 115 (1968).
Sugarman v. McDougall, 413 U.S. 634 (1973).
Sun Ray Drive-In Dairy v. Oregon Liquor Control Comm'n, 517 P.2d 289 (Or. App. 1973).
Taylor v. City of Pine Bluff, 226 Ark. 309, 289 S.W.2d (1956), *cert. denied* 352 U.S. 894 (1956).
Terry v. Ohio, 392 U.S. 1, 88 S.Ct. 1868 (1968).
Thompson v. City of Louisville, 362 U.S. 199 (1960).
Thornhill v. Alabama, 310 U.S. 88 (1940).
Udall v. Tallman, 380 U.S. 1 (1965).
United States ex. rel. Accardi v. Shaughnessy, 346 U.S. 260 (1954).
United States ex. rel. Guy V. McCauley, 385 F.Supp. 193 (E.D. Wis. 1974).
United States v. American Tel. & Tel., 567 F.2d 121 (D.C. Cir. 1977).
United States v. Barbera, 514 F.2d 294 (2d Cir. 1975).
United States v. Brignoni-Ponce, 422 U.S. 873, 95 S.Ct. 2574 (1975).
United States v. Bryant, 439 F.2d 642 (D.C. Cir. 1971).
United States v. Caceres, 440 U.S. 741, 99 S.Ct. 1465 (1979).
United States v. Cassiagnol, 420 F.2d 868 (4th Cir. 1978), *cert. denied* 439 U.S. 1051 (1978).
United States v. City of Philadelphia, 482 F.Supp. 1248 (E.D. Pa. 1979) and 644 F.2d 187 (3d Cir. 1980) *aff'd*.
United States v. Consumer Life Ins. Co., 430 U.S. 725 (1977).

United States v. Cox, 342 F.2d 167 (5th Cir. 1965).
United States v. Dougherty, 473 F.2d 1113 (D.C. Cir. 1972).
United States v. Gordon, 580 F.2d 827 (5th Cir. 1978).
United States v. Grimaud, 220 U.S. 506 (1911).
United States v. Harris, 347 U.S. 612 (1954).
United States v. Leggett & Platt, Inc., 542 F.2d 655 (6th Cir. 1976).
United States v. Mississippi Power & Light Co., 638 F.2d 899 (5th Cir. 1981).
United States v. Nixon, 418 U.S. 683 (1974).
United States v. O'Neill, 619 F.2d 222 (3d Cir. 1980).
United States v. Pastor, 419 F.Supp. 1318 (D. N.Y. 1975).
United States v. Perry, 449 F.2d 1026 (D.C. Cir. 1971).
United States v. Seeling, 627 F.2d 206 (6th Cir. 1980), *cert. denied* 49 U.S.L.W. 3249 (1980).
United States v. Steele, 461 F.2d 1148 (9th Cir. 1972).
United States v. Wade, 408 F.2d 1230 (D.C. Cir. 1968).
United States v. Wayte, 549 F.Supp. 1376 (C.D. Cal. 1982).
United States v. Wayte 82–1699 (9th Cir. decided July 10, 1983).
Utah v. Gallion, 572 P.2d 683 (1977).
Vander Linden v. United States, 502 F.Supp. 693 (S.D. Iowa 1980).
Vitarelli v. Seaton, 359 U.S. 535 (1959).
Wagner v. Northeast Farm Service Co., 177 N.W.2d 1 (Iowa 1970).
Warren County v. Judges of the Fifth Judicial District, 234 N.W.2d 894 (Iowa 1976).
Washington Mobilization Committee v. Cullinane, 400 F.Supp. 186 (D.C. Cir. 1975).
Wayman v. Southard, 10 Wheat. 1 (1825).
Webster v. City of Houston, 689 F.2d 1220 (5th Cir. 1982).
Winn-Dixie Stores Inc. v. FTC, 377 F.Supp. 773 (D. Ct. M.D. Fla. 1974).
Yellin v. United States, 374 U.S. 109 (1963).
Yick Wo v. Hopkins, 118 U.S. 356 (1885).
Youngstown Sheet and Tube Company v. Sawyer, 343 U.S. 579 (1952).

GOVERNMENT DOCUMENTS AND UNPUBLISHED MATERIALS

Constitutional Convention Commission. *Report of the Constitutional Convention Commission*. Baltimore: King Brothers, 1967.
Des Moines, Iowa, Police Department. "Regulations." Des Moines, Iowa, 1979. (Mimeographed.)
Heiges, Ralph E. "The Office of Sheriff in the Rural Counties of Ohio." Ph.D. dissertation, Department of Political Science, Columbia University, 1933.

International City Managers Association. *Municipal Yearbook, 1966*. Washington, D.C.: International City Managers Association, 1966.

Iowa Advisory Committee to the U.S. Commission on Civil Rights. *Race Relations in Tama County*. Washington, D.C.: U.S. Government Printing Office, 1981.

Iowa Department of Justice. *Attorney General Opinions*. 1911–1912.

Jackson, William A. "The Office of Sheriff in Iowa." Ph.D. dissertation, Department of Political Science, University of Iowa, 1924.

Kansas Advisory Committee to the U.S. Commission on Civil Rights. *Police-Community Relations in the City of Wichita and Sedgwick County*. Washington, D.C.: U.S. Government Printing Office, 1980.

Massachusetts Criminal Law Revisions Commission. *Proposed Criminal Code of Massachusetts*. New York: Lawyers Co-operative Publishing Company, 1972.

Missouri Association for Criminal Justice Survey Committee. *The Missouri Crime Survey*. New York: Macmillan, 1926.

Missouri Committee to Draft a Modern Criminal Code. *The Proposed Criminal Code for the State of Missouri*. St. Paul, Minn.: West, 1973.

Moran, Theodore Kenneth. "Police Decision Making: The Effects of Differential Enforcement Choices on Public Policy." Ph.D. dissertation, University of Connecticut, 1974.

National Advisory Commission on Criminal Justice Standards and Goals. *Police*. Washington, D.C.: U.S. Government Printing Office, 1973.

National Commission on Law Observation and Enforcement. *Report on the Police*. Washington, D.C.: U.S. Government Printing Office, 1931.

Ohio State Advisory Committee to the U.S. Commission on Civil Rights. *Policing in Cincinnati, Ohio: Official Policy v. Civilian Reality*. Washington, D.C.: U.S. Government Printing Office, 1981.

Peterson, David. "Police Discretion and the Decision to Arrest." Ph.D. dissertation, University of Kentucky, 1968.

"Police and Fire Services of the City of Meriden, Conn." Chicago: Public Administration Service, 1962.

President's Commission on Law Enforcement and Administration of Justice. *Challenge of Crime in a Free Society*. Washington, D.C.: U.S. Government Printing Office, 1967.

———. *Task Force Report: The Courts*. Washington, D.C.: U.S. Government Printing Office, 1967.

———. *Task Force Report: The Police*. Washington, D.C.: U.S. Government Printing Office, 1967.

Report of the National Advisory Commission on Civil Disorders. Washington, D.C.: U.S. Government Printing Office. 1968.

Schaefer, Roger. "The Police: Law Enforcers, Peace Keepers, Servicers." Ph.D. dissertation, University of Minnesota, 1977.

U.S. Commission on Civil Rights, *Confronting Racial Isolation in Miami*. Washington, D.C.: U.S. Government Printing Office, 1982.

———. *Police Practices and the Preservation of Civil Rights*. Washington, D.C.: U.S. Government Printing Office, 1979.

———. *Under the Rule of Thumb: Battered Women and Administration of Justice*. Washington, D.C.: U.S. Government Printing Office, 1982.

———. *Who Is Guarding the Guardians? A Report on Police Practices*. Washington, D.C.: U.S. Government Printing Office, 1981.

U.S. Commission on Review of the National Policy toward Gambling. *Gambling in America*. Washington, D.C.: U.S. Government Printing Office, 1976.

Wileman, Fred A. *Model Policy Manual for Police Agencies*. Madison, Wisc.: Institute of Governmental Affairs, 1976.

Williams, Gregory H. "Maryland State's Attorneys." M.A. thesis, University of Maryland, 1969.

FEDERAL AND STATE CONSTITUTIONS AND STATUTES

Alabama. *Code of Criminal Procedure* (Supplement 1973).

Alaska. *Statutes* (1969).

———. *Statutes* (1980).

Arizona. *Criminal Code* (1982).

———. *Organic Laws* (1901).

———. *Revised Statutes Annotated* (1956).

———. *Revised Statutes Annotated* (1969).

———. *Revised Statutes Annotated* (1978).

———. *Session Laws* (1901).

Arkansas. *Rules of Criminal Procedure* (1980).

———. *Statutes Annotated* (1947).

———. *Statutes Annotated* (Supp. 1960).

———. *Statutes Annotated* (1969).

———. *Statutes Annotated* (1976).

California. *Government Code* (West, 1968).

———. *Penal Code* (West, 1971).

———. *Penal Code* (West Cumulative Supplement 1978).

———. *Statutes* (1883).

Colorado. *Revised Statutes* (1973).

———. *Revised Statutes Annotated*.

———. *Session Laws* (1908).

Connecticut. *General Statutes Annotated* (West, 1982).

———. *General Statutes Revised* (1966).

———. *General Statutes Revised* (1972).
———. *Statutes* (1983).
Delaware. *Code* (1974).
———. *Code Annotated* (1973).
———. *Laws* (1925).
District of Columbia. *Statutes* (1980).
Florida. *Rules of Criminal Procedure* (West, 1975).
———. *Statutes Annotated* (West, 1974).
———. *Statutes Annotated* (West, 1979).
Georgia. *Code Annotated* (1969).
———. *Code Annotated* (1975).
Hawaii. *Revised Statutes* (1968).
———. *Revised Statutes* (1975).
Idaho. *Code* (1972).
———. *Code* (Supp. 1975).
———. *Code* (1979).
Illinois. *Annotated Statutes* (1964).
———. *Annotated Statutes* (Smith-Hurd, 1973).
———. *Annotated Statutes* (Supp. 1976).
———. *Revised Statutes* (1981).
Indiana. *Acts* (1905).
———. *Annotated Statutes* (Burns, 1974).
———. *Code* (West, 1950).
———. *Code* (1982).
———. *Constitution*, art. VI, §§ 2–11.
Iowa. *Acts* (1927).
———. *Acts 33d General Assembly* (1909).
———. *Administrative Code* (1981).
———. *Code* (1851).
———. *Code* (1860).
———. *Code* (1861).
———. *Code* (1873).
———. *Code* (1897).
———. *Code* (1924).
———. *Code* (1975).
———. *Code* (West, 1976).
———. *Code* (1977).
———. *Code* (1980).
———. *Code* (1981).
———. *Code* (1983).
———. *Code Annotated* (West, 1976).
———. *Code Revision* (1860).

———. *Code Supplement* (1913).
———. *Code* (Supplement 1983).
———. *Constitution* (1846).
———. *McClain's Code* (1888).
Kansas. *Statutes Annotated* (1970).
———. *Statutes Annotated* (1980).
Kentucky. *Acts* (1942).
———. *Revised Statutes Annotated* (Bobbs-Merrill, 1970).
———. *Revised Statutes Annotated* (Baldwin, 1975).
Louisiana. *Code of Criminal Procedure* (1980).
———. *Revised Statutes* (West, 1967).
Maine. *Criminal Code* (1982).
———. *Revised Statutes Annotated* (1964).
Maryland. *Annotated Code* (Supplement 1982).
———. *Revised Statutes* (1952).
Massachusetts. *Annotated Laws* (Michie/Law. Co-op., 1920).
———. *Annotated Laws* (Michie/Law. Co-op., 1973).
Michigan. *Acts* (1895).
———. *Code of Criminal Procedure* (1977).
———. *Compiled Laws Annotated* (1981).
———. *Statutes Annotated* (Callaghan, 1949).
———. *Statutes Annotated* (1981).
Minnesota. *Rules of Criminal Procedure* (1980).
———. *Statutes* (1980).
———. *Statutes Annotated* (1964).
———. *Statutes Annotated* (West, 1968).
Mississippi. *Code Annotated* (1972).
———. *Code Annotated* (1980).
Missouri. *Annotated Statutes* (Vernon, 1966).
———. *Annotated Statutes* (Vernon, 1969).
———. *Revised Statutes* (1978).
Montana. *Code* (1969).
———. *Revised Code Annotated* (1969).
———. *Rules of Criminal Procedure* (1982).
Nebraska. *Laws* (1901).
———. *Revised Statutes* (1974).
———. *Rules of Criminal Procedure* (1980).
Nevada. *Revised Statutes* (1975).
New Hampshire. *Revised Statutes* (Supplement 1977).
New Jersey. *Rules of Court* (1983).
New Mexico. *Laws* (1921).

———. *Statutes Annotated* (1953).
———. *Statutes Annotated* (1964).
———. *Statutes Annotated* (1978).
———. *Statutes Annotated* (Supplement 1982).
New York. *Criminal Procedure Law* (Supplement 1982).
———. *Laws* (1888).
———. *Penal Laws* (McKinney, 1975).
North Carolina. *General Statutes* (Supplement 1975).
North Dakota. *Cent. Code* (1960).
———. *Cent. Code* (1975).
———. *Session Laws* (1891).
Ohio. *Laws*.
———. *Revised Code Annotated* (Page, 1976).
———. *Revised Statutes* (1980).
Oklahoma. *Statutes Annotated* (West, 1969).
———. *Statutes Annotated* (1981).
Oregon. *Revised Statutes* (1971).
———. *Revised Statutes* (1975).
Pennsylvania. *Rules of Criminal Procedure* (Purdon Supplement 1983).
———. *Statutes Annotated* (1973).
Rhode Island. *General Laws* (1970 and Cumulative Supplement 1977).
Tennessee. *Code Annotated* (1973).
Texas. *Penal Code* (Supp. 1973).
United States. *Code* (1938).
———. *Constitution* art. I, sec. 8.
———. *Constitution* art. II, sec. 3.
Utah. *Code Annotated* (1953).
———. *Code of Criminal Procedure* (1980).
———. *Laws* (1890).
Vermont. *Code* (1980).
Virginia. *Acts* (1908).
———. *Code Annotated* (1973).
———. *Statutes* (1908).
Washington. *Constitution*, art. 2, 12.
———. *Justice Court Criminal Rules* (West, 1980).
———. *Laws* (1891).
———. *Revised Code Annotated* (Supp. 1975).
West Virginia. *Code* (Supplement 1983).
———. *Code Annotated* (1976).
Wyoming. *Statutes Annotated* (1959).

NEWSPAPERS

Des Moines Register. June 12, 1972.
———. June 13, 1972.
———. June 14, 1972.
———. June 21, 1972.
———. December 9, 1979.
———. May 21, 1981.
———. August 23, 1981.
———. January 17, 1982.
Iowa City Press Citizen. June 16, 1980.
———. April 6, 1981.
Wisconsin State Journal. May 27, 1973.

Index

About the Author

GREGORY HOWARD WILLIAMS is Professor and Associate Dean of the College of Law at the University of Iowa. A former law enforcement officer, he presently serves on the Iowa Law Enforcement Academy Council, and as Chairperson of the Iowa State Advisory Committee to the United States Commission on Civil Rights. His articles on law enforcement and police policy have been published in *Iowa Law Review, Law and Contemporary Problems,* and other journals.

www.ingramcontent.com/pod-product-compliance
Ingram Content Group UK Ltd.
Pitfield, Milton Keynes, MK11 3LW, UK
UKHW021905150926
475560UK00003B/187

9 780313 240706